Whispering Winds of Change

Whispering Winds of Change

Perceptions of a New World

Stuart Wilde

Nacson & Sons, Pty.

WHISPERING WINDS OF CHANGE
©1993 by Stuart Wilde

Edited by David E. Dondero—Taos, New Mexico
Illustrations by Robyne Wilde—Sydney, Australia
Cover Art by Greg Harlin, WRH Inc—Annapolis, Maryland
Photograph of Author by J. Rigler—San Francisco, California

Library of Congress Cataloging-in-Publication Data

Wilde, Stuart, 1946-
      Whispering Winds of Change/Stuart Wilde

      ISBN 0-930603-45-1
      1. Conduct of Life.   I. Title

International Standard Book Number (ISBN) 0-930603-45-1
Printed in Australia
First Published in 1993.

Published by:
Nacson & Sons, Pty.
Sydney, Australia
Phone: (02) 2816179
FAX: (02) 2812075

Distributed by:
White Dove International, Inc.
P.O. Box 1000
Taos, New Mexico 87571 USA
Phone: (505) 758-0500
Fax: (505) 758-2265

Other Books By Stuart Wilde

I dedicate this book
to all of our
brothers and sisters on the planet,
with the prayer and affirmation
that one day—some day—
arising from the
divine order in all things,
we will see the evolution
of our people expanded and blessed to the point
where every
woman,
man,
and, child
will finally be set free.

Our time will come.

Contents

Death of the
World Ego

CHAPTER ONE

W e live in exciting times. The next twenty years will see the greatest change in Western civilization since the Industrial Revolution.

Traveling 'round and 'round the world as I do, talking to many thousands of people each year, I am convinced that only a small percentage have a broader view of what is going on.

Teaching people inner power and personal freedom has been my thing in life. I'm concerned that people get so overwhelmed by their lives and obsessed with their immediate circumstances that they loose sight of the overall energy shifts that are happening all around them. If you work upon yourself, and you become a wonderfully spiritual and psychologically integrated person with great charisma and potential, what will it do for you if, through a lack of perception, you find yourself in downtown Sarajevo and the Serbs are bombing the hell out of the neighborhood?

Information, knowledge and perception are king nowadays. Developing a personal strength and balance is important, but having an overview is now equally important. The world is shifting quickly. It's vital to have the right energy, but you also have to be in the right place at the right time.

This book is comprised of a series of essays and ideas on the inner energy of events and issues prominent at this time. You may not necessarily agree with every stance I take, but the basic tenets are clear and hard to deny. Once you look for the hidden currents of life you can then watch the world and know where it's going. This ability allows you to camp at the winning post of life, and it also helps you avoid delays, dead ends, and trouble. All of mankind's inner feelings eventually manifest themselves as an outer reality. That applies to the development of cities, nations, and continents, as well as individuals. You don't have to become a great visionary—just watch the inner flow and you'll know what will happen next.

To understand the unfolding destiny of the world, the first thing to look at is the nature of power; its concentration, its flow, how people relate to it, why they seek it. Power can be divided into two main categories: inner power and external power. Inner power is personal fortitude, strength of character, discipline, psychological integration, and a spiritual serenity. External power, which is mainly the power of the ego, describes most of the power in the world. It is military strength—which includes the police force and security agencies—political power and influence, and financial clout, both corporate and private. External power also flows from social position. Sometimes power is expressed through one's physical being by sexual control or just brute force.

Why do individuals seek external power? What does it do for them? A few seek it because they are megalomaniacs, and they get off on dominating others. Others seek power because it allows them to embrace an elitism from which flows social benefit, privileges, financial gain, and the ability to maneuver events to one's advantage.

Beyond the most obvious reasons for power is a hidden reason explaining the form and the basis of people's psychological need for it. If you can maneuver yourself into a position of power, it will automatically carry you up and beyond the common man. You are elevated and separated by the power you exert and the elite position you enjoy. Power allows you to enter the illusion that you are more important than others. And from this elevated position you are safer, you control your destiny more effectively—certainly more so than the common man who, in the external sense, is essentially powerless.

To the ego, securing a position above others is a valuable prize; it allows the ego to believe that it is immune from the destiny of man. The destiny of man is to die. If the ego garners enough power, it may rise above death and become immortal. At least in the exercising and the experiencing of power, the ego can temporarily forget about death.

5

It is elitism's illusion of immortality that drives people. The belief is that fate or God will not take out special people. Individuals pay large premiums to fly first class, partly because the seats are more comfortable, partly because the food is better, but mostly because it is elitist. Flying first class feels safer. First-class passengers are special and important and godlike. First-class passengers can't possibly crash, burn, and die. Only the hoi polloi in coach submit to that possibility.

Once you are above the crowd and perhaps even in control of them, you take on a godlike nature. You make decisions. You control people's destiny. You act as god for them. You may possibly have the power of life-and-death over them. Or you may be the head of a corporation; you are the one who hires and fires people. It is you who decides who gets the valuable contracts and who doesn't.

Once the ego establishes a godlike position over others it begins to feel better about the terrible insecurity it feels about its eventual demise. Have ever asked yourself the question, "Why are our governments so obsessed with controlling every minute aspect of people's lives? What satisfaction or pleasure could they possibly derive from such control?" The answer is, in part, that it makes them more godlike and as a result more secure.

Establishing control and influence over others form a vital supporting scaffold in the ego's life-and-death struggle. The more control it exercises, the more it can rise above the herd, and the more possible its survival.

So then you might ask, "Given that the world is becoming less and less secure, and given that the control and interference of governments has brought nations to their knees, will those governments now realize that control is folly? Will they agree to relinquish some of their control and liberate the people?" Answer: "No. Not voluntarily, they won't." The more unsettled things become, the more insecure people in power will feel, so the more they will seek absolute control.

There's a second aspect to power that allows the ego a further godlike experience. One of the main lessons we come to learn on earth is the process by which thoughts are transformed into reality. An idea is born in your imagination and then, through concerted action and applied diligence, you hopefully get to experience your desire as a benefit manifested in your life. In the first part of this process you come to understand that your thoughts, feelings, and actions—not luck—create your reality. Then, through trial and error, you step to the second part of the process, which is to make the transition of ideas into reality as efficient as possible. When you become responsible and develop an expertise in the thought process, you will learn to exercise control over your destiny. Once you have done that, you have graduated from the earth plane.

Power allows individuals to circumvent the normal learning process by offering attractive short cuts. Wielding power is a way of short-circuiting the system. It allows the ego to believe that it's beyond that dimension of human affairs which requires mundane effort and diligence. Power often allows the individual to manifest their desires with only minimal or even no effort. If, because of external power, you don't have to go through the normal process of consciousness and action to materialize your wishes, then it follows from the ego's illusory viewpoint that you must be unusual, special, above it all, and therefore godlike. Gods are obviously higher and more secure than regular folk.

So, for example, if the police chief in a small Third World town wishes to own a house, would he scrimp and save and work on his building lot in his free hours until his dream is manifest? Or is it more likely that he would use his power over the community to ensure he receives enough large backhanders and payoffs to instantly manifest the house he desires?

When someone drops ten thousand in the chief's lap for the use of his blind eye, doesn't that of itself confirm to the chief his special status as a human god? Because his power allows him to imprison some and liberate others doesn't he, in effect, command their destiny? And if he does command their destiny, it's only natural that he might conclude that he is a god or at the very least, an extremely important person who deserves the people's tribute. (What is more valuable to an individual than his freedom?)

So now the police chief's power magically transforms from an evil that is perpetuated upon his people to a "good" performed for the citizen's benefit. Namely, for a price, the police chief will save them from the worst excesses of his office. So the additional benefit of power is to remove the holder of that power from the tedious manifestation process that is the lesson of this physical dimension, and the lot of common folk. Thus, the government of a country does not have to mess with materializing its wishes through effort. It has only to issue proclamations declaring its wishes into law. It can order the civil administration to follow through, and it can coerce citizens into paying for its desire to be manifest.

Anytime you use power to infringe upon others, or when you coerce people by fear or the threat of retribution into any agreement or contract that they would not normally be a party to, you infringe upon your spiritual integrity as much as theirs. You move from the natural godlike nature that is your spirit to an evil nature that is egoistic and self-aggrandizing. An energy shift that's prevalent in the world today sees one group of people moving gradually from ego toward the spirit, through the realignment of their consciousness, while another group is threatened by changing circumstances and moves increasingly in the opposite direction, toward the ego, seeking greater manipulation, guarantee, and control over human affairs.

That's why our ego oriented governments are ideologically distant from the spirit oriented people. That's also why there are a thousand and one movements that push for various group's rights. It's the different indigenous peoples and social or commercial groupings attempting to materialize their freedom. That is the flow of the world mind—the spiritual yearning of the people toward liberation. Those on the ego parabola, who travel a discordant pattern to the general inner evolution, will find themselves isolated. Given long periods of time, it's a proven fact that those who move toward God and liberation gather life force, and are sustained and persist. Those who imprison, consume, and ravish mankind, exhibiting the most base instincts of man, eventually perish. This is why none of the great empires exist today—each was consumed in its own filth. The ego which travels away from God eventually suffocates itself to death for a lack of energy. That's also why the world is in turmoil; you are watching the ego devour itself—not a pretty sight, but very interesting.

How you feel about the ego's demise depends on your stance. If you are a spiritual person you will not care very much if the world ego destroys itself or not. You will see that eventually its destruction will benefit us all. If you are on the egotistic side of power, the idea of the system being destroyed will be terrifying. Any loss of power and influence will cause great insecurity, and your natural tendency will be to try to save your position by exercising more control or appropriating your neighbor's position. That way, at least you will have more than enough to guarantee your immediate survival.

The process of the ego and the external manifestation of power unfolds to a majestic pattern of predictability when you track it back through history, so much so that you can closely predict what will happen next. Follow me, if you will, and I'll paint you a picture of how history unfolds to a specific pattern, how the ego is currently in a noose, and how we are poised just a split second before the rickety chair upon which this whole illusion balances may be kicked away by reality, honesty, and truth. If you're a bit of a scamp, this kind of stuff is a lot of fun!

Here is what has happened in the past and what will probably unfold in the future.

The Industrial Revolution took the peasants out of the fields and into a monied economy. With a little money comes a little status. Money takes you from being a helpless victim of fate to the possibility of controlling your life. Once the peasants moved into the cities, they were now close together—they could organize. The union movement was born and pushed, winning improved conditions for the workers. Suddenly people were no longer expendable. They became something. They had a voice. They won a limited respect. But having only just left the land, their dreams were simple dreams. From those simple dreams and from their contact with each other came the idea that all men and women are equal—the seeds of socialism. In its essence, socialism is a spiritual idea, it rises naturally from our humanity. In its pure form, it is compassion. It was appropriate and it fitted at that point in history. How could anyone say the workers were not linked to each other by a common responsibility, standing shoulder to shoulder, experiencing the energy, emotion, and feelings of one another at the conveyor belt of industry? But socialism is a stepping stone in our society's empowerment. It is not, as many would have us believe, the final liberation or the panacea for all ills. While the working classes woke to new possibilities, the Industrial Revolution made many people rich. The aristocracy had previously carved out empires by taking land and resources from less developed souls. Now, through finance and trade they could carve out even greater empires, which they used to control governments and to develop a command over nations.

Even the artisans and middle classes, which were fairly small in number at the time of the Industrial Revolution, suddenly became prosperous. The aristocracy generally did not get involved in manufacturing, they preferred to own land or resources, or to concentrate on finance. It was the artisans and the middle class that opened the factories to become the household names we know today. The *nouveau riche* stepped up to join the social elite. Monopolies and cartels were created so that all the spoils could be divided among the main players. Meanwhile, socialism and democracy were developing as powerful ideas among the common people.

Eventually, the sheer number of people that now stood for democracy and freedom forced the status quo to give some of its political control to the unions, and some basic rights to the workers. Everyone gradually got the vote. In theory, people could decide what kind of government they might like, and possibly set the agenda for the nation's legislation.

Although socialism and democracy became accepted as the norm, the ruling elite (which now included the *nouveau riche)* made sure that democracy would not get in their way. Look at our representatives. Are they one of us? Do they speak for us? Or have they set themselves up as kings and queens in marbled palaces? Do they enjoy the privileges of elitism or are they obliged to operate as we do? Of course not. President Clinton spent twenty-five million dollars of public money on his inauguration parties. Never mind the national debt, mate—let's party! Democracy is nothing more than a guise rubber stamping an alternative royalty into power. If it were anything more, the leaders would have to rule according to the will of the people. I can't think of one example in the last one hundred and fifty years where any government has ruled to the will or benefit of its people. Governments rule to the benefit of kings, the elite and the status quo.

The aristocratic and capitalist power base did change after the Industrial Revolution because it had entered into a power-sharing agreement with the unions. Those same unions soon took on the role of being very important people and formed a socialist status quo. In the end, all that really happened was that the cake was carved into slightly different shaped slices—the leaders of socialism now sat at dinner with the aristocrats and the capitalists. It didn't take the union leaders very long before they began to enjoy what they saw, and they became just another part of the power structure controlling us all. The bulk of the feed and the nourishment that the national cake offers never really reached the common people and it still doesn't. Only a very small percentage of our total national wealth is in private hands. Most of the resources and wealth of the nation is under the ownership and control of governments, corporations, churches, and various institutions. Ordinary people exert little or no power.

The best way to understand the spiritual evolution of the world is to look at how the politics of power and money affect it. That probably sounds odd. How can the flow of power and money in any way be connected with things spiritual? It is. You are obliged to live and express your humanity and your spiritual self within the context of the power structure into which you are born. It forms the playing field on which you exercise your ideas and, hopefully, prosper and nurture your spirit. However, when power is exercised over you it naturally restricts your spiritual development and creative potential. To develop fully as a human being you have to have freedom of movement and enough money to purchase the experiences of life, otherwise you've come to the planet and missed the ride. Money controls the wherewithal to mobility, personal expression, and creativity. It acts as the brake or the accelerator to the evolution of our mass spiritual dream.

Those that have money can experience the full potential of their lives; those that have no money experience the same lack of freedom as did medieval peasants. The top of the hierarchy understood, that apart from exercising power and enjoying short cuts in the evolutionary learning process, they knew that if they really wanted to secure an immortality for themselves and their families, they had better control the country's money. Until then money—and therefore worth—was described in the gold and silver coinage of the nation. The new game was to convince people that a receipt for gold was as good as the real thing. Once that idea was forced upon people the next step was to kid everyone into accepting the idea that the receipt itself had value, that you really didn't need the gold. At that point, all the real wealth of the world was captured at the top of the hierarchical monopoly. The top of the hierarchy controlled the government, owned most of the land and almost all of the resources. They owned the factories, the banks, and all the financial institutions, and now they had captured the gold by simply exchanging it for paper. Many countries, including America, passed proclamations prohibiting ordinary citizens from owning gold.

Now those at the top of the hierarchy, their families, and their friendly governments had the whole system bottled up. They owned everything. They controlled the flow of money, interest rates, and capital. They were above the law for the most part, and through their control of money had complete dominion over everyone's actions and mobility. Nothing relevant could occur without their say so. So when you dropped upon this planet on your birthday, believing perhaps that your spiritual heritage was to express yourself as a human, you were surprised to find that all the avenues of expression you might wish to travel were already carved up and controlled by someone else.

If you were lucky enough to be born into the ruling elite, you could express yourself through the exercise of power. Everyone else would be obligated to express their humanity only under license from this controlling elite. This point is vital to understand as it explains everything.

In the same way that each human has a personality that forms his or her soul, I believe the collective consciousness of our world has a Planetary Group Soul to which we are all contributors. It evolves as we evolve. It develops through the collective thoughts, feelings, and actions of humanity. Prior to the Industrial Revolution, the Planetary Group Soul of our humanity rested in its embryonic tribal stage, expressing itself in simple, immature, and unassuming ways. The planetary soul, its imagination undeveloped, yearned for little. Its dreamtime was primordial, resting in the spiritual purity of the land and the changing seasons. Once the Industrial Revolution gave us motorized transport, mechanized production, and the paycheck, the Group Soul of our humanity grew rapidly. It was able, given the time in history, to dream of expressing itself in a more complete and independent way.

The Industrial Revolution showed the peasants, who were now mainly in the factories, how each had the possibility of acquiring wealth if they could manufacture and trade. It was a massive leap in consciousness for mankind. Never before had the possibility existed for ordinary people to improve themselves, evolve, move up. Previously the peasants had only a scant idea of how wealth was acquired. They had no access to those mechanisms under the feudal system. The divine right of kings had emerged because the people were so poor and all land was owned by the king. Nourishment came from the land, and so nourishment came from the good grace of his or her majesty. Few ever saw the king or queen; royalty lived in a different dimension from the common folk. It was natural for peasants to believe their kings and queens to be gods or at least the embodiment of God on earth.

The divine right of kings began to die out once the common folk closed the spiritual and psychological gap between themselves and the monarchy. After the Industrial Revolution, the evolutionary process of winning freedom was no longer restricted to gods; gradually it opened to anyone with drive and talent. That's why America fought the war against the King of England. The founding fathers in their great wisdom could not accept the idea that the King or the British aristocracy should have precedence over the new world to lord over people who lived in what was basically another dimension across an ocean. The founding fathers wanted a system in which anyone could empower themselves to complete spiritual, financial, and religious freedom.

As the Planetary Group Soul progressed through the Industrial Revolution into the 19th century it became more aware. It developed confidence from which came a need to express itself. Gradually the Group Soul saw that it could possibly free the major part of itself (the common people) by uncoupling itself from the control of its minor part, represented by the elite. The hierarchical elite that has always controlled information and knowledge, and has retained all of the power, is in fact the world ego of the Planetary Group Soul. It controls and dominates the global playing field, and therefore the global soul, just as an individual's ego normally controls his or her life. The common people represent the spirit of the Planetary Group Soul which unpretentiously expresses the aspirations of humanity. The spirit of the Group Soul is required to remain silent and passive until the power of the ego is tamed.

The desire to liberate the people from under the dominance of the world ego was first taken up by the Anarchists. The word "anarchy" has come to mean civil disorder and terrorism, but

the original concepts of anarchy were very spiritual. The idea
first came from two Englishmen, Gerrard Winstanley who was
an agrarian reformer who wanted to return ownership of the
land to the people, and William Godwin who wrote *Political
Justice* (1793). He argued for the abolition of government,
saying that all authority is unnatural and that people should be
free to live their lives according to the dictates of reason.
However, the father of anarchy is considered to be Pierre-
Joseph Proudhon, who was born in France in 1809. His book
What is Property? (1840) gave birth to a loosely knit political
movement based on the belief that if government and the status
quo were abolished people would live in natural harmony. The
anarchists originally expressed a compassionate and spiritual
ideal. It was only later that their ideas were picked up by the
more violent revolutionaries like Mikhail Bakunin and Errico
Malatesta, who pushed against the status quo, threatening its
stability with terrorist acts. It was the revolutionary anarchists
who helped trigger the First World War with the 1914 assassination of Archduke Francis Ferdinand of Austria in Sarajevo,
by the Serbian terrorist, Gavrilo Princip.

15

Ironically, though the anarchists never made any real impact
on the power structure of that time. The First World War set us
upon the path of the Proudhon's vision. The war was a turning
point in the spiritual evolution of the western people. It was an
inevitable outcropping of the European and world ego out of
control and under threat. In human terms, the war was looked
upon as tragic, but in metaphysical terms, the war was the great
liberator of humanity. The conflict was a painful experience for
the masses (eight million died) sacrificing themselves for the
cause of the Planetary Group Soul, but it was an equally painful
experience for the ego of the ruling hierarchies. The aristocracy
was wiped out on mainland Europe and the English aristocracy
suffered great losses as well. The war so devastated Europe it
had the effect of forcing the ego of the status quo into retreat.
Many things changed after the war. The dominance of the
European elite was loosened. This was of great benefit to the

survivors of the war and to those who came afterwards. The spirit of the people was released to flow upwards.

You can't underestimate what both the two world wars did for the spiritual evolution of the people. Any time the ego gets a whack in the mouth, the spirit finds room to move. The first great war of 1914-1918 eliminated the Victorian era and set people on the road to freedom. The Roaring Twenties was an expression of that new found liberty. Women in Britain got the vote. But, the upward mobility of consciousness was checked by social factors and economic woes. This resulted in the Nazis providing the next great enema for mankind. Anytime the world ego suffers the kind of drubbing as it did during the two great wars, the fear that mentally binds and dominates the common people is loosened. Suddenly people won't accept the old order any longer—they see what little it did for them. The Planetary Group Soul had won a great victory.

The Second World War wiped out almost all the remaining European royalty and so once again the status quo had to give up more of its control. In the nineteen fifties the movement to establish freedom became a powerful spur. Suddenly we were able to dream. We dreamt a bigger dream—the dream of a society based on merit, not birth right, with equal opportunity for all. This bigger dream looked as if it might be possible. But within every success there is the embryo of failure. The post-war years were prosperous and the working people began to do quite well. They bought houses, moved to the suburbs, and expanded their possibilities. Socialism took care of the less successful and everyone became reasonably comfortable. But the hierarchy still controlled and dominated almost every-thing. In effect, they had bought off the rising consciousness of the working people by allowing those individuals to rise a notch or two. Many moved up from the working class to the middle class, and the rest were better off through socialism even though they had to stay where they were. Everyone forgot about freedom for a while, and ignored the fact that the elite still dominated. Common people fell for the illusion that by moving up they were headed for the social strata of the elite. Everyone was happy just to be going in the right direction.

However, once the initial flurry of consumption was over, people once again began to question. The Planetary Group Soul, having rested upon a comfortable plateau, was now ready to climb once more. It knows that its heart and spirit are embodied in the mass of humanity. If it wants to grow spiritually, it has to liberate itself from the dominance of its ego. This uncoupling is a natural progression for the Planetary Group Soul to make. It is a macrocosm of the same process that goes on within you in your own spiritual development. As you looked within and meditated upon your life, you took on spiritual ways. Soon you realized that if you wished to progress as a conscious being, you had to control your ego and allow your heart and spirit to win back influence over your life.

17

The uncoupling of the Planetary Group Soul from under the hierarchy's thumb is still only a thought-form in the collective dreamtime of mankind. But because it is there, and because people think about it, a distance has developed between the people and the system. Millions of people are disenchanted— they are mentally walking away, even if reality forces them to stay and play the game. The grandiose and magnificent process that you will witness over the years to come is the heart and spirit of the Planetary Group Soul breaking free from the dominance of its ego.

The Group Soul of our planet is only now waking to that magnificent new idea. Like a giant prehistoric creature rising up from its primordial state, it has become aware, stretching itself to realize that its destiny lies in a higher consciousness. Its eyes are now open—it can see itself. It understands that it is in fact one soul, as well as five billion separate parts. The brotherhood and sisterhood of our people has finally been conceived, and will be birthed and made real. Its conception was expressed after the war with the formation of the United Nations.

Next came Martin Luther King and the civil rights movement. While initially Martin Luther King spoke just for his people—insisting that the Afro-Americans were equal to the European-Americans—he also came to speak for the brotherhood and sisterhood of all humanity. He said the things he did because there was truth and justice in the vision that the Group Soul had created through its realization of itself. Somehow Martin Luther King knew the contents of the dreamtime, wherein lie the unconscious thoughts of humanity. Before King, and before the Planetary Group Soul began to consider uncoupling itself from its ego, no one had a definite idea of the Group Soul's inner direction or its dream. Yes, people had had inklings, strange unusual thoughts about freedom had dribbled into their waking consciousness for a hundred years or more, but now the time had come. Previously, people were still evolving. They were too busy fighting wars or recovering from wars to take much notice of the Group Soul's direction. You see, before Martin Luther King, no one had spoken for the Group Soul for a very long time.

Then along came a very humble black man, closely connected to the tribal heritage of man, who knew what was in the dreamtime of the Group Soul. He stood tall in the authority of that vision and called upon us to remember the dream. He told us what he had seen. King had been to the dreamtime—he knew what the Group Soul of humanity wanted. So he stepped forward proudly and fearlessly, and began to utter the most powerful and immortal words spoken this century. He called out saying, "I have a dream..." As he began that memorable speech, his words exploded, touching the hearts and souls of many millions of men and women. He was the voice that spoke for us all. His ideas flowed through the minds of his listeners, beyond ego, race, and power—touching the spirit within. He spoke directly to the very core of the collective unconscious of

Death of the World Ego

America and beyond—to all humanity. Martin Luther King was for a brief moment the collective unconscious made manifest. He said that the spirit of humanity would from that day forth insist that every part of itself be equal. He said that the dream demanded we should all be free. When he spoke out against the Vietnam war the ego panicked and shot him.

Jesus, too, had spoken for the Group Soul, saying to his people that they didn't need the Jewish religious hierarchy to worship God, for God was within. The energy of the early Christians must have been too unassuming for them to accept that message completely. The Planetary Group Soul wasn't ready—it couldn't run with the idea. Absolute freedom was too scary. So people translated Jesus' marvelously liberating idea into the need for a different hierarchy, one that people could use instead of Jewish law. So, just as the socialist unions became part of the status quo, the Christian church evolved the same way.

Kennedy began to speak to the Group Soul of his people in his famous "Ask not..." speech. He said that Americans should move from the perspective of the ego that asks, "What am I going to get," to the larger viewpoint that asks, "What can I contribute?" But Kennedy, though a great man, never really spoke for the world vision. Unlike King, President Kennedy was part of the elite, and adulterated as he was, by the influence of his brother, he succumbed to the corruption of power. He infringed on the South American people and did his best to assassinate Castro. I believe the Group Spirit left him. He became exposed. Those at the top of the hierarchy took umbrage at his policy to reduce their armaments, and so Kennedy was involuntarily graduated to the next dimension.

Meanwhile, the Group Soul of our humanity continued to grow and learn about itself. The Western world has, for the most part, moved through the Industrial Revolution into the age of information and technology. The Asian world has graduated out of the tribal sector into the industrial sector, and

Africa, Pacific islands, and remote parts of our planet hold to the nature spirit for balance.

Technology allowed the controlling hierarchies to expand their ability to create phony money by expanding debt via a few digits on a computer. Money went from real worth to a receipt exchangeable for worth, to the receipt itself as worth, then to a thought-form punched out on a computer terminal that credits brand new money to someone's account. As paper was eliminated as too slow and cumbersome, the flow was no longer inhibited by the speed of a press. Now money could move at the speed of light. But it was still mostly in the hands of the status quo or in the hands of those who had joined the status quo through their commercial efforts. When people began to object to the monopoly of power and affluence that had been created, the government rolled out their spokespeople to sell everyone on a new idea called—"trickle down economics." The theory claimed that crumbs which fall from the banquet table will eventually reach the people, making everyone better off.

The people munched the crumbs and enjoyed them, but it gave them no real power. They could see and hear those at the top of the hierarchy enjoying a banquet far above them, and the people naturally wondered if the trickle down effect included a second course. Unfortunately, the banquet cost such a prodigious amount of money, those at the top of the hierarchy began to hold on to what they had and the trickle fell to silence.

Meanwhile, the consciousness movement has brought millions in touch with their inner selves. It is in this way that the Group Soul of our people will eventually have a voice. It is as if the myriad of parts that make up the Group Soul are now looking within and are beginning to speak of what they see in the deepest recesses of the inner mind and its dreamtime. Soon people will see the vision and will recall its images, speaking of the contents of that dream. Then everyone will know the truth and they will see how the people of this planet will eventually grow and evolve.

That's where we are today, in the mid-nineties. Now here's how power, money, and the evolution of the Planetary Group Soul will unfold given time.

On the surface it seems there is no way to break the power of the megapolitical monopolies or the control of money and information which governments and the status quo enjoy. It would seem that the Planetary Group Soul is doomed to rest inside the clutch of that one minute part of itself that imposes its will upon the greater whole.

But all extremes of power expressed through ego eventually destroy themselves. When a political or social system enjoys unbridled power there's no realistic check to the limit of that power. Expansion by the ego is compulsive. It has to reach continually for an unreachable immortality. It has no way to stop because it cannot see clearly outside of itself. In its blindness, it has no accurate point of reference; like travelling on a train at night with the curtains drawn—you can't tell where you are or how fast you are going. When the ego expands further and further beyond itself, it begins to lose control.

If Hitler had stopped the war at the end of 1940, fascism would have controlled all of mainland Europe. He could have made peace with England and isolated it, and simply left the Russians alone. He could have done a trade deal with the American hierarchy— they usually follow the money trail. I doubt if America would have attempted to liberate Europe if trade and a modicum of freedom had been restored. Europe might still have been fascist today. But power will not voluntarily suffer limit on itself, because the ego can't limit its need for importance and immortality. Ironically, it was the march to Moscow in a blizzard that felled Napoleon, and then Hitler, and it's the same allegorical march through the cold winds of realism that will topple the modern echelons of power. The huge volume of debt that socialism and government spending requires eats into large chunks of the total money the government squeezes from the people. Right now, some governments are paying up to forty percent of their national income just in interest payments on their national debt. Every currency unit they pay out in interest is a unit over which they have no control. Debt gradually loosens the grip of the status quo and its ability to manipulate affairs.

22   When you read in the papers that the government has just spent twenty or thirty billion dollars or pounds or whatever, that it doesn't have, rather than getting depressed and worrying where the nation is heading, you should rejoice. Put pen to paper, write to your political representative, congratulate them on their foresight, encourage him or her to spend even more. Insist on it—you'll be doing us all a favor. The more they spend money that they haven't got, the better it is for us in the long term, even though it may cause problems in the short term. However, the important thing to remember is that having them in power causes a perpetual problem for us—short term and long term!

Power comes from the ability to legislate, but without money, legislation is useless. It is money that glues countries together. Once the money stops, the separate units that make up a country move away from the influence of central control. In the US, for example, the Federal government has begun to return power to the states. This is because the Federal government does not have the money to impose the control it once enjoyed.

Given the US government's current differential between income and spending, by the year 2118 it will need one hundred percent of its income simply to service the national debt. It follows that the top of the political hierarchy is bound to lose control of America. Unless they change their ways, they're trapped. They can't stop spending or they'll lose influence and political power—but as they spend, they lose power anyway by creating more debt that must be serviced. They have no real choice other than spend, spend, spend until there's nothing left. That is the nature of ego; it can't accept a voluntary lessening of its godlike influence. If those at the top of the hierarchy gave away their power, they would have to return to a mortal world, to be cast down into the hellish dimension of realism—the lot of common folk. We know that by the year 2118, at the very latest, the union of the United States of America is bound to undergo tremendous change. It may very well unravel if it doesn't change its ways. The individual states will take back their power and probably vote themselves out of the Union. Smaller groupings may form a confederation of states to replace the United States, but the country as we know it today may cease to exist politically. Its controlling power structure will be decimated.

American history books tell us that the Union of the United States of America was a natural, voluntary process whereby the states cheerfully agreed to unite under the control of the government in Philadelphia—when in fact, the Union was created by force. Anyone wishing to leave the Union was shot. The Civil War started when South Carolina and the other southern states seceded to form the independent Confederacy (1861). The Union is not a natural alignment, it is one created by war, just as the Soviet Union created an unnatural coalition of states, united by force under Moscow's dominance. The eastern states of America captured the south, then extended their power base by annexing Indian or Spanish lands that they didn't already control, incorporating those lands to form the western states. There was nothing voluntary about the process at all. Washington's dominance over the American people is only sustained by force and money. It has no real authority other than the authority common people are obliged to offer autocrats in return for their lives. We ridicule Third World military dictatorships as being rinky-dink. But there is almost no Western nation that was not originally established as a military dictatorship. The only difference is that our dictator-ships are old, whereas African or South American military dictatorships are new. Otherwise they are exactly the same.

Some might argue that our rulers have the legal right to impose themselves upon us given that we have granted them the power to do so via the electoral process. But "legal" is just a way of describing the process by which the ego of the status quo enacts its will. There is no basis for it, in my opinion. The democratic hoodwink offered to the electorate is a scam. People are not allowed to make real decisions. There are no proper choices. What kind of democracy is it when your choice is simply who among two or three political parties will feed off you and the country for the next two or four or six years? If there was a little box on the ballot form which allowed people to check "none of the above," and that meant we could get rid of the hierarchy, then you could say we have a democracy. However, the system has ensured that we can't get rid of it by keeping all the power and the decision-making to itself. The electoral process—of which we are all so proud—is nothing more than the process by which we choose which part of the nation's mostly male ego will impose itself upon us. We are voting for prison guards. We are not voting to open the gate.

People are only now waking up to the idea that they don't have to be victimized by the system. There isn't a good excuse for it. Tax is mostly theft. Laws are manipulations. Neither are com-pulsory and neither have any intrinsic spiritual worth. Legisla-tion bends reality and the overall evolution of our people into an unnatural state. As the status quo steals the people's money, it elevates itself to safety, relegating many of the common people to a zone of economic activity where survival is precari-ous. So while two or three percent of the population remain secure with little effort, the rest are disempowered and stressed by their vulnerability to real dangers and financial collapse. That is why you see such social chaos.

Death of the World Ego

Up 'til now, money flowing out of the government has allowed most people to simply survive. But that proximity to danger is so uncomfortable and unnecessary that sooner or later our people won't stand for it any more. So far there have been a few minor popular revolts, like the property tax roll back movement in California in the 1970's and the Poll Tax revolt in Britain—where people had courage to look down the barrel of the gun and tell the government to piss off.

But, as governments run out of money, the economic uncertainty of those at the lower level of society will soon bring them out into the streets. They will see that the right to a stress free existence is not the exclusive right of a white male status quo, nor is it a right granted from above. It is a right we all have by virtue of our abilities. If a man or a woman needs twenty hours of diligent effort to secure their livelihood for a week, that's all they should have to put in, if that is all they want to do. By creaming and manipulating and terrorizing people, the government requires the nation's workers to put in forty hours per week, or more, to reach minimum economic safety. Government deductions and imposts are cleverly calculated to ensure that no one ever really gets too far ahead. Each week the nation's workers are in as precarious a position as the week before. They are forced to go out and work forty more hours just to stay in the same spot. This allows government and industry to control the nation and dominate the supply of labor and people's actions. But as people become more aware, they won't tolerate scrimping by each week. People need money to establish a spiritual strength. It's very hard to grow spiritually if you are forced into *tick-tock* for most of the week just to survive. This leaves you without extra money to purchase life's experiences and develop ideas. In the olden days, lobbing the peasants a few pennies so they wouldn't starve was enough. It bedded down the peasants' survival issues. That same principle still applies for many people today who don't look far beyond surviving and having a few beers on the weekend. But as humanity expands its consciousness, and millions of people move from ego to spirit, being financially secure becomes only a part of the issue. Empowering your quest in life and having freedom of action is equally important.

Once our population grows beyond survival issues and begins to look at what it really needs for spiritual advancement, it will see that the world ego pillages and disallows that advancement. You can control people only so far through intimidation and the control of economic opportunity. If you attempt to get in the way of their spiritual beliefs and personal advancement, they will rise and fearlessly swamp you. History is replete with examples of holy wars.

During this time, there are massive, often unilateral national groupings forming the political divisions of our planet. Vast tribes have been united by force or through the influence of money. At times they were united by the need for a common defense, but when the cold war ended that need went out the window. Many national groupings have become stale and unnecessary. Once the central grip is loosened, the various tribes will split away. Nations will explode, separating into smaller and smaller parts. That's the only way to create fresh new possibilities—and the only way power can be returned to the people.

The process has already begun. People don't quite understand what it means. They think that the troubles in Europe are ethnic wars. They are, in a way. But more than anything else, it is the process whereby groups attempt to unravel the unnatural borders forced upon them by treaties and agreements to which they were not a party. The blame lies with the manipulators who carved up populations to their benefit. Across the world, groups are beginning to pull away from hierarchical dominance and are attempting to establish autonomy over their affairs. The Scots and the Irish are trying to get out from under the English. The Basques are giving the Spanish government a hard time. The Czechs and the Slovaks have already split.

Northern Italy, tired of being milked by a corrupt government in Rome, is trying to disconnect itself from the south. Russia and Yugoslavia have already exploded into many parts. The process is well and truly under way. People realize that they'll never be free as long as large central governments and national groupings are forced upon them. Europe may eventually split into myriad autonomous states.

The Maastricht Treaty, which is supposed to unite Europe into one great homogeneous blob, is bound to collapse eventually. It is contrary to the wish of the Group Soul. Europeans have been manipulated and lied to by their governments. The treaty has been sold as a manifestation of the brotherhood of Europe; offering a common currency, a common passport, a common defense, and common goals. People have bought it, trusting it, believing it to be a part of the greater vision.

But the treaty is not a spiritual idea from the collective dreamtime of the people. It is legislation imposed from above that would subject the Europeans to unbridled control and manipulation. The brotherhood and sisterhood of mankind cannot be a political grouping enforced through power. It must rise naturally as a collective spiritual identity coming from the love and the humanity we share. It will only happen once everyone understands and agrees that we are all part of the one spiritual soul.

Politics will always go for an evolutionary short cut that offers them control. John Major, the British prime minister, refused to allow his people a referendum on the treaty for fear of jeopardizing his political future as a puppet for British power. If he'd lost the Maastricht issue he'd be gone. Seventy percent of Brits hated the treaty and wanted no part of it, but they were denied a vote. Again, the ego of the nation overruled its heart. When the bill to ratify the treaty came to Parliament, the issue was hotly debated and the parliamentary vote looked very close. Dissident MP's in John Major's party were threatened with retribution and exposure if they didn't toe the line and vote with their wimpy leader. The bill passed with a slim majority. The Maastricht Treaty is a magnificent piece of skullduggery and power brokering. It has been sold to the Europeans in a blanket of lies. Europe has a parliament that people vote for, but the control of the Economic Community is vested not in the parliament but in the hands of the EEC Commissioners. The commissioners don't face election, they are appointed by the respective governments that make up the community. Power in Europe has moved from a democratic totalitarianism in which each country elects its own parliament, to a European democratic totalitarianism embodied in the European parliament. From there it has been moved one step further to an absolute dictatorship, imposed upon the European people by various elite hierarchies who rule over them and select the Commissioners.

I'm sure most Europeans would agree with the economic union and the idea of a greater Europe embodied in the spirit of friendship and cooperation. It's the subtle, often secret transfer of political power under the guise of these ideals that threaten their freedom. Half the time you can't really find out what in hell's going on. Most of Europe didn't even see the Maastricht Treaty. When the Danish voters did get to see the treaty, they turned it down, quite naturally. God bless Denmark. Unfortunately, the Danish government wasn't happy with the "no" vote, so another referendum on the Maastricht issue was ordered for the following year. The Danish media was cranked into overtime, and scare stories were run on television for months prior to the vote. Finally, a "yes" vote was procured with a comfortable majority. Which only goes to show that our leaders don't let democracy get in their way. However, once the voters of Denmark and the rest of Europe get a real taste of Brussels and Strasbourg's unilateral utopia, they'll get sorely pissed off. Heads will roll. The scam will be exposed and the basis of the treaty will be thrown out.

As the Group Soul grows, people are beginning to see that giving away your freedom and heritage for the prospect of better conditions or a free handout doesn't really work. It's not spiritual. Socialism initially helped people, but extreme socialism—whereby you sell your soul to the state which then controls and supports you for life, regardless of input—is an idea whose time has passed. It was a product of the Industrial Revolution. It doesn't belong to this age and it is contrary to where the Group Soul is going. Modern socialism cannot survive; its effect is to create the same short cut across the evolutionary lessons of this plane as that enjoyed by the power hierarchy. Socialism allows an individual to circumvent the spiritual lesson of transforming thoughts into action to manifest his or her dream. Under socialism, sustenance, and creative possibilities are granted by others. Providing for people hand and foot kills their spirit and disempowers them, creating slaves to the state bribe. It robs them of incentive and compromises their integrity.

The Group Soul cannot evolve properly while socialism binds millions of people into perpetual disempowerment. Eventually each has to become self-sufficient because first, it is spiritually correct and second, because the penalty of extreme socialism falls upon those who are creating energy. It drags them down and that stymies growth and the overall well-being and advancement of the Planetary Group Soul. Further, socialism gives our governments another excuse to meddle with people's lives under the thin guise of charity. This will be modified. Partly through the pressure of mounting debt and partly because it no longer exists as an agreement with the majority of people.

As people grow and become more courageous, they will pull away from the government nipple that controls them. They will heed the spirit calling from within themselves. They will want their freedom and spiritual birthright more than any pittance offered for their allegiance by the controllers of Animal Farm. People will burn with desire to fulfill themselves.

Of course, if the government didn't cream the people all of the time you wouldn't need socialism, you could have personal savings instead. But the impact of taxes is enormous. It impoverishes people, slows their evolution and forces them to work up to half of every week for the state. For instance, if you start your employment when you are eighteen and pay $3,000 in various taxes the first year, you are denied that money for life. If, instead, you could keep it on deposit, tax free, at eight percent per annum until you are sixty-five, you'd have $111,000. Now if you added the same amount the next year, that would give you an additional $103,000. By the time you reach twenty-one, the tax you pay in just your first three working years denies you the massive sum of over $310,000 at age sixty-five.

The money that is squeezed out of the people over their working life would easily make everyone millionaires upon retirement. You wouldn't need the pittance offered by the state; senior citizens would be rich. Then the unspent part of those fortunes would go to their heirs, who would become even richer. Power would gradually move from the top of the hierarchy to the people. In reality, the vast majority of people die with little or no substantial assets. Of course, we are sold on the idea that if we don't have income tax, the government can't run the country. That is precisely my point. We only have income tax *because* the top of the hierarchy wants to run the country. In fact, we don't need income tax or the government. You could unwind socialism, reduce state control, privatize most of the government's functions and through a goods and service tax, you could run the country with a small but efficient civil service. A group of representatives and wise people could oversee various parts of the bureaucracy to make sure it did what the people wanted. But their function would be supervisory, not legislative.

The Planetary Group Soul is not yet sophisticated enough to toss out the idea of government, but it will come to that in the end. Structures will gradually unwind; it's inevitable. The reason I can say that with certainty is that, through inner perception and discipline, much of the population has risen metaphysically above its leaders. Though the common people exert very little external power, their inner power has grown silently and rapidly. Our leaders, focusing almost exclusively on external power, are being left behind on an inner level by the advance of spirituality in the nation. Once the gap grows big enough, the hold government has over the people will snap. The catalyst for this divorce will be the day the welfare checks begin to bounce. Purchasing people's docile acquiescence is the only way power is currently sustained. If the checks are reduced—or cease completely—the truth will suddenly dawn upon our people and they will challenge the legitimacy of the authorities.

You are an eternal spirit; you were free before you got here and you will be free once you leave. There will be no government over you in the celestial worlds. Meanwhile, you have accepted this compact state of spiritual existence inside a physical body so that the spirit within you may better strengthen, understand, and perceive itself through the increased gravity that the density of the physical state offers. Then, as you turn within, developing silence and serenity, you'll feel the spirit and see the dream. You won't seek external power, for you will have a real immortality that comes from the control of your ego through discipline. You will reconnect to your spirit. Teach that to others and soon the idea will reach critical mass, then it will be "Over, Rover," for the system as we know it today.

Thereupon, us dear, sweet humans, who have for the most part a great deal of goodness inside us, will be able to get on with our spiritual understandings. Once the dreamtime of the Group Soul spreads over us all, any idea that is contrary to the spiritual tenant of the dreamtime will sound so repulsive it will not have a basis upon which to establish itself. The kingdom of heaven will finally be made manifest upon earth. The idea that you have to struggle to earn your freedom from the repulsive ego of the state is rubbish. It's the same as the police chief exercising his largesse by not imprisoning you. It's crooked and phony. You don't have to earn your freedom—you are free. You can't imprison the God Force forever.

Unfortunately, the process whereby the ego gives up control to the spirit usually takes place only through collapse. It's almost impossible for the ego to release its grip voluntarily in the same way as most individuals don't begin their inner spiritual journey until disaster strikes—be it illness, financial collapse, mental stress, or perhaps a marriage breakdown. It will take a crisis to shrink the world ego to the point where the spirit can begin to win back control.

The initial reaction will be that the system becomes more oppressive. You will see great social upheavals and an expansion of surveillance and the police state. But eventually it will all melt away. The ego is cowardly; it cannot face the light of God, for if does, it will see itself reflected there. It will not care for a close look at that image. Once our brothers and sisters around the planet represent a large enough quantum of spiritual light, the change will take place. Why? Because there are natural laws that guarantee it. Dr. Wayne Dyer writes in *Real Magic*: "According to the laws of physics, when enough electrons line up within an atom to form a position, then all the rest automatically line up in a similar fashion. This is called *phase transition*, . . . our world is experiencing phase transition. The invisible force that aligns the electrons within an atom, that spiritual intelligence that flows through all form, is reaching critical mass in large enough numbers of humans, and the results are to be manifest in our world. The force cannot be stopped. Some will try, but they will be swept away . . ." All the major political and spiritual developments in the next twenty years will stem from the tussle between the world ego and the spirit of the Group Soul of our humanity.

Death of the World Ego

Here, in this first volume of *Whispering Winds of Change*, we can look at many of the overall issues which will dominate the battle of consciousness between ego and spirit on a personal, national, and international level. Hopefully, I can offer you some ideas that will help you enjoy the process. Nations will give way to states, who in turn will give way to small municipalities. Eventually, when we all grow a little more and take full responsibility, each person can potentially become a nation unto themselves. The power and the ecstasy of the Planetary Group Soul will be immense as each human touches and expresses his or her personal light.

There is no longer any reason for us to suffer the forced march imposed upon us. We can have our own drum. We're bigger now than we were before. They still don't get it. We are going to have to tell them. I don't believe in violence. However, I do believe we have to take an assertive approach. It has to be spiritual, polite, and loving; remembering, of course, that the hierarchy is the ego. We can't completely kill off the ego of the Planetary Group Soul just yet, we have to get it to move over.

Each conscious person can help the process enormously. Let us set aside our differences, and come instead from the spiritual connection that the Planetary Group Soul offers. Give it voice. Stand fearlessly and call out to others saying, "I, too, have seen the dream. I, too, speak from the authority of that vision and I say, 'Sir, Madam, blessing and peace. We want our people back—every man, woman, and child. We want them and we want them now!'"

From the mouths of babes....

The Tribal
Folk Spirit

CHAPTER TWO

T o understand how the spiritual part of the Planetary Group Soul will gradually flow over the world ego, we have to go back momentarily and look at the components of the planetary soul and how each of us evolve within it.

The Group Soul of humanity is made up from the collective mind and spiritual identity of everyone that has ever lived, and those who are living today. I believe it is the inherent, immortal memory of our planet, as well as being the collective unconscious. I see the Group Soul as a personality evolving in the same way as you evolve, albeit over a greater length of time.

Although humans are individuals, they tend to evolve in groups, especially in ancient times, when people were less independent. The old tribal groupings created a defined quantum of energy with its own particular characteristics. The spiritual identity of a tribal grouping is referred to in ancient teachings as the "folk spirit" of the tribe. It is said the folk spirit of each clan contains its tribal memory. What Australia's Aboriginal people would call their "dreamtime." For tens of thousands of years the population of our world, whether princes or paupers, evolved inside the mind set of these confined tribal units. Sure, some individuals wandered off and traveled, but when they did so they carried with them their tribal culture and heritage. So even though Marco Polo went to China he never ceased to be a Venetian.

Though tribal members are separate personalities, and each have their individual potential within tribal structure, they have no real way of fully expressing that individuality. They all dress and speak the same. They eat the same food. They have shared common thoughts, religions, and customs. They mimic each others' actions. Spiritually you have difficulty in telling them apart.

Imagine an Amazon tribe that has had no contact with the outside world—it evolves as one unit. The tribe has one voice that describes its collective unconscious, its heritage and customs—the ideas it believes in. That tribal quantum, or identity, rests inside and forms a part of the collective identity of the Planetary Group Soul. Imagine the Planetary Group Soul as a large fishing net. And imagine that inside that net are one million tennis balls—each ball representing one of the world's tribes. Prior to the Middle Ages the Planetary Group Soul was almost entirely constructed of just these tribal quanta. Each clan providing one word in the cosmic sentences that the Planetary Group Soul might utter when describing itself. Now imagine if one man leaves that Amazon tribe, goes off and finds work, and marries a Portuguese girl. Previously in his dreamtime—his subconscious memory—he was a part of the folk spirit of his people. He was inside their "tennis ball." Because he now has a separate existence, bit by bit his tribal memory wanes and is replaced by a new memory which reflects his new circumstances and attitudes. That man's children would be born outside the Amazon folk spirit. They would evolve inside their mother's and father's new identity. His children's children would be even further removed, even though some customs and traditions may be passed down from generation to generation.

So in this example, the Group Soul of our planet now contains all the tennis balls it had before, including the one marked "Amazon Tribe," but it now has a brand new spiritual component, embodied in the man that departs to form his own breakaway tribe. It is as if the original tribal quantum has now emitted a separate electron creating two distinct units, and therefore more energy.

The Middle Ages saw the beginning of this process of individualization, but it wasn't until the Industrial Revolution in the 1800's that people really began breaking free from the grip of the ancestral mind. The European diasporas began with troubles in Russia and ethnic pressure in the Austro-Hungarian empire, along with economic pressure, such as the Irish famine of the mid 1840's. This forced a mass migration of people from their homelands to other places, including America. The geographic separation of people from the lands of their dreamtime caused an elasticity in the folk spirit of tribes. The folk spirit began to stretch, loosening its grip. Prior to the 1800's, the idea of a person having a separate destiny—that is, an individual evolution outside his clan—was rare. Few even considered the idea. The feudal system and the lack of physical and economic mobility required everyone to stay within their social and tribal units. Where you were born was often where you spent your life.

But the restriction was greater than that. Most people could not read, there was very little dissemination of information and hardly any influence from outside forces. Whatever the tribe knew and believed is what formed the dominant strain of a person's thoughts and personality. There was very little free thinking. Certainly, there were philosophers, scientists, and a few books offering new ideas, but a lot of this "new" thinking was just sophisticated variations of religious or tribal thinking; it did not impact the mass of humanity since most could not read. New ideas and scientific discoveries rested among the intelligentsia, which numbered relatively few people. While Isaac Newton was formulating his laws of gravity, peasants in the countryside went about the same as ever. It wasn't until the time of the Industrial Revolution that science began to have real, practical applications that could affect people and their consciousness. Until that time the mass of humanity was never exposed to anything that was particularly different or new. They didn't want to be exposed. People weren't ready. The communal mind of the old tribes were very disturbed by unusual thoughts. Suspicion and ignorance dominated. That is why loners, eccentrics, and outsiders were considered a threat. Tribes are usually xenophobic. Foreigners and strange ideas are viewed as compromising the psychic integrity of the tribe and a threat to its safety.

Everything remained as it was until the beginning of the last century when the Planetary Group Soul went through a "big bang" much like the universe did at the beginning of time. Industrialization and mass migration caused the tribal units to separate into more and more parts. Individuals left to find work. Once the people exited *en masse* from the immediate grip of their tribal folk spirit they were partially liberated. They could imagine and dream more freely. They began to hold independent thoughts and express themselves in a liberated and less restricted way. Philosophy, inventions, and ideas spewed forth at great speed. The mind of man was slowly being set free. Now, the Planetary Group Soul contained millions of partially independent electrons in addition to all the original tribes. That gave the Planetary Group Soul a previously unknown velocity.

Yet tolerance was a new idea. It only came about once people left their tribal homes and began developing true individuality. As long as the world rested in its tribal state the idea of one planet, one people, was impossible. The tribes and various developing nations were too insecure and deeply entrenched within their own perceptions to accept others. Tolerance has only taken on real meaning in modern times, as businesses became multinational and ordinary people were exposed by communication to a global scenario.

The Tribal Folk Spirit

The process is very slow. It has taken a hundred and fifty years
to date, and it is not complete by a long way. Even today only
about twenty percent of Americans have passports. Most
Americans live inside the American mind. They have little or no
real knowledge or interest in the outside world. Global events
are not discussed unless they are in some way connected with
America. However, the people of the world are gradually
getting out from under the dominant strain of their cultural
programming. The continued mass migration of people since
the Second World War (after which many immigration controls
were relaxed) has eventually led to the creation of multi-
cultural societies. In the same way that the European diasporas
forced people to migrate—thus stretching their psychological
and intellectual boundaries—intermarriage between people of
different cultures created a "big bang" in the tribal gene pool
(which contains the genetic part of the tribal memory). Previously, the gene pool rested almost exclusively in the tribes, as
marriage to outsiders was frowned upon or strictly forbidden.
Cross-fertilization of genes from different tribes has created
another subtle but important stretching of the folk spirit. It has
assisted the one-world, one-people idea. Education and information is also prying open the cultural grip. As it does, more
and more people find the courage to step toward freedom. This
mass exit from the folk spirit will eventually allow the people
of our planet to become spiritually free.

The way to understand it is this: Each person has an immortal
spirit within them. While people rested within the tribes that
immortal spirit had no way to fully realize itself. It could not
express a complete independence. It could only passively
contribute to the folk spirit of the tribe. Most individuals are not
strong enough yet to walk away—they need the tribe around
them and the cultural familiarity it offers to give them security.

The process of individualization is a major step for humanity.
Until you break away from your tribal heritage you cannot see
yourself properly. You don't have enough space between you

and the tribal folk spirit to observe yourself. Initially, the space you create may be geographic, but eventually it has to become a clearly defined psychological and spiritual distance. You may have already moved to the outer edges of your folk spirit, but until you break away completely, you can't become a fully independent spirit with an independent destiny. You are still partially in the communal tribal mind.

Think of it like this: You have personal thoughts, but your thoughts are not vastly different from others of your culture. Each morning a million tribal members rise and think, "Breakfast." If you are French, you will express what you consider is your individuality in the language and context of French culture. You will adopt the idiosyncrasies and nuances of French thinking and French pleasures. You will emotionally embrace French ways. You will probably consider French ways superior to those of other cultures. You will be familiar with other French people, and so on. Your individuality is expressed through the French folk mind and all things French. The same rules apply to any other cultural grouping. While in the emotional, intellectual, and social link of your culture, your individuality is limited by that very culture. Sure, you can put a gold staple in your nose and consider yourself a radical, cool dude. But in the end, it's a gold staple in a French nose, on a French face, behind which you express a French mind. Absolute spiritual individuality is not, as yet, *there*.

I have a notion that the spiritual process is similar to the laws of quantum physics, in which atomic and subatomic particles appear as waves of energy. Until you make the conscious decision that you wish to know a particle's exact position, then and only then does the particle in the wave individualize and become solid and independent, acquiring a definite position and a separate identity.

It seems to me that there is a correlation between our journey out of the folk spirit to individuality and the behavior of atomic and subatomic matter. While atoms oscillate together grouped in hazy, ill-defined wave patterns, it could be said that they exist in their tribal state. In that state they have no mass nor any absolute position, only the probability of a position. The wave is not made of solid matter, and of course it is not the atom itself that is undulating, but an amorphous disturbance of information. The way that a particle becomes solid and independent is through the conscious volition of an observer. Through and because of observation, the particle graduates from an evolution in the wave-motion state to become a separate identity that has mass and a definite place in the infinity of things. You could say it has taken on character and won its freedom from the influence of the wave to which it formally belonged.

Thus, it follows that the gap or space between a particle and its observer is a vital component in granting that particle a solid individuality. For if an observer were *inside* the particle when attempting to observe it, he could not establish a gap or space between himself and the particle—thus the particle could never become solid. Imagine the tribal folk spirit and its culture as a subatomic wave. While you rest inside the wave, it is impossible to observe yourself properly because what you are—your total energy—is oscillating as a component of that folk wave. There is no gap! Your spirit and the tribal folk spirit are mixed. You are spread throughout the wave and it, in turn, is spread through you. Your spiritual identity rests in a hazy probability pattern that constitutes the wave-motion of the cultural identity and folk spirit that is your tribe. Under these circumstances you can never become a separate particle. Thus, to particularize yourself, you have to stand back from the influence of the tribe—the wave interference that muddies your identity— creating a psychological and spiritual gap between you and it. Without the gap there can be no observation. Without observation you can never define yourself spiritually to a precise location or independent destiny.

When waves of subatomic particles cross each others' paths, they set up interference patterns; emotionally you could say they irritate each other. In fact, the waves could not be detected by scientific equipment if that interference did not occur. Thus, people in the tribal wave have to create agitation to be noticed. That's why moaning is a national pastime. Particles don't moan much, they just go fix their lives. Wave energy seeks others to fix things for it. While the mass of humanity rests inside the wave state of the folk spirit, world peace is unlikely. The subatomic nature of the interference patterns created by waves precludes it. Cultures oscillating in close proximity to others are bound to irritate each other, which eventually leads to trouble.

However, when enough people individualize to become separate spiritual particles, then each human in that state can coexist with others peacefully. Particles in the solid state, because they have a definite mass and an absolute and defined position, are more detached. There is an absolute space between each of them, so they don't irritate others. Generally, they exist without even touching other particles. Sure, on occasions, some subatomic particles may collide with others, but when they do, the explosion creates a burst of energy rather than the interfering, often deprecating energy that is in the wave state.

It is only through the particle state that we can have world peace. Detached harmony is a function of the solid state. That's why the center point of my philosophy has always been introspection, which establishes observation, and emotional detachment, which creates space. Then, through the discipline of not infringing upon others, you can disengage from the wave and the turbulence it creates. It, in turn, is liberated from the turbulence you create for it.

The ego's image of its separateness is only an aspiration, an illusion at best. It's not a real spiritual separateness that comes from establishing the inner solid particle state via observation and contemplation. The ego, existing in the wave, has no solid identity. It is bound to feel the insecurity and contradiction of the hazy state in which it oscillates. This is the exact opposite of what the ego hopes for. So the ego projects outward along the wave lines to others, seeking reassurance. "Tell me I'm OK, Tell me I'm right. Tell me I'm special. Define me through your observation of me."

Doing this, the ego is reaching for the particle state, hoping to establish a solid independence. When that doesn't work, it looks for oblique strategies that might establish it as special, usually through status and position. Thus, the ego seeks to differentiate itself from others, using the gold staple in the nose or by joining an exclusive club or, perhaps, an elitist religion.

That is why religions are successful in spite of the often simple and childlike nature of their teachings. They offer the ego— which is trapped in the wave—a spiritual transcendence by offering it the gap. "We, of this religion, are separate and distanced from the rest of humanity (the wave) whose destiny it is to be lost in the heat of hell's fire" (that is, in the oblivion of the hazy energy that defines the oscillation of wave-motion).

The whole object of elitism and status is that someone external to the holder of that status observe it. Otherwise, it's useless to the ego. That's why it's considered important for people of a church to come together regularly—so that they can practice their elitism, and more importantly, observe each other doing so. This establishes the illusion of each member's solid state. The futility of this practice is that you can't have a solid state in a wave pattern—tribal, religious, or subatomic.

That doesn't stop the ego from giving it a good try. Through elitism the ego hopes to establish its separateness and the presence of observers to that separation. That's why celebrity status and glamour are considered so important nowadays. The principle is right. It's the execution of the principle that's

43

wrong. So the ego spends $75,000 joining an exclusive country club hoping that might work. Unfortunately, the gap the ego has to establish between itself and others is not a social, external one; it's internal.

Introspection is the only way the gap can be truly established. Through introspection you establish mental control, denying the ego some of its outward projection. The ego doesn't like to lose influence which makes it insecure. The ego cannot allow itself to be killed off. So it will wrestle with you all the way. Sometimes winning, sometimes retreating, only to assert itself once more. The irony is that in order for the ego to attain its spiritual dream of a separate identity, it has to lose to the battle. Poor ego. It's stuffed.

Unlike a subatomic particle, the human mind—in which the ego dwells—can observe itself. So it doesn't need the love (concentration) of a scientist to make it solid and real. It can detach from the tribal wave and, rather than loving (concentrating) on the external world to make that reality solid, it can love itself. Through observation the mind can establish an independent identity in the inner spiritual world. By processing your mind and your emotions, you can liberate yourself from the anguish you inherited from the tribal wave. It's what psychologists and spiritual counselors call releasing. Once that psychological and spiritual discipline gets under way it creates an absolute space between you and the wave-like interference of the tribal folk spirit. Detachment further heightens the process, creating an absolute space between you and the emotions you inherit from others, and a further absolute space between you and your own emotions. You detach to become a particle. Your are now spiritually individualized, matured into an independent evolution of your own beyond the wave.

Interestingly, you can see the human progression from wave-motion to particle, as expressed through the evolution of dancing. Sacred tribal dances are group events. The participants bob up and down in wave-like motion, often in a circle, which is an externalized symbol of their conjoined spirits. They all perform the same movements. Sure, the tribal leader may put on a solo performance because of his or her special status, but the main body of the tribal dance is expressed as a wave

From there we developed what is now known as Old Time Dancing, like the Scottish Reel. Again it is a group dance where the participants follow set rules—there is no room for free expression. Ballet is a more sophisticated and liberated form of the group dance. The *corps de ballet* is the tribe; the soloists are their king and queen. Then ballroom dancing was developed. It has formally defined steps and rhythm, but now the group is down to only two members. The woman has little liberty as she is controlled and guided by the male. She goes backwards and he goes forwards, which is symbolic of our tribal traditions which say women should subject themselves to the male's vision. But there is some room for interpretation within ballroom dancing. When the two dancers finally separate, as in the Charleston or the Twist, each dancer performs almost the same movements, but the woman has her own vision free from the male's control. Finally, we progressed to modern disco dancing, where both parties are completely free to boo-ga-loo any way they wish. I see a transition in dancing that follows the journey from wave-motion to independent particle.

If only it were as easy as learning a new dance. In fact, the transition to complete personal freedom is not a simple one for people to make. Their clan offers security and a solidity that comes from familiarity and close friendships. Life in the wave is less exacting. Its hazy nature allows for a shared responsibility. The life of a particle is immediate and more clearly defined. It can't really shift personal responsibility as there are no hazy wave lines connecting it to others along which the transfer might be made. Therefore, the path to complete individuality is rather lonesome. It forces one to become self-sufficient. In the subatomic world, a particle's transcendence from wave-motion to the solid state is instantaneous. In our time world, the shift is slower and more gradual. The difficulty of making the shift has caused people to look for stepping stones between the safety of the tribal folk wave and the completely free particle state of absolute individualism.

Our Amazonian man who left the jungle to marry a Portuguese girl is no longer supported inside the safety and evolution of his tribe; he has formed a subculture. His subculture being small and new and lacking self-confidence, it would be surprising if the Amazon man and his family would have the power to exist psychologically on their own. So naturally our tribal man looks for a new alignment to which he and his family can belong. He probably finds a reassuring alignment inside a larger national identity which, in his case, would be Brazil. As time passes, he begins to consider himself Brazilian rather than Indian. His wife, who may have been a part of a Portuguese tribal grouping, has moved out of that molecule by marriage and she also would gradually look to a Brazilian identity. The man's tribe back home, resting inside the folk spirit of their people, would still consider themselves Indian.

So, too, the people of the west of England who for a thousand years considered themselves Cornishmen, have through the passage of time come to see themselves as Englishmen first and Cornishmen second. As the population drift continued over the last hundred and fifty years, a national spirit grew out of an amalgamation of tribes. Most people shifted their allegiance to the new national identity. Some tribal memory was sustained by the people who remained on ancestral lands, and ethnic cultures held together somewhat as tribal groups gathered to live in sections of urban cities. But over all, much of the tribal cohesion in our societies has fallen away to become a national temperament.

The drift from tribal alignment to national identity created the possibility of our modern nations. The process was partly social as well as political and military. The creation of a nation-state was the first step the Planetary Group Soul had made in thousands of years. But there is was no complete freedom of expression inside the nation-states, as tribal leaders were replaced by modern governments. The national culture is not as controlling as a tribal culture, but it still dominates people's thinking. We have moved towards autonomy, but by no stretch of the imagination could one say that we are free. In effect, we have shifted from a tribal wave to a bigger, more energetic national wave.

47

The two world wars decimated and scattered many ethnic groups. The First World War began the process, which continued after the Second World War, whereby many national units came together into clearly defined countries. Many of our national boundaries are fairly modern, most of them having been decided by conquest—many in this century. After the wars, much of the control vested in royalty and the upper classes unfortunately shifted into the hands of the government rather than to the people. What was left were governments in partnership with an industrial, commercial hierarchy. In England, part of the aristocracy survived, especially those families who had large commercial interests, but generally the social and economic grip of the aristocracy waned. During the fifties and sixties the consciousness of the people changed, as the country became more egalitarian and various Labour Governments wiped out hereditary wealth with swingeing death duties. What remained was government and big business.

The global mind is not yet a reality. People talk about it all the time, but in truth, the mass of humanity is poised somewhere between the tribal and the national mind, though there are millions who are beginning to separate from that to embrace a global view. They represent a small minority in the total world population.

Tribal and even national views are often jingoistic and very discriminatory. It stands to reason that if people exist partially or completely inside the wave-motion of their folk spirit, or even in the wave-motion of their national spirit, they would not have enough separateness to create a formal spiritual individuality—only the potential or probability of one. Having not yet separated to become a particle, they could not possibly fully respect or appreciate the individuality of others, since they have not achieved it themselves.

48

Though television has opened people's minds, the globalization process will still take time. It is all very well seeing others on a colored screen, but to understand the concept of the global family you have to expand your energy, travel, and meet your relatives. You have to experience the world. That's why people who take to the spiritual path travel a lot. But extensive travel is not possible for most people. The remnants of the psychically insecure tribal mind is still with us—though each generation is less discriminatory than the next.

The process isn't helped when governments use the media to glue their populations together by appealing to national pride, thereby hoping to foster loyalty to the nation and allegiance to the governing body. It is a way of keeping people locked in the national wave. One of the tricks constantly used is where the government of a country juxtaposes itself with the national identity, creating a hazy line in the minds of the people between two very separate components—the government of a nation and the nation itself. It is implied that allegiance (or at least passive acquiescence) to the government is required as a component of allegiance to the nation. The inference being—if you don't support the institutions of the nation, you are a traitor to your country. The lie is very subtly put. It speaks directly to the tribal or national mind, requiring citizens not to rock the boat and destabilize the integrity of the national wave.

The Tribal Folk Spirit

Appealing to the national pride, and thus bolstering its ego, is a propaganda industry unto itself. Vast media coverage is given to sporting events in which the nation is represented. Everyone is pumped into believing that the antics of a man or woman on a track is somehow the outcropping of a nation's greatness—that it is somehow a reflection of individual worth, and the by-product of the wonderful actions and policies of government. This is the reason why sports are so heavily promoted. Give people a little dancing ball to follow and they'll forget about that big ball which is the circumstances of their life. Jerking the national ego is a surefire way of distracting people from the real issues. Why are millions of people 'round the world, who may normally have no interest in sport, mesmerized by the Olympic games? It's because the vestiges of the old tribal mind, which has grown to become a national mind, is bolstered by even the slightest success. So a bronze medal in Ping-Pong creates a national hero in some places, and makes the people of that nation feel better about themselves. The remnants of the tribal mind are still very present. If your mind is global, you may watch the table tennis for the pleasure of it, but you wouldn't care much who won or lost. You certainly wouldn't go potty if a man or woman you have never met—who happens to have the same citizenship as you—does well. Their success would mean nothing to you because you're not programmed inside the national molecule. Most people are. A lot of care is taken to ensure our national leaders are linked in photo opportunities to sporting heroes—the basketball team on the White House lawn, the cricket team at Number Ten, Downing Street and so on. It's a propaganda ploy that seeks to link a political leader with the national triumph, implying that the leader was somehow responsible for that success. The international fervor over sporting events endorses the national ego, bolstering the illusion that the people of one country are special and separate from others. We won. The foreigners lost. We're better.

These rather stiff and childlike values are breaking down, and the development of a twenty-four hour global economy is showing people that they can't exist in national isolation. We have to reach out to others. Doing so, we have to learn about other people and respect them in order to trade with them. Trade develops friendship and trust, and so over time the clamp of the national mind set will loosen. Individuals can never be free until the national mind set is expanded to where we accept ourselves as a global people. The controlling hierarchies will always be able to depend on small-minded people, and the national ego in general, to endorse their power base and their actions. By pumping national pride, the government tethers people inside the national mind set, where it can sell them on the idea that whatever the government says is good for the country must also be good for the individual. You can sell that idea to people in the tribal wave because of the hazy connection they have with others in their wave-like existence. Of course, very few people have a precise idea of what actually is good for the country and what is not. They have little or no independent information. They tend to take the government's or media's word for it. Although they may not derive any personal benefit from some proposed legislation they submit, believing that if it benefits the whole it must also be said to benefit them. Cranking the concept of the collective national mind and its purported good, and playing on nationalism is how leaders control and manipulate the people. It is also the process whereby they get you to go to war to implement their policies.

Just as we had to eventually go beyond our tribal identities to evolve, one day we will have to release our national identities to be free. The political explosion of Eastern Europe and the coming devolution of many nations is a vital part of this overall process. By retreating into smaller political units we establish control over our affairs. Though smaller political units may initially impact us economically, in the end it's the only way we will ever control our destinies.

The Tribal Folk Spirit

The irony is that, for the Planetary Group Soul to grow, we have to learn to think globally and to act locally. The movement for higher consciousness is already creating the global mind. Political and economic upheaval will result in smaller, more controllable local units. Over the long term, the large nation-state is a dead duck.

If you discipline yourself and begin to control the ego by developing serenity and introspection, the spirit within grows. Its energy pervades your attitude taking you out of small-minded tribal ideas to a wider more expansive outlook. Our world now has many millions of conscious people who are moving past an allegiance to a national identity, toward a planetary identity born of spirit. It's through this shift in consciousness and the death of the world ego that the nation-state will gradually change and eventually disappear. You can't imprison a global mind in a national wave. In the long term it can't work. I think it's fair to say that the ecology movement is partially an outcropping of the global mind. It attempts to establish a global responsibility that can only be fully realized over time as we eventually become a global people.

The quest for a higher consciousness is very powerful if you think about it. As people begin to look within, what they are saying is, "I have gone beyond my tribal folk spirit, and I have progressed through the tick-tock rhythm of the Industrial Revolution, and I'm now placed beyond my national heritage, stepping toward the infinity of spirit within me." Turning within is the act of leaving the evolution of the earth plane.

The spiritual identity of the planet has gradually grown. Each person who has taken the journey influences others to do the same. Not just through example and personal contact, but because the Planetary Group Soul is in communication with itself. Thoughts and ideas silently leap from one human to the next, without us realizing it. We are all in a dialogue deep within the collective subconscious mind. That doesn't mean you can't be an independent particle out from the wave, it just means that we can communicate with each other. Nothing happens in a vacuum. If you drop this book on the floor it affects the whole universe, which adjusts for the change in the book's position. Everything is linked. There are tribal links, national links, universal links and probably links beyond that. I imagine the whole thing is just one vast mind with each component liberating itself so that eventually the whole mind can be set free. So back on our planet, if you come up with an idea that no man or women has ever considered, the very fact you have had that thought will allow others instantaneously to think the same thing. We are interconnected, because we come from the same place. Your body exists in the modern day, but its components are very ancient. For example, take a molecule of iron in the hemoglobin of your blood. That molecule was formed fifteen billion years ago at the time of the "big bang." It traveled across the universe from the beginning of time to the present day to perform a useful function in your blood stream. At a fraction of a second, 10^{-35} after the instant of the "big bang," the whole universe and the components of that iron molecule were compressed into a space about the size of a grain of brown sugar. Every human came from that highly compressed place, as did every galaxy and all of the stars. We are one. We straddle time from its inception to this day. The world mind, which exists as ideas and memories in the Planetary Group Soul, is also one.

To give you an example from my own experience, I'd like to explain how I feel certain that as humans we silently intercommunicate. Heat leaving the body stretches out like solar flares to a distance of about an inch. Beyond that, the electromagnetic energy of the body and mind stretches to a distance of about two to three feet. It is less pronounced in the lower part of the body and most pronounced in the area of the chest and around the head. The old writers called this electromagnetic field the etheric, a term they borrowed from Homer, and which I understand derives from a Greek root "to blaze." The etheric is easily visible to the naked eye providing you engage your peripheral vision. The rods of the eye are situated to the side and are more sensitive than the cones of the eye, which are in the center. So peripheral vision is more sensitive to subtle light and energy than direct vision.

By concentrating on your peripheral vision over a period of time you activate it. You have to remind the brain that you want that information. Over thousands of years our peripheral vision has weakened as we no longer need it to save us from predators. If you concentrate on your peripheral vision it will become more sensitive. Eventually, you will see the etheric energy that shines from people as they walk along. It doesn't take any particular psychic gift or spiritual quality; it's more a function of training your eyes to look for it. You have to tilt your head slightly so that light strikes the side of your eye as well as the center. Peripheral vision is affected by bright sunlight and unnatural light, such as neon. Dusk is the best time to see etheric energy.

The human etheric has distinct striations and patterns which are created by thoughts and emotions. You can't see the actual thoughts, you can only see the patterns they make. Broad bands and flashes of energy pass very quickly like mini-lightening bolts from the scalp to the outer limits of the etheric and peter out as their energy wanes. Along the front of the body the energy reacts mostly to emotion, and unlike the mental flashes leaving the head, the frontal movement tends to roll in waves that ripple from the neck and chest area downwards, fading to nothing as it passes the knees. Often the rolling motion is in a forward direction rolling away from the chest. This is also true of etheric energy in the genital area, which has a forward rolling motion, rather than a downward motion.

The rolling motion sometimes occurs over the head but is more pronounced down the front of the body. Energy flashing to the back of the body travels less far, usually not much more than from six inches to a foot. It is often much less distinct than the energy we project above us and in front of us. All of the energy moves when the individual moves. As we walk along we momentarily leave a ghost image behind us which delineates the space through which we have just passed. When two people in the street cross at close quarters or bump each other, the etheric of each leaps across to the other. An intermingling takes place. You can watch it. Then as the two individuals separate again, the etheric of each tries to stay in that intermingled state until the distance becomes too great, and the two energies pull apart. It's really interesting to watch. If a pretty girl passes a group of men you can actually see their etheric try to follow her up the road. Under normal circumstances, if you look at a person at a distance with normal vision, occasionally they'll notice you staring at them, but usually not. However, as soon as you "click" to your peripheral vision and pick up their etheric and hold the sight of it for even a split second, they will immediately notice you, even if you have not projected any particular thought or sound toward them. Ninety times out of a hundred, the person will feel your perception upon them and will turn slightly or completely in your direction. They don't even know why they are turning—it's instinctive. Exceptions occur when they are deep in thought, or if they are in the midst of an emotional wave, reacting to a feeling they are experiencing.

Recently, I was sitting at a hotel in Hawaii. Between the hotel's restaurant and the sea is a foot path that holiday-makers wander along, going from one end of the beach to the other. Sitting there at dusk with friends discussing the etheric phenomena, I started to lock on to the passersby—what I call "tapping." I'd point out a passerby to my friends and then I'd tap that individual and make them turn toward me. I counted as I ran through about forty people. Only four failed to turn.

Now, if I were projecting a particular thought at those people, you might say that the fact they turned was as a result of some form of thought transference. Or, you might say I experienced thirty-six coincidences. But I've played this game often and showed it to others so many times that it's gone past the possibility of chance. I know for certain that in just perceiving or looking at a person's etheric they feel it on an inner level, and they turn to wonder where the feeling is coming from. This phenomena makes me sure we are all interconnected at a deeper level. Under certain circumstances, of which we are not sure of yet, our thoughts travel.

The distance for visual etheric perception may be limited to forty or fifty yards with accurate sight, but, in the collective unconscious of humanity, I believe there is no limit. We are all part of the same dream. Again, don't get confused between the idea of our planetary interconnection at the unconscious level and the idea of spiritual evolution following the rules of waves and particles. The solid identity of an evolved human is not compromised by the communication that might exist between all humans.

It seems to me that this communication is quickening and the Planetary Group Soul now has a mind of its own, and it's going places. You can see its evolution as a child's journey to adulthood. For the first two years of a child's life, it doesn't have an experience of being separate from its mother. At about two years old it begins to identify with its father and other family members. In doing so, it begins to mature and gradually it separates from its mother. By the age of twelve or thirteen the child moves out of the family alignment to where connection with friends of its own age is the main preoccupation. These teenage friendships form the makings of new tribal associations. The friendships usually last until the child matures and marries to form a new family unit, or until the person wanders away from that grouping to live alone.

The Planetary Group Soul, through its individual parts, has gone through the same maturing process. Beginning its childlike experience in its tribal state (the earth mother), where it had little or no realization of itself, to where it progressed into a national identity (the extended family), and out through that to an international identity (the friends), and finally out beyond that to where many hold a global view.

Of course, the Planetary Group Soul does not move along a linear time line, as humans do from birth to death. Instead, it's spread across the various states simultaneously. Part of our world population is still in the tribal experience; most of the population is in a national alignment and large numbers have now moved into an intercontinental or global perspective. This stretching of the Planetary Group Soul has given it perception and strength. The "big bang" that occurred on a socioeconomic level in the 1800's created energy, but without the stretching that has occurred across the four evolutionary states mentioned above, the Planetary Group Soul could never see itself as a complete being. It could never reach fulfillment. Millions have now passed along the evolutionary path from tribal to global. These evolved people know how to exist at the outer edges of the planetary mind—beyond the normal evolutionary process of humanity. I call these people the *Fringe Dwellers*.

As these people disengage from the wave vibration, they look back at the tribal tick-tock world and have difficulty relating to it. Much like a rebellious teenager who is attempting to set up his or her own life and identity, and who doesn't relate well to the parents whose influence he or she is trying to leave, the Fringe Dwellers push against the authority of the status quo. It doesn't frighten them anymore. They see it as rinky-dink. They begin to see themselves beyond it—tick-tock and life.

There is another fascinating aspect to the empowerment of the Planetary Group Soul—the influence of modern women. In the same way as the Amazon man who broke away creates a new energy, modern women have created the same burst of energy by becoming more powerful and independent. They are breaking free from the age-old domination of the male.

Visualize the process. The Planetary Group Soul explodes out of its tribal compaction but half the population is dominated by the other gender. The two genders evolve through history in lock step, with one part always controlling and dominating the other. Suddenly the female wakes to her own power and breaks away from domination by the male, creating further space in the planetary mind and a brand new source of energy—an even heightened spiritual velocity. In the same way as the Amazon man had to break away to form an independent electron, the women of the world are breaking out of the restrictive confines of male domination. The reason for it is not just to grant social justice to females, it's a vital part of the Group Soul's evolution. Our planet cannot evolve to completion unless the two polarities of itself—male and female—step slightly away from each other to create a proper synapse of energy. Remember, without the space between men and women there can be no proper observation for either one of them. The world cannot evolve to its full potential while women are trapped. The world ego is mostly male. It will take the power of women to help the spiritual identity of the people override the world ego.

Meanwhile, two generations of children have grown up since the Second World War. The first generation, the Flower Power children were well removed from their fathers and mothers. The second generation is even more distant.

That is why the present generation of teenagers is so listless and hostile. It's not just the normal process of disconnection from their parents—it goes further. The modern generation is far removed from the tribal spirit of their people; they don't relate well to the tick-tock world of the industrial sector and anyway, they have their mums and dads to do the drudgery for them. They see little alignment to the national wave. It offers them little other than the opportunity to subject themselves to an allegiance to those at the top of the hierarchy, the act of which gets them nothing they don't already have. This leaves them in a desolate place.

They don't have the metaphysical sophistication or world experience to move forward, and any backward movement subjects them to control—forcing them to give up their independence. Our children have been given independence on a plate—they were born to it—with little concept of having to win it by effort. The television shows them the benefits of emotional and financial freedom, and many, whose parents are well off, have some experience of it. They have reached the end of evolution without going through the middle. Much of our youth exists at the outer edge of the evolutionary experience, outside the main body of society. In a way, they are the most free people to have ever walked the planet, but in that freedom they have nowhere to go. So they wander about. Additionally, there is often no work for them to do.

Technological advances in productivity and government mismanagement have placed them in perpetual limbo. In socialist countries kids leave school and go on the dole; many of them are still on the dole ten years later. Many of our youth now form a part of the Fringe Dwellers. They haven't joined life's game, and there is little indication that they ever will. As a result, they don't belong, and many of them don't accept the authority of the system over them—there is no reason or benefit for them to do so.

In the Western democracies we have more and more people—millions of them—leaving the system everyday. Either they literally drop out or they remain loosely connected to the system for economic reasons. Either way, they are emotionally and spiritually detached. Then there are millions more who are still in the system but have politically distanced themselves from a game to which they would prefer not to belong. People are sorely pissed off and disenchanted. They want the opportunity to leave the wave and become particles.

The alienation of the people is fueled by economic woes. If the rules of the game are stacked against you, if conditions prevent you from making headway, it is very likely that you will eventually lose interest. Further, there is one other remarkable thing that affects this whole process. For young people to get going in life they need capital. Almost all available capital is tightly controlled. If you want to rent money you have to play the game, which is controlled by those at the top of the hierarchy. But today even that is not enough. World debt and the servicing of that debt has created a cash crunch. Capital is now being hoarded by those in control so that they may use it for their own survival. There is almost no money to finance the ideas of the younger generation. These young people have no work, they have little motivation, and there is no capital available to them that might inspire them to seize opportunities and attempt to contribute. What capital there is, is tied up in the corporations. If they want the use of capital to express themselves they have to join the system. Given that option many vote "No." The voluntary, often apathetic acquiescence of millions of people under the system's thumb is no longer guaranteed. People see the alliance of big business and politics as stifling their ability to evolve. Democracy is defined as government "by the people." But we are coming to realize that we don't have government "by the people," we only have government by representatives that are part of a corruption we don't relate to. The authority of the system is being questioned—quite rightly so.

The idea that a group of people that you've never met and who have none of your interests at heart should rule over you is ludicrous in this age. The wave theory doesn't allow for particles. When you think of it, there's no basis for that authority. How can the ego of the status quo threaten and control the spiritual evolution of five billion people? It can't in the end.

Look at China, it makes up twenty percent of the world population. It is currently run by a dozen doddery old fogies who pull the strings behind the scene, hoping to manipulate the Chinese people indefinitely. What do you think their chances are? I imagine that the memory of the millions that were killed by Mao Tse-Tung, and others who perished in Tiananmen Square, has not been forgotten. When the people get their chance, I would fancy that membership papers to the Chinese Communist Party would be a very life threatening document.

Once the divine right of kings disappeared to become a relic of history, the only basis for the status quo's manipulation of its people came from habit and threat of retribution by the state. The organism of our modern state is a violent institution. It kills people it doesn't like. Lots of them. I don't know about you, but I, personally, am not standing for this nonsense anymore. I think murdering people to keep some arrogant ponce in power is evil. It goes against the spiritual tenant of the Planetary Group Soul and deep-rooted feelings of all conscious and decent people.

We know that if our planet is to survive, we have to evolve to a better, more loving way of resolving issues. We also have to break the self-serving monopoly of the few over the activities and resources of our planet. We can't allow approximately two or three percent of the people to pillage the planet to oblivion while the mass of humanity is enslaved by the system.

Some would say that these ideas will lead to mayhem. But that is just a standard defense that is rolled out by those who have a vested interest in maintaining the current system. Further, I'm not saying we shouldn't have any formal administration of our countries. I'm just saying we don't need these modern so-called democracies anymore. We have grown beyond them. We need smaller units—oligarchies that are managed by conscious, loving people who will respect each other's ideas and independence.

The Tribal Folk Spirit

We will have to create small, direct democracies so people can choose what they want, and so individuals can create and experience life to its fullest. We are mature enough to know what we want, and what we want is a supportive system that represents us. We don't need the double-speak telling us how wonderful it all is. We have to agree to be realistic and look at the facts. We can see with our own eyes that reality dramatically contradicts the official version.

There will be a moment in the not too distant future, when everyone in the Western world will get it all at the same time. They will suddenly see that they don't have to endure the ego anymore. Once that moment occurs, the strength that flows to the Planetary Group Soul by millions of people having the same idea simultaneously will give courage to those people and others, and people will stand in front of the tanks and they will refuse to move. The military will not act; many of the soldiers are coming to feel as we feel. They will step aside. The soldiers are also the people.

These ideas may seem radical, but only to the ego mind that forbids any threat to its dominance. These ideas are not radical in the mind of the Planetary Group Soul, where they form a vast band of truth deep within most people's hearts. It is not a political revolution, it's a spiritual one. People yearn for the freedom of expression, but are frustrated because they don't know how to get it. But the wonderful thing is that if they are patient, it will be given to them on a plate. All we have to do is wait. Our brothers and sisters will get it any moment now. Meanwhile, we can give the Planetary Group Soul a voice for its truths, and we can stay busy working on ourselves while we connect with others to assist the global process along.

Our time will come as sure as tomorrow follows today. If you don't believe me, there's nothing I can say—other than to politely point out that you are extremely wrong. Who, in the early 80's would have laid money on the collapse of Communism in the U.S.S.R? Very few. Who in the mid-90's would lay money on the collapse of our Western democracies or the devolution of the American union of states? Not many.

That is because the ego has no real connection to the heart. Economic problems will open the channel. There will be a rush of blood to the head and the ego will be swamped. If you accept this to be true and you know it will happen, all you have to do is maneuver yourself to be in the right place at the right time. It's all so incredibly easy. Ignore the official news and the hype, and don't be confused if in the mid-90's things improve temporarily. Just watch for what is being expressed from the heart's of the people and you'll more or less know what's about to happen next.

There are things we can do to help the Planetary Group Soul to reach its new evolutionary plateau, but before I go into that let us look at the Fringe Dwellers phenomena in more detail. It helps to understand the massive strata of energy that is being laid down as a wedge against old-fashioned thinking. That strata of higher consciousness now forms the power and the foundation of the Planetary Group Soul as it expresses itself through the heart and spirit of our people.

The Fringe Dwellers

CHAPTER THREE

The spiritual Fringe Dwellers are an interesting bunch; they are the first large group of people in our history to make the inner move from wave to particle *en masse*. In doing so they have created a split in the evolution of our world—which I'll explain in a moment. Of course, in every society there are many types of eccentric characters, social misfits—hoboes, hermits, dopers, bandidos, terrorists, and a host of others. But these categories are very different from the spiritual Fringe Dwellers I speak of. Most misfits are on the fringe because of their lack of economic status or because their psychology plays an important role in sustaining them outside the system. These groups may seem different from the rest of society, but often they are very much a part of the wave-motion of human experience. You'll find them still intimately involved in the rough-and-tumble of life. The hobo is busy surviving, the doper is on the street looking for drugs, the bandidos are occupied stealing things, and the terrorist types are plotting their next move.

But the Fringe Dwellers I speak of are those whose spirit—the very core of their being—is leaving or has left the system. They have detached and projected themselves out of the destiny and evolution of the common man, and the tribal or national folk wave. These spiritual Fringe Dwellers usually have an alignment to the universal God Force, which comes from their own sense of spirit that is now individualizing from the tribal wave. It is through the development of a real sense of spiritual identity that the Fringe Dwellers come to an understanding of the infinity of all things. It seems a contradiction. You have to leave the crowd to understand that you belong to everything and everything is connected to you. Initially, you experience only a connection to your tribe; you don't usually appreciate the larger spiritual alignment we all have. But once you individualize to become a particle, you gain enough distance from the tribal wave to appreciate a deeper sense of your connection to all things. It's the difference between the limited view one has from within the hazy wave of a tribal alignment, and the uncluttered view of a true particle whose destiny is outside the wave. Gradually, your former tribal belonging is replaced with a silent, infinite belonging that comes from an inner knowing not easily described in words.

Are the Fringe Dwellers just a few mystics, ascetics or hippie wackos? No way. Millions of people all over the globe have now taken the step. Many are very normal and socially well adjusted. They often live ordinary lives. They go through the motions of fitting into society, and from all external indications you often can't tell them apart from the rest, but in their minds and in their hearts they are on the outer edges of the world mind, in a dimension of consciousness that is removed from the mainstream.

As one who presents seminars and lectures around the world, I have talked to thousands of people who describe the same strange, almost mystical feeling of being alienated from the normal process of humanity. They exist in an evolution that is clicked off to one side, like a cog that has slipped its notch, and is now rotating on an adjacent wheel. This doesn't mean that the FD's are antisocial. In fact, many of them have a deep love and respect for their fellow men and women. It's just that they have detached from the emotional alignment of common concerns and interests. I am a fully paid up member of the FD's group— perhaps you are also. I remember as a teenager—several moons ago—waking from a dream in which I was protesting my presence upon the Earth. In my dream I was trying to gain someone's attention; I felt I had been banished to this weird corner of the heavens in error. I was protesting my innocence. My resounding feeling was one of a great injustice. Have you ever had a dream like that?

I began to wonder if the feeling of distance comes up from some deep spiritual heritage that the Fringe Dwellers have, or do they gradually process themselves out of life by working on themselves over the years. My conclusion was that some are born to it because their Higher Self or spirit is very active and present in their life, while some come to it via their upbringing or other influences. Gradually, through esoteric practices and disciplines, the power of their Higher Self is forcefully manifested in their lives, influencing the way they feel spiritually.

In my case, I think both examples apply. From the age of about seven or eight, I felt that strange sensation of not being a part of humanity's process. I'm sure a lot of people feel like that sometimes. I remember walking in the woods with my father or being with him out in a boat at sea, and spending hours looking skyward waiting for something or someone to come and get me. But aside from these feelings, I feel my upbringing detached me from the steadying influence of belonging somewhere. I was born in England, but spent no time there as a child. My parents lived in Germany, and when I was two my family went to Africa, where we moved around quite a lot, never living in the same house more than a year or two. I started off in Tripoli, Libya, and wound up in Tema, Ghana, where I remained until the age of eleven, when I was shipped back to England to attend boarding school. My mother was Sicilian, but I'd never been to Sicily. I wasn't African—though I felt more kinship with the Africans than I did the English—but I didn't belong to the black man's world, and I didn't belong to England either. I didn't even learn English properly until I was five or six—my mother and father spoke German and Italian at home.

During my seven years at boarding school in England, I was away from my parents and my home in Africa. I felt disconnected and cared little for the school and its ideas. While my classmates took on the social molding offered by the institution, I resisted all the way. I caused an endless stream of trouble attempting to ensure my heart wasn't captured by the system.

It was a marvelous running battle; I can't say I won all of the time because the system wielded authority over me, but I scored some good hits. Of course, I had to pretend to fit in sometimes, otherwise my troubles got too intense. But for me it was like making promises and keeping your fingers crossed behind your back so that you have an "out." Including my school years, I spent a total of twenty years in England. But in the end, I declared myself, "Not really English." Once I did that, circumstances allowed me to emigrate to the United States. Americans are very friendly, but I didn't belong there either, although I did have a good time. When I got into metaphysics at the age of twenty-eight and listened to Taoist principles of detachment, it all sounded so natural. It's not hard to be detached if you have never belonged anywhere. So in my case, the Fringe Dweller aspect of my consciousness came partly from my upbringing and partly from a deep inner force that pulled me out of the system. It could just be that our upbringing molds our inner feelings, which choose circumstances that align us to the Fringe Dwellers' path.

Here's an interesting point: In my seminars I have often asked people, "How many of you feel that you have more or less completed your evolution as a human? That, in fact, there is not much more for you to learn?" About one third of the room will put up their hands. One might be tempted to say that they are full of their own importance—and how could anyone dare to suggest that they have learned the lesson of humanity? But in talking to people, you can see that they are mostly humble and genuine in their views. They have no ax to grind or cause to expound. They honestly believe that either they are in their last

The Fringe Dwellers

human experience, or that they have completed all that there is to learn in this one. In questioning them, they all say they don't want to come back. They know they have finished.

Of course, the idea that you can't learn the lesson of humanity quickly and simply comes from organized religion, which has a bit of a vested interest in saying so. I think the Buddhist teachings are neat and have a lot to offer, but I have never bought the view that it takes a thousand incarnations to go beyond the earth plane. When Buddha said that (if he did say it at all) sitting under the Bodhi tree was the only game in town, it's natural Buddhist writers thought it would take ages and ages to understand ourselves and our environment. But nowadays, we pretty much know all there is to know; there aren't too many mysteries left. What you don't know, you probably don't need. And what you do need, you can take it on at high speed. The whole world and all of its possible experiences are theoretically available to you at the flick of a switch. Psychology and our knowledge of human ways have become so sophisticated that there really aren't any human ideas or behavioral patterns which haven't been studied and explained a hundred times over.

The various religions teach that our goal is to seek to emulate the perfection of the masters, but deep within us we know that the masters were probably not quite as perfect as the writers made them out to be. It is not perfection we seek—just peace, understanding, and the sweet embrace of a personal reconciliation.

I'm convinced that the lessons of humanity aren't so complex. If they really were beyond us, no one would be here on the planet learning them. Meaning that, as an eternal spirit, you wouldn't put yourself into an evolution on the physical plane if the lessons offered were impossible to comprehend. So it follows that there must be a way to eventually get the message.

In the wave-state, transcendence looks and feels wildly impossible. How can an individual get past the interference he or she feels and eventually evolve? The interference pattern of the wave-state is perpetual, so it gives the impression that our lessons are eternal, perpetual, and incomprehensible. But once out of the wave and in the detached free particle state, there is no interference; suddenly you see that the lessons are not lessons to be learned, but more a subatomic state to achieve. You don't have to learn the lessons—you become the lesson. You are the lesson. A fairly instant enlightenment is possible.

In my book, *The Force*, I assigned a hypothetical vibrational speed to modern humanity. I picked twenty thousand cycles per second: meaning that the totality of an average person—physically, mentally, emotionally, and spiritually—oscillates his or her etheric at this hypothetical twenty thousand cycles per second. Of course, the real speed must be much higher, given that light oscillates at the very high frequency of about 10^{15} cycles per second, but we don't need the real speed to understand the concept. A hypothetical speed will do.

As you raise your consciousness and become stronger and more open, those cycles per second move up—you oscillate faster and faster. In the etheric state you can see it. Some people's energy is dim and travels only a short distance; it has a dull opaque quality, while others you see are very bright and clear. Their etheric energy is vital and booming out from them. In some rare cases it travels a long way, that is, farther than the normal few feet.

In recent times, the total average vibrational speed of humanity has been steadily moving upward. But for thousands of years it remained more or less stationary. The difference between the lowest and highest levels of consciousness was never that great. The aristocrat and the peasant oscillated fairly close together, even though usually only the aristocrat could read and write. They were both in the tribal mind. What the aristocrat believed, and the metaphysical power he exerted, was much the same as the peasant, because both were spiritually powerless. There was little introspection, so almost no independent particles existed. There was no analysis or psychology, or any perspective from outside the tribal mind. Everyone lived at various social levels of the same collective ignorance and fear. All were victims of historical circumstances. The upper classes with their access to knowledge, and who might have furthered their spiritual evolution, had no hope of exiting the wave because they were so obsessed with status and ego. In those days there was nothing to suggest a person might possibly individualize and control his or her life. The idea would have been considered ludicrous and seditious. Instead, trust was placed in religion and one's relationship to an emotional God. You either made it or you didn't. There was no security, little justice, and science was in its infancy. Fear, ignorance, and bigotry pervaded every level of society.

So if you look at Figure 1: Say the average speed of humanity in the year 1700 A.D. was lower than today's, perhaps hovering at twelve thousand cycles per second. There would be some individuals lower, and a few higher, but the band or separation between the highest and lowest was not great.

Figure 2 is placed at 1960, and you can see how our hypothetical band has widened. The lowest level has climbed a bit since 1700 A.D., but at the top end, the upwardly mobile, educated

Metaphysical Vibrational Speeds of the Etheric and Human Understanding

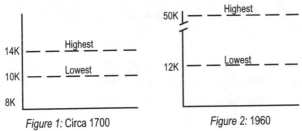

Figure 1: Circa 1700   *Figure 2:* 1960

types have climbed a great deal. Of course you can't say what the bottom or top level is, but you can see the difference in real life. Think of the knowledge and power an atomic scientist has at his or her fingertips compared to a worker in a paddy field. Or take a highly mobile, self-realized conscious being hurtling through the modern environment and compare them to a native in the forests of Papua, New Guinea.

In the sixties, a great shift happened. The young of the postwar era would not align to the prewar ideas of their parents. The mass use of mind altering drugs changed things rapidly, mainly because it turbo-kicked people's imagination. Besides fear, the reason people get stuck at the top of the consciousness band is often because of a lack of imagination. There are a lot of very bright people whose energy could climb a great deal further if they were not dominated so much by intellect and the stifling effect of the tick-tock mind.

The overall shift was assisted by other factors. When Armstrong landed on the moon in 1969, organized religion momentarily took a whack in the ribs. Suddenly man had progressed out of the earth's influence (reaching heaven metaphorically) and the need for religion was diminished. The restrictive views of many religions looked small and unsophisticated when an entire universe seemed available to us without their help.

The psychedelics of the Flower Power era acted like steam, blowing through the consciousness of humanity. It affected society at all levels, creating a new dimension of consciousness that was not stuck or held back by the boundaries that the world mind had created for its people. Gradually, many were released to float upwards. (See Figure 3.)

Flower Power created the basis of the spiritual Fringe Dwellers who came later. That's not to say that today's Fringe Dwellers are all acid heads or hippies from the sixties. It's just that the flower children opened the door and many followed.

The Fringe Dwellers

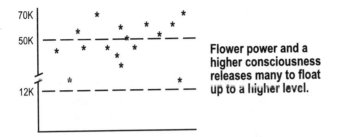

Flower power and a higher consciousness releases many to float up to a higher level.

Figure 3: 1960-1975

Now you may wonder: Since drugs have been around from the beginning of time, why didn't the transformation happen sooner? For some it did—but the numbers were not great. It's interesting to note that the tribal cultures that had psychotropic drugs also had some of the most metaphysically advanced philosophies. The Mayans and the peyote culture of some Native Americans are two that come to mind.

The Flower Power subculture of the sixties, with its emphasis on hallucinogens, was different than the drug culture of the twenties, which was based mainly on opiates that numb the senses rather than elevating the imagination. Additionally, Flower Power had more room to move in a social system liberated by the war.

In the 1970's, the new consciousness that Flower Power had set in motion began to exert financial strength, and suddenly the hippies had clout. They had the know-how to influence others. They could stand outside the system and thumb their noses at those inside. When others saw that this fringe element came to no harm and that, in fact, most prospered, vast chunks of the population went beyond their fear of alienating or abandoning tick-tock and the tribal mind. The status quo appeared as a toothless tiger. Embracing your own individuality brought you no harm or retribution. Millions worldwide followed the Flower Children out of the mainstream evolution of mankind and people began drifting off toward the margins. Once liberated from the clamp the conservative system places on people, they found room to experiment and develop a higher consciousness.

Don't get confused between a higher consciousness and intelligence, status, and money. In the tribal wave, intelligence and money separate you from others. But now there are a lot of people whose metaphysical energy is higher than the top band of tick-tock or anyone in the tribal wave, because they have a new consciousness and individuality. The very rich or very bright tick-tockers who haven't worked on themselves are usually still in the tribal mind. In the wave there's a limit as to how far your energy can climb. In fact, if you are very rich it's most likely you will be deeply in the tribal wave, as that is where you will be making your money. A modern technocrat who might be a living genius, may have a very limited spiritual identity, in spite of his or her great intellect. The nature of the profession requires him or her to fit into the boundaries of the tick-tock mind. Even though the technocrat may be at the top of the tick-tock scale there is a limit to how far he or she can go. Sometimes being very bright can hinder your spiritual evolution, because intellect and logic dominate your vision and lock you in.

Gradually, the band of energy hovering just above the main evolutionary process (shown in Figure 3) began to coalesce into a loose knit identity. That was how the New Age movement and alternative culture was born. As it became more cohesive, it began to drift upward. The faster molecules, rising in an arc-like curve, moved rapidly away from tick-tock. The lower end consisted of newcomers or the unsure, who were still influenced and anchored by the psychological gravity that the tick-tock band exerts below them.

Now something very interesting happened. As one curve rose and drifted away to form a crescent, the main tick-tock band changed shape as well. Part of the slower band regressed and fell backwards, curving back and imploding on itself towards a slower evolutionary path. (See Figure 4, below)

Gradually, the two curves more or less separated, and the world mind, which had been skidding along at speed, began to experience disequilibrium, confusion, and fear. People in the tick-tock wave felt out of control and overwhelmed much of the time. As they resonated that idea or feeling for a number of years—through the late '80's early '90's—you saw their collective insecurity manifest as reality. The cohesion of tick-tock unraveled economically and socially.

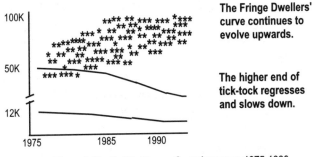

The Fringe Dwellers' curve continues to evolve upwards.

The higher end of tick-tock regresses and slows down.

Figure 4: The Split in Human Consciousness, 1975-1990

The top end of tick-tock, which usually consists of those more socially or economically advantaged, was also affected by the speed of things. Many suffered financial setbacks; much of the upper echelon came unstuck. So they turned downwards, lowering their expectations—not so much for protection but because they couldn't hack the speed. The boom of the 1980's meant that a lot of very mediocre people did well. Once the lush business conditions changed, much of the mediocrity and the hype was wiped out. Executive unemployment rose sharply. The curling down of the tick-tock band seen in Figure 4 is the reason you see the rise of right wing parties in the Western democracies. People have become more conservative and reactionary.

The rising up of the Fringe Dwellers' curve has many interesting aspects worth considering. Now there is a gap between that curve and the upper strata of tick-tock. That is what I mean by the split in our evolution. The bottom of the tick-tock band is still very tribal and fearful, whereas the middle and upper part is less fearful, but they are often deeply locked into status and material things. As economies deteriorated, their expectations and their energy fell in unison.

I know that I often ridicule tick-tock in my books, but you do have to respect its individual members when you meet them. After all, tick-tock is a part of everyone's evolution—we have all been through it. The problem is that in tick-tock the tribal mind and the ego reign supreme. These two features of the tick-tock's mind make it very vulnerable to changing conditions. The day-to-day dimension of ordinary people is taking a terrible whacking. Old tribal values and ideas are breaking down under pressure. People feel lost and many find it hard to let go and move from that band of consciousness and into spirit. But the Fringe Dwellers' curve has a way of sucking people up through its spiritual energy. More and more will follow as people begin to question the validity of the old ways.

The upper end of the Fringe Dwellers' curve is now outside the evolution of the earth plane. It's as if those people have died, to begin an evolution in another dimension, even though they are still alive in the physical plane. They have projected themselves out of the destiny of the world. Essentially, they are karmically and spiritually free.

You have to wonder what their function is. Sure, the climb is a natural progression for humans to make. But why have so many made the journey at this time? Obviously the conditions are right, but is there a higher reason? Why does the Planetary Group Soul need to create a powerful group of solid, independent particles outside the mainstream wave? Certainly, it would be handy to have a large group of fairly stable, conscious people

The Fringe Dwellers

to act as a steadying force while the world bounces around through the choppy conditions of the '90's and beyond. And certainly one might be tempted to argue that the function of the Fringe Dwellers' curve is to elevate the rest of the world. However, you have to wonder if the constituents of tick-tock need elevating, especially when many are choosing to turn downwards, to a slower, more comfortable vibrational level. Any attempted acceleration would probably drive them 'round the bend, given that they already have plenty to worry about.

Beyond the obvious reasons for the evolution of such huge numbers up the Fringe Dwellers' curve is the fascinating idea that having so many outside the world mind set preserves that very same mind set from self-destruction. It acts as a safety valve. Here's my explanation: The tick-tock mind and its ego looks out from itself, to a God above it, to an experience beyond it, to the future, to the next pleasurable sensation, and so on. Its power is dissipated by its perpetually outward view. Its focus is to permanently yearn for things it doesn't have. Daydreaming is a feature of life in the hazy wave—it's simpler than concrete action. That's why the dreams of the common man are not often materialized.

The Fringe Dwellers also look outward as they climbed up and out of the mainstream, but at the top of the curve they have no place to go. They can't step into another dimension without dying. They possibly can peer into other worlds, but they don't belong there as yet. In the end, the Fringe Dwellers have to turn and face back down the path they just came up. First there is mountain, then it becomes a holy, mystical mountain—the lap of the Gods, the playground of angels—then in the end it's just a bloody mountain . . . period . . . full stop.

Now that might seem a little disappointing but spiritually, it's not. In making the journey you touch the real essence or spiritual reason for all things, which is, of course, the celestial radiance of the light of God. You are happy to turn back because you now have a spiritual vision of the correctness of things. Your whole mind is bathed in the grace of God's light, and the spiritual beauty of that will remain with you forever.

The effect of the Fringe Dwellers turning and looking back, creates a force field that acts both as a boundary and a buffer for tick-tock. Remember, the Fringe Dwellers aren't out on a starship some place; they're standing next to tick-tock at the bus stop. But the effect of the Fringe Dwellers' collective power encircles the mental projections of the tribal mind and its ego, silently reflecting back to it what is truth and what is illusion. Gradually, everyone is forced to look at themselves. The movement for a higher consciousness has already made quite an impact on the world in many fields. Health and diet, ethical investing, the liberation of educational curricula, conservation and ecology, world peace and so on. But most of all, people are taught that there is a personal bliss beyond the mayhem and troubles that dominate the lives of many. As the movement for a higher consciousness penetrated more deeply, it allowed ordinary people to embrace introspection, meditation, and fringe ideas without being pilloried by their associates as weirdoes.

Higher consciousness is the way we gradually heal the planet from the pollution that the status quo has bombarded us with. Over the last forty years television has helped people by teaching them about the world we live in, but it has also created a great angst. It offers the ordinary man or woman a glamorous world that is worshipped as a paramount need. The effect of bombarding the world mind with a sweet smelling, Porche driving, abundant, idealistic vision titillated the ego, creating a warped expectancy.

Toward the bottom end of the tick-tock range—at the twenty thousand cycle level, or below—there is almost no way a person can materialize much of that TV heaven. But the religion of glamour and status fuels the ego none the less, and so the world

The Fringe Dwellers

mind has bought the idea that everyone is terribly important and that we all should have the benefits of the TV vision as a constitutional right. It is the mind of humanity stretching for the particle state in the external world. Glamour is an illusion. Television and the media fuels that illusion because it has to pander to people in order to win their approval and to sell things. By pumping the illusion, the idea was born that you don't have to work on yourself or put out in any way to obtain the product of your dreams . . . all you have to do is want them. Something or someone from within the wave will give it to you. It's the idea that a separate individuality will stem from the glamour of the vision.

The highly sophisticated, bejeweled lady that strolls through a TV commercial or lolls at the poolside seems to make no effort. She is a product of the ego that likes instant recognition without effort. They don't show you the ten years of heartache and consistent effort that it might take a real person to achieve such a material heaven and ease of life.

Once the world mind was titillated, glamour became vital to everyone, where previously it was only vital to a few. Now we have a star struck mind set that says, "Gimme, gimme," so society and the politicians attempt to do just that. But overall wealth can only be created gradually, a few percentage points per year. Meanwhile, the people's egos were inflated by television at speed. Millions now demand a free ride; why not? Their electronic teacher said it was fair and possible. The common folk demanded that someone should raise them up. The intellectuals demanded power and respect, regardless of whether their offerings were valuable or not. Mothers were no longer prepared to just nurture their families, they wanted a place in the sun and the material benefits that the commercials said they should not live without. Quite naturally, wives went out to chase the dream, while the kids stayed home with the electronic baby-sitter feeding them a lot of half-truths. It's no wonder the young are a bit mixed up, poor dears. The glamour of the effortless TV heaven turns out to be very different from the reality teenagers confront when they hit the streets looking for a job. Realism often denies the vision; so realism is brushed aside while everyone seeks instant gratification—the one that they have been promised. The fast-buck-at-any-cost message became religion, and with that came all the lies and deceptions needed to endorse a hopelessly unrealistic vision.

Faced with the prospect of disappointing the tribal wave and the negative reaction that was bound to follow, our institutions embarked on ways of granting to as many as possible, as much as possible, in the shortest period of time. The Good Fairy was cranked into overtime. It didn't matter if the wealth generated wasn't real; what mattered was that it got to everyone before they ran amok. So government spending rocketed through the roof, and where there was not enough money, new, fake money was invented. Credit cards, promissory notes, shares, junk bonds, mortgages, hire purchase—you name it and someone, somewhere made sure the ego got its regular fix. For a while the TV dream looked as if it might become a reality. Young bucks straight from college were making $500,000 a year working on Wall Street, transferring illusions from one part of the world ego to another. Everything was possible. You could have a new heart, silicon breasts, a new and younger face, even immortality. All you had to do was say, "I am special. I am a true-blue particle. I deserve immortality." You didn't have to do anything; at worst, it was a lie guaranteed to last a lifetime. Ticktock was quickly polluted with a great falsehood.

That illusion could only be sustained by more lies. So we developed a society where everyone demanded the dream regardless of the facts. It became compulsory for everyone to have money, a home, and a future, and if they couldn't manage it through their own efforts, money would be appropriated from others to provide it. Those that diligently worked to acquire a home and the good life and a vision were lashed by repeated guilt trips. The TV pulpit ran stories of beggars as if somehow your wealth caused the beggar's poverty. It was implied that you were responsible for materializing every beggar's dream. The ego of indolent people loved that. It shifts responsibility from them to others in what is, in effect, a collective, psychological communism. No mention was ever made of work or diligence or output, because that contradicted the lie. You can't suggest to the homeless that they get a job, save money, and rent or buy a house like everyone else. It is sacrilegious. It smacks too much of realism. The ego will offer excuses instead. The homeless can't work, there are no jobs, there is not enough money. In some cases that may be correct, but the implication is that if you have worked to acquire your vision, then you are personally responsible to guarantee at least a minimum level of the TV dream to everyone that happens to live in the same country as you. In addition, you are responsible for an unspecified number of others that live elsewhere.

Energy is the only real currency; everything else will collapse in the end. But in the meantime, the silliness of the lie is everywhere; in our religions, which offer us heaven if we join their elitist system and follow a few simple rules; in our governments, which promise everything in order to buy power; in our schools, which teach and endorse the lie by pumping kids' egos with propaganda and information that they can't use in real life—everyone graduates nowadays even if they can hardly read or write. The Great Lie is the central theme of the New World Religion that television has created. No part of our society is free from it. No one dares to tell people the truth.

But the Fringe Dwellers are different. Seeing life as energy and looking at themselves they begin to embrace the truth. They move from ego to spirit. It hurts at first, and there is much to process and to go beyond, but gradually we accept what is real. We see how truth is both humbling and empowering.

But what is important is that by climbing up and learning the lessons, the Fringe Dwellers have affected the rest of the world on an inner level. The tick-tock mind is changing even though it does not realize it. It is being processed and influenced by a higher vibration. That silent, subliminal injection of power offers a psychological protection to the world mind as circumstances change.

The effect of this happening *en masse* is to temper the world ego and its hemorrhaging of energy. The Fringe Dwellers' power gradually plugs the blood flowing out of the wounded brain of man and reflects energy back to people. The total power of the world mind becomes less dissipated. The healing is under way. I don't buy the idea that the planet is a victim, or that the collective inner mind of mankind doesn't know what it's trying to achieve or where it's going. On the contrary, I see order and a natural progression through history. I feel that the Planetary Group Soul knows what it's doing. Just as biology shows us that this lump of rock hurtling through space is more than just solid matter—it has an intelligence that is aware of itself and it adjusts to biological and environmental changes—so, too, the inner mind of the world also shifts periodically to adjust for the collective feelings of man. In my view, it is not an accident that the consciousness movement has placed over a hundred million people up the Fringe Dwellers' curve, while many more are moving up to join them. That body of energy is there for a reason.

Being on the path ahead of tick-tock acts to delineate the outer edge of our vision at this time. It requires that humanity stop reaching forward; that we now assimilate what we have learned. The Fringe Dwellers' curve hauls people up, but at the top end of the curve it actually inhibits people from traveling further. That is why so many New Age people have come to a grinding halt. The Fringe Dwellers act as life guards, saving humanity from destroying itself through disappointment and sorrow.

In the end, everyone has to turn around, and rather than facing upward and outward, pleading and begging, they now face inward. At the moment when they truly acknowledge them-selves as a part of the God Force, they look only within for power, exhilaration, teaching, and strength. Gradually, even tick-tock understands the futility of a hedonistic, madcap world that rushes along at breakneck speed to acquire stuff that is not real and serves no lasting purpose. Eventually, everyone will have to agree to discard the TV religion and accept alternatives—seeing beauty and sustenance in little things, tempering their desires, moving ever so gradually toward truth. We should be encouraged by that. We should show people that in abandoning the lie they suffer no great loss. Does it mean we cannot dream? Not at all. You can have anything you desire, providing you have the tenacity and energy to pull it off. That's reality. If you lack things in your life, point the finger at yourself. Perhaps the quality of your energy won't sustain the breadth of your vision.

As the Fringe Dwellers' curve went through its journey of self–discovery, it shot through gestalt, gurus, extraterrestrials, me-diums, crystals, shamanistic practices, and whole bunches of other good stuff. But in evolutionary terms—where a thousand years is but a second—the Fringe Dwellers' curve ran out of ideas in a heartbeat. This is why the top of the Fringe Dwellers' curve is flat—they are running out of things to do.

It's interesting to note that so many spiritual teachers have fallen by the wayside over the last few years. Very few new ones have emerged, with the exception of a few rather dubious gurus who are making headway offering tick-tock an alternative to worship. But most of these Johnny-come-latelys can't hold a candle to ol' Bhagwan, so I doubt if they will last. The Hindus gave us a lot of valuable esoteric information, and they laid the groundwork of modern metaphysical knowledge, but they also gave us the strange notion that holy men and women should be worshiped by their students. The idea comes from the Hindu caste system, which elevates some as Brahmin, who enjoy a godlike status, while relegating others to a place so low they are considered untouchable. That notion is fraught with peril and belongs to the ego. Certainly, one can admire wise teachers, but the idea of worshiping some dusty little fellow on a cushion looks really silly. Still, it usually takes people a while to understand that the power is within them, and it can never be granted by someone else.

Once you make the final turn and particularize your destiny, part of you will face perpetually within; it's a process of collapsing inward upon yourself. Once you no longer face only outward, you project less and less mental and emotional energy away from yourself. In all practicality you begin to disappear from the tribal vision of itself. Is it surprising therefore that tick-tock often won't acknowledge you? How can it? It can hardly see you ... you're poised between two worlds. The final turn may take a few years, but once you commit to the idea, it can show you new and delightful things about yourself.

If you are a spiritual Fringe Dweller—or if you are becoming one—the first point of reconciliation is to admit it. You have to understand that you have projected yourself out of this world, so you may never really fit. People will mostly reject your ideas. You may never gain the recognition or acceptance to which your talents may suggest you're entitled. But you don't need recognition, and to crave it only fuels the ego and affirms a lack of acceptance of self—so why drive yourself crazy? Just agree that the life of a Fringe Dweller is a wonderful place to be. At least you are not earth bound.

Trying to fit in is silly ... it burns energy. Wake up to the weirdo within you and don't apologize for it. Just be it. Love it. Nurture it. Look within it. It has value; it serves in a silent way. If people don't agree with you—knickers! You're not in their game; you have scooped up your marbles and invented a game of your own.

The Fringe Dwellers

Sure, admitting you're weird is difficult. Conformity is a tenant of tick-tock's hold over people. But, when you think of it, how many people in the world do you really need? Conformity sells us the idea that we can't make it without a whole bunch of morons who agree with us. But isn't it the morons who are selling us that idea? How many people do you actually need? Perhaps there are none that are absolutely vital, or very few anyway.

Now, if you have to win over the entire tick-tock mind—all five billion people—that's tough. But what if you only have to win over four people or six or a dozen? That's simple. Perhaps you have to play their game a bit to keep them on your side . . . so what. If you're a fully paid up loony twenty-three hours a day, and straight as a die for one hour, that's probably good enough. Perfection is only in the mind; it's not real. When you think of it, attaining perfection is mostly the ability to get comfortable with compromise.

For years I fell for the commercial trap of trying to modify myself to fit into what I felt people wanted. There was a time when I was involved with others trying to develop a TV talk show with myself as the host. Looking back, the idea was so utterly ludicrous it would make me roar with laughter if I hadn't wasted $50,000 on the dumb idea. The TV companies are just parrots in tuxedos—they sure as hell don't want any spiritual terrorists alienating their couch potatoes. I wouldn't have lasted five minutes!

It was only a few years ago that I finally understood the complete futility of trying to fit into the mind set of a people to whom you do not belong. It takes a while to believe that you can create a brand new genre; in my case, *Wildeism*. In your case, just add an "ism" to your name. But once you step up to bat, you get a personal shelf at the library, even if it is marked "Caution. Incomprehensible Weirdo."

Dear scamps, if you are a Fringe Dweller or you're on the verge of becoming one—admit it! Then try to develop a lifestyle in which you need as little as possible from others. That sets you free to be yourself. Everyone wants something all of the time, so they are trapped by desire. They need support, recognition, and encouragement; to get it they have to act to please others— it holds them down.

Once you're up on the Fringe Dwellers' curve you probably won't need recognition, and you won't need much encouragement—you can encourage yourself. You may need support from others to finalize the last of the reconciliation, and you may need others to help materialize your dreams, but you can rent your helpers and pay them in a way that incurs no personal debt. In materializing your needs silently on your own, you become your own boss. Once you have tempered your needs and you have supplied for yourself all that you really need, then dismiss all the things you haven't got and become permanently comfortable. You'll be one in a hundred thousand who isn't pleading, begging, hoping. That's a powerful strength. You have to be patient, but patience is a learned skill. In one of my writings I talk about the concept of the professional waiter. That is, someone who is not an amateur waiter who waits in their emotions, but the professional waiter, who is so composed and in control that they can wait forever. If you don't want anything and you're a professional waiter, how can anyone touch you? They can't.

The world of the Fringe Dweller is individual and different. Be yourself. Allow the world to bitch and moan. It's their right, but they have no real power over you. The possum can't tell the kangaroo not to hop—so hop on regardless. It's better to hop down your own path than to cling to a branch, comatose, with a possum that doesn't know diddly-squat from shinola anyway.

Plateaus of
Higher Consciousness

CHAPTER FOUR

B efore we go on to discuss how we can create energy shifts that will benefit the world, let's look for a moment at the process by which you have shifted—or will shift—your destiny by journeying out of tick-tock into a higher consciousness. Understanding this process at a personal level will give you insights into what is happening on a global scale.

Our life's journey of self-discovery is not a straight-line rise from one level of consciousness to another. Instead, it is a series of steep climbs and flat plateaus, followed by further climbs. Although we all approach the journey from different directions, certain of the journey's characteristics are common to all of us. We begin our spiritual understanding in a mundane place: The ordinary world of survival—that dimension of tribal or national consciousness, where the intellect and the ego reign supreme, and tribal attitudes and ideologies are promoted as the only knowledge one will ever need. The humdrum plane of the day-to-day existence most experience as "life" is what I call "tick-tock."

The people who taught us the rules and methods of tick-tock brought us through our childhoods and dropped us off at the doorstep of adulthood. They were, for the most part, sweet and kind, and they loved us and did their best. But from the perspective of a higher understanding they were often as thick as two planks. They rarely gave us the necessary tools with which to proceed. Then, suddenly, the day came when we began to question the validity of all that we'd been taught. There had to be more. Once we began to question and to seek, we started to climb out of a slower evolutionary rhythm into a faster, more rarefied alternative.

If you accept that your destiny is mostly formulated and controlled by your mind, with its mental and emotional projections, you will see that as you climb out of tick-tock you change your destiny away from the evolution of the common person (who belongs to the collective destiny of either his or her tribe or nation). You step into a separate reality, which is the feature of the inner particle state. It's a reality driven by your hopes and dreams, rather than one belonging to the collective reality of the tribal wave and its limited attitudes.

The vast majority of our world focuses entirely on the intellect, so all of their life's experiences are external—they have no inner journey to speak of. Life is often very emotional and traumatic for them. It is very real. Life's circumstances are all they have. If your focus is tuned only to the outer conscious world then your subconscious inner world will be nearly dormant. It will passively reflect the programming offered it by the intellect, communicating back to that intellect mostly via the dream state, which is often ignored as unusual or quaint or too scary to look at.

In these circumstances the subconscious mind is blind. It cannot see out except through the intellect's vision, so the subconscious is fearful. It only has the memories of an individual's past experiences to select from and to guide it. It can do nothing but repeat what it already knows. It is powerless—like a baby in a cot. It has no volition. It can only react. It doesn't really contribute other than as a memory bank.

In my experience, the first part of the inner journey begins through focusing silently inwards. Your subconscious mind is transformed from just a nebulous cloud of memory to having a real inner identity. Once the Inner You is activated by your observation of it, the journey becomes more and more real, and your inner identity develops a proper voice. Not just the negative dialogue of the subconscious mind that you are used to, but a spiritual voice, one that establishes itself very slowly via symbols and pictures. As the Inner You gains strength and is empowered to become real, it eventually can set off on a journey of self-discovery through inner dimensions as you continue journeying outward via the intellect. Of course, you are not two separate people, you are two aspects of the same person.

If you want to successfully make the transition from tribal wave to inner particle, you eventually have to control and dominate your ego. As you do so, the spirit within you begins to shine through the Inner You. It is the light of the spirit molecule deep within you that grants your inner self perception. You suddenly acquire a heightened sense of feeling. So when we refer colloquially to a "conscious person," we mean they have heightened feelings, compared to the rather dull or dormant perceptions of an unconscious person. Some of the subtle feelings emanating from within will relate to your external life, the rest will correspond to your inner experiences. In this way, you can follow your inner journey and learn from it, while enlightening your external life with new perceptions.

Through discipline you can control the ego, and through meditation or quiet contemplation you begin to soften the electrical field of the mind, which normally swamps the spirit. You allow the spirit molecule to shine through the Inner You—sparking it to life. You empower the Inner You by really believing in it, so that your inner identity gains courage and strength, taking on a whole gamut of new possibilities. A part of the subconscious mind always remains as the memory bank, but a part of it now begins to climb out of its alignment to tick-tock via the newly formed Inner You. That inner climb usually takes a thousand days—which is not long when you think of the years we spend asleep coddled in the humdrum world.

The vibration of tick-tock is low. It has little or no spirit, and what little there is gets drowned out by the cacophony of the intellect. But at least you know how to operate within its confinement, and you can see possibilities for yourself. The familiarity of being attached and linked to tick-tock emotionally gives you strength and confidence. But once your inner self begins the climb to self-discovery, your attitudes change. Your energy rises quickly, and soon you realize that to sustain your upward progress, you must discard much of the mental and emotional encumbrances acquired in your formative years.

As you review and release those encumbrances, your connection to tick-tock is loosened—it becomes harder to relate to issues that others feel are important. You begin to see your external life as less of a drama because you now have an inner self with a life—and a destiny. Before your inner self had nothing. It's a very exciting experience for most people. However, most of what you have at this early stage is introspection—new ideas and disciplines perhaps—but nothing much else as yet. That is why the climb out of tick-tock feels, on an inner level, like scaling a rock face. Much of the stability you were used to—mundane as it was—is now gone. All that holds you is your expectancy of greater energy up ahead and your belief in self, driven by your desire to discover a new way.

During the thousand day climb, the Inner You never sees further than a few yards in front of itself. Your imagination and intellectual ability to formulate and materialize plans was originally developed at a lower energy level, developed by someone who was, in effect, a different person—the external you. The Inner You may not know yet how to make the currency of a new vibration work at this higher level of being. It has only been awake a short time. The only thing you can be sure of is that each step you take on your inner journey carries you away from the security and linkages of the old world, upward toward a place that is faster, and more complete, a place of consolidation that I call the First Plane of Understanding.

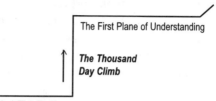

The First Plane of Understanding

The Thousand Day Climb

Plane of Survival (Tick-Tock)

Figure 5: The First Plateau of Higher Consciousness

Your spiritual perception and inner development is empowered by whatever disciplines or teachings you embrace—meditation, contemplation, vegetarianism, shamanism, spiritualism, or whatever "ism" takes your fancy. Primarily it is empowered by your ability to establish observation, which allows you to begin to release from the tribal wave and the inherent baggage you have acquired.

As I traveled through some of the inner worlds, I discovered that what you are unfolds into more and more components. We are a myriad of parts and identities—each one inside another. Beyond those that I have discovered so far, there must be many, many more. Each part is laced and interconnected to every other part, so terminology can get a little confused. To clarify things, let me take a moment to review the words I use so that we can understand them in the context in which I use them.

The External You, which operates through the intellect and forms the basis of human experience, is the main contributor to your personality. Personality is stored as memory in the brain, which also holds your subconscious memory, much of which lays hidden from view. You only have the one memory—part of it is conscious and most of it is unconscious. The ego, the intellect, and the subconscious make up the mind, which forms the personality. The human personality, its attitudes and actions in life, is what Christians call the soul.

Historian Tevor Ravenscroft pointed out in his book, *The Cup of Destiny*, that for a thousand years our entelechy consisted of the three components of body, mind (personality or soul), and spirit. In the year 869A.D. Pope Nicholas, who must have been quite an intellectual chap, decided that spirit didn't exist. He stated that we are just body and mind. So the Eighth Ecumenical Council decreed it so, and the spirit was banished. Thence forth, our Western people had to make do with just body and soul (mind). "Spirit" deteriorated to mean charismatic features of the intellect or personality. So when we say a person has spirit, we mean strength of character. Mind won—spirit lost. Over a thousand years later, the intellect is still worshiped as the preeminent force.

But behind the mind there is a door. If you open it, there sits your spirit, twiddling its spiritual thumbs, oscillating quietly, waiting. . . reading "The Life and Times of Pope Nicholas." I believe the spirit is a molecular quantum of the same celestial light or energy that we call the God Force. Your spirit is the God Force and the God Force is your spirit. What is the God Force? As I see it, it's an energy that pervades all things—a celestial light. The nearest thing in Christian terminology is grace. The difference between the God Force and regular light is that the God Force emanates feeling. Humans call that feeling love. I don't know why celestial light causes humans to feel positive emotions in that way, but I wouldn't be happy with some twee answer about "how nice God is." There has to be an explanation. When you walk in a forest you feel good. But do you feel good because the forest is intrinsically good? No. You feel good because the environment is highly charged with negative ions which are refreshing to the body. In other words, is the celestial light intrinsically good or does it exude some hidden force that makes you feel good? Are there circumstances when those conditions change? It's hard to say. But if celestial light didn't exude feeling it would be regular light.

Let's leave the God Force for a moment, as it gets into complicated speculations of space/time cosmology and religious arguments from which there are no real conclusions. Let's return to the spirit. I believe the spirit molecule radiates energy, and in the same way as you need nutritional energy to run your body, the Inner You needs spiritual light to give it perception, because the Inner You starts off completely blind. The Inner You also needs light to give it power to travel inwards. I think there is at least one more vital function of the spirit quantum and that's to retain an eternal memory of you after death. The mind, or soul, has no way of remembering itself without a brain—at least none that we have discovered as yet.

It seems to me that the spirit within you is ancient, probably eternal; it has memory that seems greater than the contents of the subconscious mind. It knows things that your mind or even the Inner You—which, after all, was birthed from your mind— could not possibly know. What it knows and remembers is very hard to access. I used to think it was impossible to reach the spirit's memory while still alive in the physical body—I've changed my mind—but still it is vast. That is why some call it the Higher Self. I use the terms Higher Self and Spirit interchangeably. It's impossible to say if the spirit quantum's memory is stored within that quantum or if it somehow accesses a greater memory stored elsewhere. The Planetary Group Soul that I referred to in the previous chapters is the group mind or soul of humanity. In Jungian terms it is the collective unconscious wherein lay all the archetypal symbols and thoughts of mankind. But beyond the Planetary Group Soul there has to be at least one more component to hold the memory of that Group Soul, and I believe that's the Planetary Group Spirit, which is all of the spirit quantum that have ever existed inside each human, interconnected to each other via their God Force quality.

By now you may be a little confused. And you might be wondering: Am I body and soul? Or spirit and mind? Am I an inner being, a Higher Self, a quantum of God Force, a celestial light and/or a Planetary Group this or a Planetary Group that or even Paddy McGinty's goat? Fret not. It all becomes clear as we move along. The fact is, you are all of the above, except for the goat. Each piece is inside another.

What's important to remember is that through introspection you create the inner particle state—the Inner You. It gains strength as you focus upon it. By quieting the ego, the celestial light of the spirit shines through, giving your inner self life. The spirit is immensely powerful, but it has little influence in your life until it is freed from the debilitating racket made by the intellect. Then it can pervade your inner self, which in turn, pervades your outer conscious self. It's the spirit that gives the Inner You energy and provides vision to your inner and outer self through a heightened sense of feelings. Spirit grants you feelings because everything is energy, so everything radiates a message. The spirit is connected to everything via the God Force. The spirit can connect your inner self or your conscious outer self to the energy signals emitted by every aspect of life.

Suddenly, your inner self is no longer completely blind. It now has heightened feelings provided through the grace of spirit that illuminates its path. Prior to its awakening, it's impossible for your inner self to begin the journey. Without inner perception it would not even conceive of it, anymore than a baby would rise from its cot to hitch a lift downtown. After your inner self gets perception, via spiritual feelings, it experiences a great rush of joy and excitement. It is now alive. It has a purpose.

Realizations come thick and fast; now your intellect is no longer denying your inner self its proper spiritual destiny. By birthing the Inner You and infusing it with spirit, you begin to extricate that identity out from the tribal mind. It teaches you things. Your perspective becomes more and more infinite and nondenominational. Your power grows because your intellect no longer dominates. You are no longer in your own way. You are inspired to climb. Each step invigorates you. You want to align to a new energy, possibly a new career—one that is more spiritually aligned or has more meaning, except you don't clearly see what direction to take. The question common to us all at this stage is: "What the hell do I do next?"

As you begin to exit the wave to become an inner particle, it's likely you will want to help others make the same transition. The problem at this early stage is that your inner vision is literally up against the rock face of your climb from tick-tock. So when you ask yourself, "What next? Which way?" You often get no real answers. Things don't open for you as you feel they should. This is because you only have a very limited depth to your perception while on the climb. Though there may be opportunities and new associations, and though you may be experiencing a lot of psychic activity, unusual coincidences, ESP, and sometimes even strange phenomena, there is nothing very concrete or obvious presented to you. As you search for a new, higher place in which to slot into life, this can cause you a lot of confusion and heartache.

The secret is this: While scaling that rock face you need every ounce of energy to hold on. Through a simple lack of determination you can easily fall back to the mundane plane of tick-tock. As you try to leave the wave it has a way of reaching for you, attempting to call you back, sometimes ridiculing you for what it perceives is the silliness of your attempts—which it doesn't understand. Wave cannot comprehend inner particle. Like Lot's wife in the bible, you will have a desire to look back, because after all, tick-tock was home for a long time. So your tendency to drift back, plus the psychological tug of the tribal wave, may disrupt your climb and rattle your security. If you're not careful—down you fall.

Anytime you make transitions in the inner world, you will be doing the same in your external life. Transitions place one in a vulnerable state and they should be taken on with diligence and a heightened awareness. The process requires patience. You need time to become comfortable with new ideas and beliefs. It's easy to comprehend a new concept intellectually, and to agree with the idea, but it takes much longer for that concept to become real in your heart, so that you can live and breathe it naturally.

98 There is a tendency for people to get so carried away with their inner journey and the sheer exhilaration of the climb that they become hyperenergized by their own enthusiasm. They immediately discard their old systems of financial support and wander off like pilgrims, hoping that from within their inspiration they'll discover a way of making a living that suits their changing consciousness. In their effort to open up a new path, they often succeed in decapitating the old order to such an extent that they soon face financial hardship or worse—complete ruin.

Please box clever—the lessons are simple: While you are climbing the rock face, recognize it as such. Understand that because your vision is limited, you will not see far into the future. The best thing to do is to concentrate on the climb, rather than trying to carve out a new career for yourself just yet. If you head out too early, you will very likely shoot yourself in the foot. I have seen it happen a thousand times—an individual becomes so inspired by the climb and their desire to quit tick-tock that they set themselves up in a new business (usually related to self-help, alternative healing, or assisting others in some way) before they really have the energy or perception to pull it off. Invariably, the business ends in failure, which further pressurizes them. Their progress up the rock face is stymied because their belief in self is temporarily shattered. In addition, their finances are decimated, greatly inhibiting their ability to purchase the knowledge and experiences needed to complete the climb. To really change your consciousness and to create a consolidation of power within, you need peace, balance, and time to reflect. A lack of money at this time is detrimental to the process.

Instead, do one or all of the following things: First, recognize that you are on the climb, know that it is important and sacred, and that what you are doing at this moment is climbing— nothing else. Simplify your life and support yourself anyway you can, providing it does not take too much of your time and energy. Fry hamburgers, pump gas, whatever. Be satisfied in just climbing. Be patient; all will come in time.

The second option is to think twice about chucking in your tick-tock job while making the climb. Even though you may have to grit your teeth and suffer, it's better to have strong financial backing for your quest, than to be terribly spiritual and potless. It's almost impossible to stabilize yourself at a higher vibrational energy if you are being harassed by mundane stuff like making the rent. The last thing you want to do is to fall back on having to accept people's charity or government handouts to sustain you. That acts as a contradiction. You can't embrace freedom and individuality if you have to trot back and forth to the nipple to sustain yourself.

It's best to keep your former means of financial support in place and begin a new venture, perhaps on a part-time basis. That way you have both things going for you simultaneously. Once your new, chosen direction becomes strong enough to support you, you can discard your old tick-tock money sources and step to the new career in a balanced way.

Once the thousand day climb is over—and you'll know almost to the exact day when that is—you reach the first plane of understanding. Because the changes within you are now consolidated, they belong to you, and they are you, instead of your attempting to belong to them, as is the case during the climb. Now you will have breadth of vision. At this stage it will probably still only be feelings, rather than inner sight expressed as visions, but those feelings will be able to pull information and energy from a greater distance. People and opportunities will be attracted to you. There is a peace and a naturalness within you that comes from consolidation, which exudes inner strength and stability of character.

When you look back at your climb, you'll see how during that crucial time you were too uncomfortable with yourself to be of much use to others, and because you were changing, you often lacked complete confidence. It's common for your overenergized obsession with your new discoveries to actually push opportunities and even people away. Remember, the world is intuitive. Opportunities move toward order, balance, and power; they move away from scattered, overenergized people, and they flee at high speed from confusion and a lack of consistency.

There is one more caveat. When you make the turn within, the psychic phenomena, strange coincidences, and heightened perceptions that you experience may kid your ego into thinking that you are some very special wizard who has been chosen by God to lead the ignorant to the promised land. I'd be careful not to be suckered into that idea. It's not a good time for the ego to get into a power trip. You need humility and introspection, not a rise in self-importance. After a while, all the whizzbang ESP stuff will quieten down; there is nothing more comical or open to ridicule than a wizard with no whizz. If you really want extraordinary powers you will have to travel a very long way to get them. Once you are upon the first plateau of understanding, opportunities will emerge. At first they seem rather small and relatively unimportant. Follow them; they will lead to greater things. Invest in yourself and try things out. It doesn't matter if you head up the wrong path; with your higher level of perception you'll soon see if a particular direction is for you, and if not, you'll shift to another. Going a little way up the wrong path is not a bad thing. You learn about yourself and your needs, and if nothing else, you understand what to eliminate. Eventually, you are bound to find what you seek.

After the thousand day climb, there are other climbs up ahead, but none will be like the first. The others are more gradual and shorter. They can last between a month and six months, and though the climbs can be quite tough, and your body might ache as it reacts to the establishment of a higher vibration, you'll manage quite easily, for now you will have the tools and perception of spirit to help you. In addition, your inner self will have learned a lot in the thousand day climb and will now have a greater spiritual capacity. Prior to its absolute consolidation at the top of the climb, the Inner You has only a partial definition. Yes, it is a personality, but much of its definition is still hazy. It lacks experience, and the memory of tick-tock lingers, wafting through like a pungent aroma that reminds you of a place you once visited.

As you make the inner journey from one plateau to the next, the grip of ego on your life is loosened, and the light of spirit begins to shine through the inner self and upon the ego, melting it somewhat. The process is enhanced because your concentration is now shifted from a totally external view to a partially inner one. Your ego is disenfranchised. Once the inner particle state becomes more and more real, the ego starts to flap in the breeze. It has lived all of its life in the wave; the inner state is so foreign that the ego backs off not knowing what to do.

The intensity of the ego melt down varies from time to time; it is greater in the climbs and less on the plateaus. During the relatively flat, easy times, where you are usually traveling forward, but resting, the ego will from time to time put in a counterattack, especially if you are out of touch with your inner self, imbalanced in some way or physically tired. But over the years, the ego's efforts eventually become more and more wimpy.

When those meltdowns occur (and everyone that has ever been on the path will feel them at some time or other) they seem, psychologically, like bits of your personality are dropping off—almost like soil erosion. In those periods, you will feel overwhelmed by the thought that you are dying. But you aren't dying—your ego is. It can't sustain the idea of your living without it. So, for a time, your mind will be drenched with the most morbid thoughts, while your ego squirms like a stuck pig. If the sensation becomes oppressive, put yourself on a vigorous discipline of some kind, whether it be fasting, silence, being alone, meditating, handling unresolved problems—whatever. The bad thoughts will pass and eventually the ego will agree to lessen its grip on your life.

The nature of your inner journey will depend a lot on the issues and traits of your inner self (which you will recall was birthed from the contents of your mind). On reaching the first plateau, some choose to wander about for a while before continuing. Others make a beeline for the next climb. There is no right or wrong of it. Sometimes, if you go too fast, you may ride roughshod over some special aspect of yourself that needs attention. If you ignore it and travel too far past it, your inner journey becomes empty. In some way that I don't exactly understand your power gets snagged on the item you dodged around. If the item is major, you'll see it appear in various guises in your external life. It will keep coming back to chat with you. Sometimes, it's holding a big stick while it's chatting. On other occasions you will resolve an issue on one plateau and find it comes back on the next plateau, but has deeper qualities. Like an onion skin that peels off, allowing you to go deeper and deeper into the center of the issue, each plateau unravels only as much as necessary and then allows you to move on. You know through feeling how much is necessary.

There is one other caution that I feel bound to mention: As you climb from plateau to plateau your understanding becomes more rarefied, you will become more and more detached and distant from tick-tock, eventually winding up on strange and quite lonely planes of consciousness where few others have ever been. On those plateaus, you will get the impression that the dimension of consciousness in which your inner journey exists is becoming more and more bland. There's little there that you recognize. The symbology of the place does not compare with the familiar things of the physical plane—it's foreign. So foreign, you don't comprehend it well, if you see much of it at all. You'll get the impression there is nothing much there. Up on those higher plateaus, there is a small but real possibility that, having completed your exit from tick-tock and understanding things to such a level on the inner journey, you may accidently project yourself out of the physical plane. That possibility exists because, in essence, you'll have completed your experience here on the earth plane, and great chunks of your ego will have already fallen away. Because the Inner You is in such unfamiliar territory, the emptiness of its surroundings flows into your external life. You'll get bored and you may find it hard to keep your mind on anything in particular. The ego's primary function is to keep you locked in the physical plane. When it melts, your grip here becomes more tenuous, and you may for a while feel rather listless. Sometimes the thought comes up from within you—without your even being aware of it at first—that perhaps it might not be a bad idea to quit the physical plane and head off to another evolution, given that this one seems to offer so little that's new and different.

The danger lies in your lack of imagination and your belief that there is nothing left to do. If those thoughts become a perpetual part of your thinking, your conscious self will begin to loose its grip on life. Remember, by then the ego will have suffered such a terrible melt down that it can't see much point in continuing. So it may try to quit. The inner self does not care much if you are alive or dead. It has an eternal journey and a solid destiny of its own, empowered more and more by spirit. In fact, up on that plane I had the distinct feeling for a while that the inner me had traveled so far that it was not quite sure if the outer me was alive or not. I took great pains to explain to it that I was still here, a bit bored but hale and hearty, no less. Certainly, the inner self doesn't care that much one way or the other. The ego and the physical body were never the inner self's best friends.

Now, checking out is fine—if checking out is what you want. However, if you exert your imagination and expand your external vision, you will quite likely discover all sorts of things that might interest you. You may find that there are certain aspects of your life you have already completed, to which you can return, recapitulating your experiences in a more profound way. If you really don't know what to do next, ask of your Higher Self/spirit to guide you to a place where you are needed. Most likely it will.

The trick is to be inventive and keep moving, otherwise you may "twang" yourself out of the physical plane through a lack of emotional commitment to life. I just mention it in passing, as I've lost a few mates that way, and I nearly lost myself one day, when I wasn't watching my rear end, energywise.

Traveling, climbing, and traveling some more, after a number of years you'll eventually come upon a very strange place: the Plane of Desolation. It is long and wide, and devoid of any inner life. It is a twilight zone placed between our world of human images and thoughts, and the pure spiritual world that lies beyond. You won't need much up there, and the few that have experienced it won't talk to you about it, as it has way of mesmerizing one's consciousness into silence. Each step is slow and deliberate, and the quixotic nature of that eerie place—the door step of the gods—makes the inner self ever more contemplative. It is utterly engrossing, like moving across a vast empty desert in slow motion. Every step becomes an affirmation of your power. Every minute action speaks a million words, inscribed as if upon sacred parchment, describing and evaluating the level of your selflessness, the purity of your intent and the quality of your courage, determination, solidity, and strength.

I'm not sure if the length of time spent on the Plane of Desolation is the same for everyone, but in my case it took three years to walk across it. Understanding, of course, that this is an inner journey; three years describes an external time frame not internal.

At the other end is a door to another place. As you approach the door, the melting process of the ego becomes so intense it's like walking toward a raging fire. The inner pain is excruciating, and the flow of remorse and sorrow and utter helplessness the ego spews forth (through no fault of its own), overwhelms you with a sense of futility, apprehension, and fear. It is said that all travelers turn back at the first approach. Humans are just not equipped to cope. The fragility of our condition and our attitudes towards loneliness and pain overwhelm us.

Now you see why the plane you just crossed seemed so desolate. For as you begin the final traverse from our world to another, the images and symbols of the human mind—that the ego personality relates to—begin to disappear. There is nothing on that desolate plane to assist you or to support you. There's no one up there to show the way; there are no instructions. You're on your own. Once you approach the door, the disembodiment you experience is so intense you see how the Plane of Desolation, rather than being hostile, was actually a teacher. It was showing you, through its starkness and lack of things on which to hold, what to expect later. Crossing the plane strengthens you for the approach.

Each time you move toward the door the pain and fear grow a little less, and somehow the power and spiritual love that exudes from the other side of the door touches you, gradually helping you sustain your presence there. You get more comfortable as time goes on.

Close to the threshold, you will experience a compression of time. You might have already experienced it, in a mild form, on the plateaus that you crossed a while back. It is difficult to explain the process, but it's as if time becomes thicker and thicker. There's an invisible force that surrounds the threshold, which at first, seems to be deliberately holding you back. In fact, it is not.

Imagine a journey of ten thousand miles that takes ten years. Finally, you arrive at the door. It burns you with a feeling of disembodiment, and in your apprehension you retreat and return, only to retreat again. But eventually you adjust to the weird experiences that surround the entrance, and you feel comfortable standing close to the door. Several more years have passed back in the real world and now you are three yards short of the door, but you can't move yourself forward. Between you and the door time is so thick that the final nine feet of your journey take several more years to complete.

You move so slowly you get the feeling you're never going to make it, and I expect that many a traveler has quit at this point and turned back. Imagine a world where it takes you a year to lift your foot and place it in a stride in front of you. You need tenacity and patience; if you don't quit, you'll get through. On the other side is another world. It's so pure and pristine, and utterly beyond the imagination of humanity that it covers you with its presence; the first thing you do is fall asleep. I can't say how long that inner sleep lasts in the inner world's time frame, nor can I say whether the sleep period is common to everyone, but in my case, fifteen months passed on the earth plane. When you wake, perception of that new world is available to you. However, on an inner level you have to come back because you can't stay there while your main focus is the human form. Your external life would collapse as your internal perception of that celestial place swamps your feelings, causing you to lose a cohesive attitude to life. But in completing the journey you succeed in a sacred quest that is undertaken by very few. There is a serenity that descends upon you from the realization that you belong to that spiritual dimension, and that your place in the immortality of the light is assured through the heritage granted to all by the God Force. The position you establish in that world grants you the vision. Your inner being now has real sight as well as feelings.

If you look at the plateau journey on a personal level, you can see that there is a global version that the Planetary Group Soul is also going through.

The first step each individual takes in changing their consciousness is by becoming restless in tick-tock and dissatisfied with life. This dissatisfaction occurs as an individual begins raising his or her energy to oscillate at a higher speed. Suddenly, the circumstances of life, and the idea and habit of tick-tock feel extremely restrictive. It's not that the circumstances are wrong of themselves—they may suit others just fine—it's just that they become wrong for a large group whose energy has gone beyond those circumstances.

On a global level, we rested inside tribal ideas for thousands of years. The collective energy of mankind wasn't going anywhere, so tribal circumstances suited us. But after the Industrial Revolution, everything acquired velocity. Expansion gave our people hope. However, after a hundred and fifty years, the remnants of the old ideas have now run their course. People are looking for answers. There is a dissatisfaction with restriction. I'm talking about life in the Western democracies. I'm not referring to other areas like Asia or Africa.

Technology is allowing many to work from home; the grip of the unions is being loosened. The status quo is losing control and acting erratically, causing a tremendous volatility in society. Our reality is wobbling. Nothing is certain anymore.

At the lower level, the moaning and groaning you hear every-where is just the ego being rattled. People are asking questions, wondering why, looking at tick-tock and seeing themselves as victims of it and its leaders. The moaning is all a bit negative, but it's not a bad thing in of itself—it forces people to seek new solutions.

People are opening up to new ideas. However, there is a long way to go. The New Age, alternative healing, and other spiritual ideas have not gained much acceptance in the mainstream of society. Sure, there's a lot of alternative people, but if you take society *en masse* the numbers are still quite small. Of the English-speaking countries in the Western world, I would say that only in Australia and to some extent New Zealand have these new ideas penetrated into the mainstream. In America it has spread well, but the vastness of the country and the strength of traditional religion prevents complete penetration at a mass level as yet. The USA is very conservative compared to other Western nations. In Canada the penetration is mainly on the west coast, while in England the movement is still in its infancy, but is growing despite the inhibiting class system and adverse economic conditions which stifle people's ability to invest in themselves, so they may grow and expand.

The climb up the rock face to the first plateau is devoid of real vision and can be rather confusing and uncertain. I believe that the Planetary Group Soul will go through the same process. That may cause a dark night of the soul for some, but it's the only way that a stifling and spent energy can rebirth itself to become something new. In the same way as your first move is to accept new ideas and to control the ego, the Planetary Group Soul will have to come to the same wider vision for the people.

I'm convinced the process is well under way, with millions of Fringe Dwellers and spiritual seekers moving away from the central control society imposes, toward the margins. It's there that they find freedom and the ability to become self-sufficient.

In this way, spiritual attitudes to life become normal rather than strange. For many this transition is not a trauma, but very natural. Difficulties occur when crises force people who are firmly in the status quo or on a personal ego parabola, to accept change against their will. But many now realize that they have to look within. So the numbers of those that are only rooted externally is declining. Gradually, we will come back to what is real and what is true. That will be a very refreshing and comforting place to be.

Let's look at truth.

Truth or Consequence?

CHAPTER FIVE

The process by which the world ego gives over part of its control to the spirit of the people is unlikely to be a smooth flowing, natural event. It could be if the world ego rested within a disciplined and spiritual world mind, but it doesn't. Your ego is vulnerable and a victim of your changing consciousness. The world ego is particularly vulnerable to the influence of spirit upon it because the power of spirit forces it to look at itself and accept the truth of the distortions it projects. But truth is hard to accept. It takes a courageous individual to look at the truth in their life, and it will take courage for the world to go through the same process.

Imagine that as if by a stroke of magic, the whole world was forced to live in truth, starting at lunchtime today. Think of the mayhem. Business people would have to pay their bills. Directors would have to stop misappropriating shareholders' money. Governments would have to stop manipulating information and live within their means. Advertising agencies could no longer hype high priced products of dubious value to unsuspecting customers. Public relations would probably die by tea time. Most of the media would fall to silence. Most of the lawyers would disappear. Real estate prices would plummet. Workers would be forced to offer a complete day's work for a complete day's pay. Spouses who cheat on their partners would have to 'fess up and so on.

Truth is not terribly attractive to the world mind. It is terrifying really. Still—not to worry—truth isn't happening just yet. Instead, copious great lies can be churned out and sustained a little while longer. People like it. They buy it and parrot it on. When enough people buy a lie it eventually becomes a truism. So, in modern society, truth is partly a factor of popularity. Popular lies are truth. Unpopular facts are heresy.

The lies have always been there, but over the last fifty years the manufacture of the Great Lie has become more and more an industry. It is so popular it's now a religion unto itself. We expect people to lie. Lying is considered shrewd and crafty. Through lies we get ahead. We even have laws that forbid openness and truth. Many facts are hidden from the people, in what is deemed to be in the public interest. Of course, a scamp might ask how hiding information is in the interest of the public Answer: It is claimed to be in the public interest when hiding information protects someone's power base. A second lie is then required to make sure no one asks any awkward question about the first lie.

Sometimes, when lecturing, I talk about the Great Lies of life. I don't do it often because people don't like it. You can visibly see your audience shifting in their seats like cattle that have been spooked by the scent of an unseen predator. The word "lie" somehow affects the human bladder. Two or three minutes after you utter the unspeakable word, a large chunk of your audience will find reason to head for the toilet. In fact, if you intend to talk about the "Great Lies" for any length of time, you might as well come off the podium and head for the restroom yourself. Sooner or later that's where all of your audience will be, with the exception of the few that are stone deaf or asleep.

But truth, my dear scamps, is a commodity whose time has come. It's a necessary good that our society will eventually have to embrace. Truth is an outcropping of your spirit. It is a vital part of establishing proper introspection and observation. We are heading that way whether people like it or not.

I believe that the immortal spirit within us is in effect a configuration of atoms and molecules trapped inside the electromagnetic force field of the body and bound by the electrical field created through oscillations of the brain. It seems to me that the spiritual self cannot lie. I'm not sure why it can't lie. I think it's because the spirit is passive. It radiates energy, but it doesn't forcefully project energy as the mind does. It is not influenced by opinions or positions it has to defend. I would like to say that the spirit can't lie because it is a spark of God, but I'm not big enough to know what God is. Certainly, the spirit is a spark of an immensely wonderful manifestation of an energy that is much bigger than us; it has no fear, so perhaps that's why it doesn't mess with petty nonsense as we humans do.

If you control the ego, and focus your consciousness on your inner spirit, it soon reflects back to you the inconsistencies embedded in your personality. Over the years, as your spiritual energy grows, lies go from a part of everyday life to unfortunate necessities, to uncomfortable experiences, to extremely pain-fully burdens that you will do anything to be rid off. If you have taken to the spiritual path you will know what I mean. You can't have observation without dismissing the lies. Transcendence is partly the process of moving from phony to real.

Personally, I found the procedure invigorating and liberating, but like ointment on a cut, it stings a bit. As a young man in my twenties, I had a Phd (Piled Higher and Deeper) in bullshit. My friendship with accuracy and genuineness was fleeting at best. Truth for me was mostly a blind date that I acquiesced to when I was very drunk. However, I was drunk most of the time. Perhaps I was closer to the truth than I remember. At the age of twenty-eight I took to the spiritual path with gusto, and by the time I did so I had already become uncomfortable with my hypocrisies and inconsistencies. It followed naturally that I would dismiss many of them from my life over the next few years. However, the complete process of going from phony to real took me about eight years. Even today I sometimes find obscure bits of myself that haven't pledged allegiance to the new order. Truth is vital if you want to progress as a spiritual being.

Of course, it's important to tell the truth to others and to be an honest person. But the reason for being truthful is not a moral issue in my view. Rather it is part of the process of developing a sensible and realistic inner dialogue that is fundamental to personal strength and spiritual well-being. It's the only way to go if you want to particularize your destiny.

If you tell a lot of external fibs, your internal dialogue will generally reflect the same inconsistency. It's hard to get a grip on your personal power and realize your full potential as a spiritual being if what you believe about yourself is highly inaccurate, or if you constantly buy the ego's story and head up the wrong path.

There is a third aspect to this. If you don't as yet embrace complete truth within you, quite often your dealings with others will be muddled. You'll hide or distort your true intentions and give people a lot of bull or an inaccurate picture. That may come home to cause trouble. Once you can fearlessly look at yourself, you will also have a tendency to dialogue with people in a direct and honest way. They may not like what they hear, but at least you have told them the truth. Your ego may not like what it's hearing either, but you must learn to control it or it will tow you around for ever.

Our inherited mental programming is often very negative and insecure, so the ego is naturally attracted to anything that makes it feel special or pumps it up, regardless if it's fake or not. The anguish of the world can be laid totally at the ego's doorstep. As people seek to sustain and propagate the phony images of the ego, almost any course of action is justified. The only alternative is to let the ego suffer its anxieties. So much of our energy is spent sustaining an unholy position that we buy lock, stock, and barrel from the ego.

If you begin to change your internal dialogue by batting down the negative aspects and replacing them with positive expectancy, the ego retreats. Much of what the ego is telling you about life and the imminent danger you face is not true or realistic. The disaster films it makes you watch are an outcropping of its library; they don't necessarily describe what's actually happening in your life. They are negative "maybe's." Eliminating them is a slow process. The ego may have reigned over your mind for a long time, but eventually your inner dialogue improves. You shift toward truth. The need for self-aggrandizement, reassurance, and ego boost wanes. You become a more attractive person to deal with.

115

The spiritual energy within you—or the Higher Self as some call it—is honest and serene. It is fair and good. Most of all, it is humble. Embracing it doesn't stop you from being assertive and concise in your approach to life. It certainly is no impediment to getting what you want—quite the reverse. However, it does require that you stand in the awe of that energy, and have a sense of propriety about your actions and what you project to the world. That is what is meant by taking responsibility for your life.

From mental discipline and an alignment to spirit, you begin to control your levels of fear. As you do, it takes you out of the normal mind set of mankind, which is very fearful most of the time. You step to a new and more courageous place. If you step toward your spirit, it embraces you and creates a spiritual cocoon that gradually expresses itself in your etheric energy, making you safer. As you touch it and feel it and live within it, its inherent serenity pervades your being. You move out of the lower oscillations of etheric which removes you from harm's way. One thing builds on another.

As I said, in controlling the ego you tend to melt it. It feels very threatened by its loss of power. But you have to lose yourself in order to rediscover yourself again. Once the security of spirit flows through you, you see how mental discipline heals your life. Eventually the ego relaxes when it sees that the new driver of your personal bus is as steady as a rock. The by-product of spirit is perception. With it, you no longer have to guess what direction to take—as the ego does. Everything radiates energy. Spirit connects you to that radiation. Through sensitivity and feeling you have advance information, so you know what to do. When you are not sure what to do it means that the circumstances you are considering are not radiating enough power, because either there is something wrong, or they haven't properly developed as yet. When you are not sure, do nothing—wait.

We have to demonstrate this mental discipline and control of the ego to our people. It's the only way the world can heal and reconcile itself. Contradicting and assailing the Great Lies is the first step. If the ego is never contradicted, it tends to soldier on, perpetuating its own myths. "Black is white. Wrong is right. Anything's fine, if it stops the fright." You can see why people need to bend reality to suit themselves—it's mainly a security issue. You can have compassion for that. Eventually, however, we all have to look at our inconsistencies. The world as a whole has to retire the Great Lies and begin to reestablish a holy relationship with itself.

What are the Great Lies of the world ego? They are the half-truths and complete falsities uttered (usually through the media) by the corporate or political status quo. It's the process which the former US President Herbert Hoover called "sustaining the moral of the people." The function is to bend public opinion in the required direction, while covering real facts with side issues that distract the populace.

Some of the lies are fairly inconsequential, like those companies that advertise mountain spring water that is actually filtered tap water, then there are the lies the media offers, which are not necessarily lies in the strictest sense of the word, just slants and distortions used in the presentation of information which establishes a fact and then excludes the consideration of other possibilities. Beyond those lies are the whoppers that governments tell to keep everyone apathetic and docile.

As I came gradually to the truth, external lies started to bug me because while listening to other people's lies, I somehow felt I might never go past my own. But I learned to disconnect, and I turned the source of my frustration into an entertainment. I love to peruse the newspapers in search of the Great Lies of life. It's much like that kid's game, "Where's Waldo?" which in some countries is called, "Where's Wally?" Kids look for a little guy in a funny hat, hidden among a hundred illustrated characters. Finding the Great Lie is a grown-up's version of "Where's Waldo?" Politically, being caught deliberately lying is a no-no. So lying through obfuscation, confusion, and omission is the preferred choice of our parliamentarians. We are bombarded by misinformation buried in statistics and half-truths. But like Waldo, if you look you'll find them.

Not all half-truths are lies. If you only know half the facts, then what you utter is all you know—so it's truthful from your point of reference. Half-truths offered by a government department that has access to all of the information available is deception. I could spend endless hours discussing the Great Lies, studying them has been one of the loves of my life. I even contemplated a small book called "My Fifty Favorite Lies." But instead of looking at fifty lies, let's look at just a couple to give you an idea of what I mean.

Each month the government announces the unemployment figures as a percentage of the work force. Let's say this month's figure is ten percent. The figure is offered as a true representation of the percentage of the work force currently unemployed. High unemployment figures are politically damaging, so the government engages in a deception to announce the lowest figure possible.

Let us say, for the sake of argument, that the Labor Department or Home Office (or whatever) doesn't blatantly cook the books in their favor. So when they say unemployment is at ten percent, it is an accurate figure of the number of people on the dole. At this point they haven't told a lie because they haven't told you very much at all.

Here's the truth of it. First, no one outside the government really knows how the figures purported to represent the total work force are calculated. An individual has to be registered in the government computer to be counted. Who's in and who isn't— we don't know. We have to take the government's word for it. What about all those citizens who have never ever been in the work force or those who don't care to be in the computer? How many of those are working or unemployed?

In addition, the official unemployment figures deliberately omit several very large categories of people who are not officially unemployed. They consist of all those people that are out of work but not on the dole, including those whose dole payments have run out. Also, they overlook all the workers who are changing jobs or moving, plus those whose pride or strength of their savings exclude them from the list. Added to the official omissions are all the people with part-time jobs who are not counted as unemployed for the part of the week that they don't work. Technically many part-time workers share jobs with other workers, and many would work full-time if there was enough work to do. If you include everyone out of work, but not on the dole, and then add the partially unemployed part-time work force, the official figure would jump from ten to twelve percent and would begin to head for the fifteen percent mark.

Official lists also omit people in hospitals or on sick pay, as well as prisoners who would jump the walls for a steady job if they could. Then add to these figures senior citizens who have been forced into early retirement. You have to count this category because if a chap is forced to retire at sixty-one instead of sixty-five, he is technically unemployed for four years. Then there's all those people able, fit, and ready to work who face compulsory retirement by the state or industry because they have reached the official age.

The list goes on to include those workers who are marginally disabled with slight back injuries, stress syndrome, and that kind of stuff, who might work if they had to or if they could, but who show up on disability pensions, rather than unemployment figures.

Now the real percentage is definitely edging fifteen percent and heading for twenty. Over and above these half dozen groups are all the small independent contractors and small business people, who may suffer losses in any one financial year. They count as employed but have effectively earned no money, rendering them technically unemployed. Many of these independent contractors don't work full-time. So if ten self-employed carpenters work on average two weeks out of four, you have, in effect, five fully employed carpenters sharing work with five others. Then add all the mothers at home who might willingly join the work force if the economy were better, but choose to muddle along on their husband's pay instead. They often don't show up on the official list, because they dropped out of the work force to have children or they never joined the list in the first place. And then there's no record of all those citizens who got fed up and emigrated to other countries to find work.

Once you have totted up all these conveniently "missing members" there are still a few more. A large number of people are in government training schemes of one kind or another. They don't show up as unemployed either. These schemes may be technical courses, retraining, and youth employment plans. In addition to all these people who are handily shunted off the list, there are a large number of students who would like to earn a wage, but stay at a university a few extra years instead because there is a shortage of gainful work.

120 Now the real unemployment figure may be up around twenty percent of the possible working population. From the real figure, you would have to subtract all those who collect dole but who are secretly working (it's safe to say twenty percent of the dole recipients actually work). So that would mean knocking two percentage points off the total unemployment figures. But in the end you'd come to some fairly accurate numbers. Ten percent unemployment is a political setback, but if the real figure were actually known to be fifteen or twenty percent, the government might collapse.

While citizens experience the reality of true unemployment in their daily lives, the government papers over the real facts by omission, dramatically shrinking the official numbers and offering instead of fact, the "happy happy" lie about how things aren't too bad. They will tell you that everything is just about to improve. It's drivel. Once people wake up to the great turd they are offered as truth, the government might have to clean up its act a bit. Meanwhile, we wait with baited breath for this month's figures.

Another one of the government lies I find particularly fascinating—because of the wonderful double-speak involved—is the issue of the nationalized industries. Because governments are going skint, they are desperately selling off assets and various government industries and utilities to stave off the inevitable. In countries other than the US, many of the industries were nationalized years ago. They were bought and developed by the state with the taxpayers' money. The idea was that the state would administer these industries—like the coal industry in England—for the benefit of the people, who would all share in its collective ownership. It's pure gobbledygook from George Orwell's Animal Farm. Dividends arising from profits these companies made were never paid to the common people. When the governments decided to return these industries to the private sector the industries were not given to the people. They were sold back into private ownership. If the nationalized industries were truly an asset of the people then the government would have had to give the shares, free of charge, back to the taxpayers whose money bought the companies in the first place. At that point, the whole nationalized industry idea went out the window and the state has kept all of the money. The idea that the state holds assets—land and so on—for the national benefit is pure drivel. Only the truly scrambled or highly misinformed could fail to see through such a blatant lie. No benefit has ever flowed to the people. What was often a publicly owned monopoly becomes a privately owned monopoly.

But the government can get away with these scams as it genuinely believes that no one will take any notice. Further, it believes its citizens are largely idiots, to be controlled, punished, and instructed in the official philosophy. This belief stems from the egotistic and arrogant nature of absolute power. Once we grow a bit more and become individually more responsible, things will have to change. The spirit of the people acts as a mirror to the status quo. In that reflection the hierarchy sees its own weakness. The process is slow because the power structure is as myopic and hardheaded as it is intransigent. This is an automatic response of a governing elite that considers itself superior to the masses. In fact, if the truth were known, the ruling elite despise the masses. They would much prefer not to have to mess with telling us anything. We're an encumbrance they are forced to pander to. Dealing with the drones is bothersome when you are a very important person who's busy running the world.

As the Planetary Group Soul evolved, people began to question the hierarchy's monopoly over information. Feeling the political pinch, the state now offers us truth in lending laws, corporate disclosure requirements, freedom of information acts, and the promise of open government—whatever that is.

Though these changes are commendable, I think it's a bit of a red herring. It's appeasement with no real change. The Freedom of Information Act offers you selective bits of what is often old information that the government doesn't need any more—but what about the real stuff? Corporate disclosure is a good thing, but does it really stop company directors from pinching your money? I think not. The accounts of public companies proves otherwise. Most directors of public companies bathe in their shareholders' money regardless of whether the company makes a profit and pays dividends or not. I'm yet to be convinced that disclosure does much for you. If I come to your house on the first of each month and rob you, and I then offer you a detailed computer printout of what I took and how I spent your money, what does that really do for you? The issue is not information, so much as—how do we stop government and corporate theft of the citizen's resources.

Don't let the issue irritate you. The very fact that these freedom of information laws have been passed shows that the spirit is eroding the power of the ego. The healing process is on its way. We are moving toward truth. It will gather momentum. As individuals, we often feel small and insignificant. But we shouldn't fall for that attitude as of itself—it becomes an affirmation of our disempowerment. The Planetary Group Soul is massive and it is right. Stand inside the justice offered by its great spiritual strength and suddenly you possess a power that is far from insignificant.

Truth or Consequence?

In the early 1400's France was in shambles. It was ruled in the north by the English who had crossed the channel and captured the lands by force. The central and southern part of what is now France was governed by war lords and robber barons who pillaged the land and fought among themselves. The country was very poor because agriculture and industry was limited to what people were able to defend. Large tracts of fertile lands were abandoned and left uncultivated. There was a ruling elite which had a court at Chinon but it was a hot bed of self-indulgence, corruption, and infighting. There was no cohesion or leadership. There was no French monarch to unify the country. The English were moving relentlessly south. The court was threatened.

In the village of Domrémy, in the Meuse river valley, there lived a young girl, the daughter of a farmer. One day she had a vision from the dreamtime of the folk spirit of her people. The young girl knew what to do and set out to travel to the court at Chinon. On reaching the court, she walked in among the courtiers and approached a rather feeble man standing there. Speaking from the authority of her vision, the girl proclaimed the man as the rightful King of France—much to the astonishment of the courtiers.

As the story goes, there was a moment of shock and surprise; many courtiers laughed at the ludicrous nature of the scene and at the presence of the poorly dressed girl in the court. A moment or two later everyone saw the correctness of it all, and they fell to their knees and pledged allegiance, shouting "Hail, the King of France." France was unified under this new king, who later became Charles VII.

The young teenager—who we know as Joan of Arc—inspired an army which won several battles against the English, including the battle of Compiègne. She began the process whereby the English were eventually removed from French soil. At that point, she should have hightailed it out of there and disappeared. Instead, she battled on and was captured by the Burgundians, who handed her over to the ecclesiastical court at Rouen. The main objection to Joan of Arc was that she wore men's clothes. I'm not sure what you'd expect a military person to wear. The church also objected to the fact that Joan said she was directly responsible to God and that she did not have to go through the Catholic church. She died at the stake in 1431, aged nineteen. But she was, briefly, the voice of the folk spirit of France, and through its power this young farm girl changed the evolution of her people.

When the time is right, anyone can speak for the hearts of the people. Three hundred and fifty years after Joan of Arc, the folk spirit of France had had enough of kings and queens and so removed them with the same authority—using the guillotine. In removing Louis XVI and Marie Antoinette's heads, the people symbolically severed the control of the ego over the heart and body of France.

The point here is that once you come out of the collective unconscious of the Group Soul—be it a national folk spirit or the entire Planetary Group Soul—you stand inside the embrace of its spiritual correctness, the justice of which lies deep within everyone. Speaking from that place no one can really deny you. If a peasant could crown the Dauphin, King of France, you or I, or the man that has the donut shop across the street, we can— when the time is right—walk up to the system and take the crown back. That's exactly what we're going to do. We just have to know we can do it.

First we have to work on ourselves a bit more by turning back to the sacred and holy nature of the spirit within us, which offers us a divine order steeped in correctness and truth. To embrace that divine order we have to accept the blessing it offers us. We have to accept truth within our own heart and we have to live inside what is real, and then we can gradually suggest that everyone else do the same. By stepping into a

Truth or Consequence?

spiritual and psychological integrity, you erode your ego's ability to manipulate your life and the lives of others. If you develop a personal truth, it's tough for others to assail that truth. The distance you create makes you less reachable. Then when you hear the Great Lie, call its bluff. The world needs a few people to stand up and shout, "Rubbish." In doing so, we challenge the right of authority to bend information in its favor. It only takes one person to point out that the emperor has no clothes.

Somehow, the ego has to realize that its reign of manipulation is over. You can proclaim the age of spirit by demanding the truth. The lies are sustained by people's apathy and the system's belief that it is immortal and immune from danger. Everyone can dish out punishment and pain with little regard for how it feels to the recipient. They can cover their actions with platitudes and reasonable arguments that will justify any course of action—genocide, fratricide, daylight robbery, you name it.

When the Ceausescu's quasi-imperialist Communist empire fell some years ago in Rumania, the Ceausescus were captured trying to escape. They were videotaped while being interrogated by their captors. Nicolae Ceausescu was defiant, falling back on the power of his presidency, attempting to intimidate his captors. Mrs. Ceausescu kept insisting how much the Ceausescu family had done for Rumania, what a godsend they had been for the country and how much the Rumanian people loved her and her husband. The ego fervently believes its own perfidy. The spirit of Rumania held a slightly different opinion, and the Ceausescus were promptly dispatched to that part of the happy hunting ground where despots get to shake hands with truth.

Ironically, the Ceausescus had a big impact in Africa, which is home to some of the world's greatest slime balls. The problem with Africa is it's not very prominent on the world stage, so its leaders can get away with more than usual. Also, it is difficult

125

to criticize black regimes without everyone taking it as a racial slur. But what the departing Ceausescus did was to give a lot African leaders a terrible fright. President Moi of Kenya suddenly got a terrible dose of righteousness and announced elections. Nobody could actually remember what elections were, so unfortunately for Kenya, Moi won. Kamuzu Banda of Malawi was another one that saw the light. We can take heart that the process whereby totalitarianism rules forever unchallenged is gradually being replaced by a large dollop of people power. Unfortunately the process is terribly slow.

The ego has difficulty seeing beyond itself. Embracing the complete truth through realization is not natural for the ego. Usually truth comes to the ego only from an outside source, or as said, through crisis which causes it to shrink and so—in stepping back—it sees itself. But the Great Lie is a balloon. One pinprick and it's gone. The pin is fashioned by the collective mind of the common people developing a spiritual vision from which flows a global truth.

The power of spirit never ceases to amaze me. Spirit halted the Vietnam war. The hearts of the people ploughed over the military, and everyone saw that butchering a million people, including many of their own fathers and sons, mothers and daughters, went contrary to spiritual truth. It was handy that Nixon was such a liar. It helped contrast the distance between the ruling elite he represented, and the spirit of the people— who were no longer confused about what was in their real interest. I think it was lucky for Nixon that he 'fessed up to the truth and showed some contrition. Otherwise, the spirit of America would have gone after him and he would have been up there, keeping the bench warm for the Ceausescus.

The world ego has such a power to manipulate opinion that it can kid everyone into supporting anything. When I used to see President George Bush on TV at the White House, surrounded by the trappings and symbols of America, talking about family values, apple pie, baseball, and all that good stuff, it all looked so homey and proper. You can easily become confused. There is a blur created between right and wrong. On the surface it all looks so right. But that homey character in the grey suit butchered a hundred and twenty thousand people in Panama and the Gulf. For what? To catch a drug dealer who worked for the government anyway? To keep a few corrupt sheiks happy? To win a few points in the next poll? I am confused about what family values the victims enjoy. I don't know about you, but there's something about all of that which assails the spirit. If it hurts my brothers and sisters, it hurts me. It's an affront to the spirit of humanity that falls upon us as a weight. I don't buy all that "rah! rah! America the brave" routine if it means decimating my people to sustain dubious political causes and corrupt power structures. Eventually, as global people, we will have to become collectively responsible for the safety and well-being of everyone. There's no more "us and them". The egotistical, jingoism of national pride that will slaughter anyone our leaders don't fancy will have to give way to a more loving and tolerant attitude. We'll show our leaders "family values" by not allowing them to shoot our families.

I was riding the elevator at the American consulate in Sydney, Australia. Two diplomats were in there with me. One said to his colleague, "I'm going down to the Visa Department to help out, there are a lot of tourists all wanting visas at once." His colleague replied. "Ah! Let's shoot 'em and go to lunch. It's simpler than doing the paperwork." Both thought that was hilarious. Of course they weren't serious, but in a way they were. It's part of the arrogance of the American government to believe that it can annihilate anyone it doesn't fancy. I kept silent and just listened. But the sight of that scrawny diplomat swaggering though the consulate like he had a two foot erection with a flag pinned to it was rather unappealing. I'm sure the Australian tourists would be thrilled to know the US government's attitude towards their holiday plans. "Come to America, spend your tourist dollars and get shot."

In the end that attitude will cause trouble for the common people of America. It's pure ego. The American military has pulled the wool over the eyes of the people so that macho and bravado are an accepted part of the national culture. According to a recent ABC poll, forty-six percent of Americans favored assassination as a way of solving the US's problems in Iraq. Do you think the American mind set has been manipulated a bit? It's all very well shooting up a few Cuban construction workers in Grenada and making a Rambo film of it, but what will America do if it ever fights anyone that can actually shoot back? The media and the military have sold the people a Great Lie which says America is invincible. But Grenada, Panama, and the starving barefoot soldiers of the Iraqi army are not realistic confrontations.

At the time of this writing, America is still considering entering Yugoslavia to dispose of the Serbs. The American public is being softened up to accept a possible invasion. I sincerely hope Clinton comes to reason and sees sense. I don't agree with the Serbian military or their political stance, but it can't be denied that the Serbs are brave and powerful fighters willing to endure endless pain and suffering in defense of their homeland.

If America goes in there, all piss and wind, after-shave and Cola Cola, and tries to take on the Serbs on their own turf, it will be a sorry day. The Serbs are not mugs. They are battle-hardened warriors armed and dangerous. They won't flinch. I personally doubt that the United States can intimidate them. An American victory would be far from certain. What is definite is that many tens of thousands of America's finest will experience the long ride home in a ziplock bag. Macho and bravado are egotistical. They kill people indiscriminately. As the world ego destroys itself, a lot of poor innocents get caught in the middle. But America doesn't have to go through a military debacle to wake up to what is going on. It can just wake up.

Truth or Consequence?

That's why, my dear scamps, truth is very important. We have to go back to a personal honor code, before it's too late. Sometimes talking about truth and honor can sound a bit pompous, but what we're offering is not a truth that we wish to impose on others by force or even by reason. It's a truth and an honor code that we internalize and radiate through the power of spirit, so that others can see that there is a new, better way of conducting our journey though the physical plane.

Individually we can work on ourselves. By working on your own ego and developing truth, control, and an equitable inner dialogue, you individualize the spirit within you through the process of observation. If you work on yourself, the progress you make radiates invisibly to others, helping them and giving them courage, which also improves the global picture. After all—your ego is a part of the world ego, and as you control it, you lessen the overall influence of the world ego while expanding the presence of truth on our planet.

There are personal benefits. Change creates turbulence. If your life contains a lot of phony or untrue aspects, or if you have an unrealistic appraisal of yourself, that acts like a sail cloth to your energy. The slightest turbulence can quickly create an extreme imbalance. By bringing in the sail—by reversing back into as much truth as is comfortable—you consolidate your power and develop much needed stability. While the rest of the world allows the ego to expand them into the stratosphere, you have settled inside what is real, what is here in the present. You have gained a solid stance from which to observe events and contemplate your next move. The trick is to dream big dreams and make plans, but empower the present by making it real through concentrating upon it.

Humility is an attribute of spirit. If you embrace truth you will become a more humble person. That doesn't prevent you from achieving what you want in life or attaining your dreams, it just means you realize the immensity of the sacred heritage we possess and that you are happy to stand inside that.

Start by developing a true positive inner dialogue with yourself. It takes a while. The mind has a lot of unhelpful images that it sells to you as true. When those negative thoughts come forward, exclude them by saying, "I don't accept that perspective. It is not the truth." Replace that thought with a positive, thruthful one. Eventually the inner dialogue changes. Simultaneously, clean up the things you utter to others. Keep it simple and share from your heart those things you know to be true.

I wouldn't worry too much about the little white lies of life that crop up in social situations; it's more important to ensure that your main actions and your words emanate from spirit, not ego. If you develop an honor code and an equitable relationship with yourself and others, it pulls you out of the ego's evolution and eventually into a sacred place. Sure, it may deny you some quick profits, but in the end you have to look back at your life and you will own every moment of it. Did you create light or mayhem? Did you contribute to your enlightenment and the consciousness of others, or did you manipulate and imprison people for your own ends? Did you offer joy and positive hope or did you destroy people and cause more misery? These are impacting questions. Ask them now. Change your ways. Flow along a new path. You don't want to end up on the despot's bench looking at the ugliness of your life.

Our mistakes and the mistakes of our leaders melt to nothing in the light of eternity. We can only grant ourselves absolution when we seek a proper and holy contrition in our hearts, and once we establish the truth of that by affirming and pledging a future goodness. Conscious individuals should take that oath today so that others may be inspired to follow on tomorrow.

Otherwise, the consequence of the Great Lies will drag our world into a very dark time. It's not compulsory. We have to speak out and show the way. Strong people should set an example for others and stand up for truth, to show the way to those of our brothers and sisters who are less sure of themselves. They have to learn that a different perspective is not threatening to them. It's just different. To establish truth we have to allow freedom of speech. People have to be exposed to ideas that are outside the tribal and national mind set. We certainly need some fresh thoughts and ideas if we are going to make it through the next hundred years.

Let's talk about freedom of speech.

131

Freedom of Speech

CHAPTER SIX

T o get to "truth" we first have to look at freedom of speech. In the Western democracies freedom of speech is taken for granted. In the United States, this right forms a part of the Constitution. The original idea was that anyone could get up on a soap box and spout their views, or write a pamphlet criticizing the government and not get chucked into the jail for their efforts. The point of freedom of speech was to allow varying political and social views to be aired so that people's desires and opinions could effect social change—it all sounded marvelous.

Nowadays, we still have freedom of speech, providing you don't disagree with or touch upon any one of a hundred or so subjects that are considered taboo. Yes, you can still get up on your soap box, but you can't effect any real social change without communicating through the national media—which is vital if you want to change people's minds *en masse*. At this point your freedom of speech goes out of the window.

In most countries, TV and radio stations are licensed by governments; in some countries the stations are actually owned by the government. The station's conduct is watched, and what they put on the air is controlled not only by legislation, but by the station's fear of alienating the authorities and big business. Sure, they can criticize the government, but they are frightened to disagree with the main tenants of the status quo. That's why TV and radio stations in America often air that bit at the front of "talk shows" which says, "The views of our contributors are not necessarily the views of this station." Stations who rely on the goodwill of the masses are terrified of creating real controversy, for fear of alienating the manufactured mind set of the viewers.

America has Public Access television which anyone can go on, but it broadcasts to such a limited cable audience (often numbering only a few hundred households) that it doesn't really mold opinion or have much impact. Regardless of whether a newspaper or station is right wing or left wing, they gradually come to express a common elitist view. After all, the status quo supports the media through advertising; how can a paper write things that criticizes its customers?

The major networks have simply become mouthpieces for the government. I saw a survey some time ago about the types of people that appear on Ted Koppel's Nightline. Over ninety percent are white, over eighty percent are male and over seventy percent are government officials. Watch the nightly news and you will see the same thing. Government officials, selling government policy, all wrapped in a logical, cozy reasonableness that no one is allowed to disagree with. When a new law is proposed does the news broadcaster come out and say "This is a bunch of bullshit, the people don't need it?" Or does he or she go along offering rational reasons why everyone is going to love the law? Sometimes a member of the opposition party is on the show for balance, but they only offer a variation on the same theme. One part of the status quo disagreeing with the other part. It's all tied up. You never ever see dissidents on TV. You are offered the impression that no one really disagrees, that the government line—or a slight variation of it—are the only possible alternatives. You are offered the wolf and the fox, but no one ever speaks for the chickens.

The brainwashing that goes on is so perverse and all encompassing that people don't even realize they're being brainwashed. They genuinely believe the opinions they hold are original and personal to them. It's very hard to see outside the quantum created by the mass programming of opinion. You are inside the train with the curtains closed.

The sanitized version of the nation's state of being we see each night on TV is written by graduates of the Academy of Positive Pleasing. People tell us what we want to hear. We hear what they want to tell us. The deputies of the Russian Parliaments were still twiddling their pubes offering the Great Lie and making happy noises right up until the day the government went bankrupt and all of the state employees' checks bounced. In the long run truth is compulsory.

135

The same fear and control exists in the film industry. Most commercial films are American. All English speaking films rely on American distribution to make it financially. Theoretically, you can make any film you want, but you can't show your film *en masse* without going through the American distribution system, which is tightly controlled by a few individuals. The people making and distributing films in America are mostly white males, and are predominantly Jewish. Make any film you want as long as it fits the distributor's mind set. But what are your chances if you are black, female, and Arab?

Suppose you wrote a satirical script that suggested that the Israeli government is similar to the Nazi's under which the Jews suffered so much. After all, the Israeli government shows many of the same characteristics: Arab ghettos, racial discrimination, property seizures, shootings, and arrest without trial. Could you get your film shown anywhere? Would a big name actor take a part in your film? Hell no. What if you wrote an article for an Oregon newspaper saying that the conservationists should get stuffed, and that we should mow down the forests willy-nilly and give the loggers back their jobs. Is the paper going to print that? These examples may seem extreme. You may say it doesn't matter because we don't want to mow the forest, and besides, it doesn't bother us what the Israel government does.

But the point here is that it's not your personal view that counts—it's the principle.

In the ten years I lived in America I can't recall ever seeing a story explaining the Palestinians' side of the argument. The Palestinians are depicted as low-life terrorists. But one man's terrorist is another man's freedom fighter. Israel itself was established, in part, by the terrorist activities of their own guerrillas—the Hagana. If you wrote an article expressing the Palestinian view it probably wouldn't get published, and if it did, you would be attacked as anti-Semitic. The manipulation practiced on Western opinion says that in order for you to respect the Jews you cannot openly criticize Israel or its government.

But what if you are not an anti-Semite? What if you do respect the Jews and all the people of the world, and you are an honest, decent person who just wants to know more? Who are the Palestinians? What is their history? What do they want? What are their claims? These are reasonable questions, especially since the problem isn't just going to go away. So why don't the Palestinians get a voice in the media? Because the status quo disallows anyone taking exception to the official view. If people knew the Palestinian side of the story—if you knew say that fifty Palestinians are killed or wounded by Israeli forces for every one Israeli that is killed by the Palestinian terrorists— then you might consider the other side of the story. Israel would be pressured by public opinion into having to make a deal. It's plain and simple. Israel is one of America's main allies. No one is allowed to take an opposing view, even if there's a modicum of justice in it.

The same laws apply to the IRA in the British papers. There are no positive stories about the Irish freedom movement which objectively discuss their claims. I don't ever recall seeing any-one on TV saying that perhaps the IRA is right—that Ireland should be reunited and the north set free from the dominance of the British government and the Protestant minority. A recent poll showed that the vast majority of the British want the government to negotiate directly with the IRA. The people also want Northern Ireland to be independent or reunited with the south. But the feelings of the people go against the official line, so the voice of reasonableness is silenced.

The control over the minds of the people is effected by bombarding them with only one side of the argument. But the Planetary Group Soul has to hear the voice of all our people, not just the ego's view. There is a spiritual correctness to things. You can't eliminate it by denying people a voice because of the political or social implications of what might be said.

Right now, Western governments are running out of money with such speed and gay abandon that sooner or later they are going to have to pass even more draconian laws. Laws controlling everything, including the right to own property, freedom of speech, and whatever else might be needed to hold onto power and avoid the mess they're creating. Does that sound unlikely? No. Some such laws already exist. Two years ago the Australian Labor Government passed a law banning political advertising in the media. A few people got on TV to say they thought the law was disgraceful, and a bevy of government sponsored experts contradicted their protests by saying that banning political advertising would be terribly beneficial for the population as a whole, and that Australians didn't need political advertising. So from that moment on, anyone opposing the government couldn't get their message out. It boggles my mind that there wasn't rioting in the street, but what can people do? A court action was brought against the government, which was finally successful in Australia's highest court. The law was overturned. But the fact that a democratic Western government easily passed an illicit decree that effectively silenced its opposition for several years, shows that the hierarchies will do anything to sustain power. I find it a bit scary.

Meanwhile, back in the US, the government passed some smashing little laws (there are over a hundred of them), under the guise of the RICHO statute, the anti-drug wars, and other legal maneuvers, which allows them to seize people's property without having to prove they are guilty of anything. In 1992, they got $400 million worth of stuff; this year it's estimated the government will seize over $1 billion of its citizens' property without paying for it. Nice work if you can get it. In my book *The Trick to Money is Having Some*, I mention that you don't really own your own stuff anyway. If you own a home, you pay property taxes. The tax is one percent per annum where I used to live—more in other places. It doesn't sound like much, but even one percent allows the Government to repossess the entire nation every hundred years—the cash equivalent, that is.

So, do you own things, or are your possessions like the TV stations—under license from the government? Try not paying the government; will they let you keep your stuff? You can keep it providing you pay whatever license fee they dream up. You can say what you like providing you don't want to talk to substantial numbers of people, and then only providing you don't disagree.

Over the years the media and the government have shaped certain ideas in the minds of the people so that now those principles are inalienable and unquestioned. If you repeat a few basic ideas often enough, eventually everyone is indoctrinated into agreeing. Criticism and dissent are immobilized. The Great Lie becomes "religion." The minds of the people, in essence, are under license from the Government—together with their possessions. There is almost no alternative voice.

Take a controversial issue like immigration. Can you go on national TV and say, "I think immigration sucks. The idea of having all these foreigners on welfare, dealing crack, and shooting up Miami is not appealing. Let's ask them politely to leave, and not invite any more." Have you ever heard anyone on TV say that? OK, I accept that most Americans would not agree with that line of reasoning, but it's not a matter of agreeing or disagreeing. It's that alternative opinion is forbidden—it's censored.

But then, so is most everything. Why do all American actors in films make love with their pants on? Is there a law against nudity? No, there's not. But there is censorship called the CODE that restricts who can see what in films. So the movie makers won't show you Al Pacino's pee pee for fear of losing their shorts.

You might say you don't want to see Al Pacino's pee pee—but again, it's the principle of it. Hollywood's version of life is not real. It's sanitized and illogical and conformist and male. Anyway, sex with your clothes on is not safe sex—you'll get your thingy stuck in the zipper.

The presumption is that the authorities knows best, and with the main principles accepted as sacrosanct, holy, and beneficial to us, why would any one in their right mind disagree? The wave-motion of the national mind set requires an absolute compliance to the tribal religion. In fact, if you look at what these old ideas are doing to us, you can see that some of them have brought the Western democracies to their knees. Someday, the freedom of speech rules will have to include hearing stuff we don't like. Otherwise, the spirit of the people will never have a voice and we'll never be able to fix the mess.

We could look at a hundred principles that have now become "religion," but there are vast areas of public affairs that no one is allowed to mention or disagree with. For example: government financing, the banking industry, computer surveillance, foreign policy, the Internal Revenue Service, the DEA, PAC money to politicians, executive power, covert actions, military spending, the rights of the police, and so on, and so forth. In the United States, if you are a member of Congress and you criticize the Internal Revenue Service, you are automatically subjected to investigation and audit. America has a system whereby the IRS is more or less outside any legislative control, and happily uses terror and harassment to cream the people for as much as possible. No one says anything. It has been irrefutably proven over the years that political activists in America automatically fall prey to IRS investigations. It's all very subtly done, and the IRS's activities are couched in plenty of legal BS. On the surface the IRS claims to be impartial but, in fact, they target anyone threatening their power or anybody the government dislikes for political reasons.

The control of opinion and the molding of public consent are intrinsic to the American system and that of most Western countries. I find it fascinating to watch how control of public opinion through propaganda pervades almost all aspects of life. Of course, there are major economic issues manipulated and bent to good advantage, like the unemployment figures already discussed, and then there are more general socioeconomic issues such as the Welfare State. All political parties around the Western world support the Welfare State spending ever increasing billions that they don't have on sustaining the idea. A politically sound way of using other people's money to keep yourself in power! But is it a good thing for the nation to borrow money to give to people for not working? Is it right that a man or woman should be supported indefinitely by diligent people who work hard? Where does charity end and political bribes begin? It is hard to say. Certainly, to borrow money to sustain the idea is absolutely crazy.

The government maneuvers the media to suggest that people who have money because they work should pay for others so they don't have to work. I have never seen anyone allowed to challenge the concept. The idea is always sold as soaking the rich and is therefore fair. But is it morally correct to soak anyone? How do you justify making people pay for things they are not getting? Most of our society is not rich, but everyone gets soaked under the same principle. Under the guise of sustaining the Welfare State, governments manipulate opinion to raise billions to sustain themselves, their bureaucracies and their military machines—all of which helps keep the governments in power. It seems to me that there is tremendous effort made to legitimize daylight robbery as charity. No one has ever been allowed to argue that the workers and small business people—and even the rich—should be able to keep their money, or most of it anyway. There is an implied discrimination that labels anyone who objects as nasty and greedy, as someone who doesn't want to help their fellow men and women. There is a further implied discrimination that suggests that all business people are feeding off the common folk. In fact, it's the government who is feeding off the common folk.

I think that some big business and monopolies do take advantage of their power, but most business people run very small concerns and work hard just to get screwed for their efforts. But is it true that all these people are scum bags that prey on little people, and therefore should be taxed, legislated, and harassed as much as possible? Or is that an old-fashioned idea which causes inventors and creators to pick up their marbles and head off elsewhere?

The state religion and the tribal mind set is everywhere. Look at the position of Christianity in our Western societies. You see endless hours of Christian TV, but what alternative ideas are ever offered? Almost none. The Christian church has a monopoly over the mass media and therefore molds opinion in favor of itself. The implication is that Christianity and its principles are good, and everything else is less good or downright evil. So why would anyone need to listen to a different opinion? Our lack of freedom in the media doesn't allow for any new ideas to be discussed—ideas that are perhaps based on energy and reality, rather than religion and emotion. Ideas that might be more appropriate under the current circumstances. You must question down to the very core of what people believe in order to find a new order and new way. Tinkering with the old systems has not got us the results we need. But can people open themselves to accepting a new idea, or is that too threatening? Denial is society's condom that protects it from being impregnated with alien ideas.

Denial is collective in the tribal mind, but it operates to a greater or lesser extent in each one of us. Right now there are messengers coming from your inner mind telling you things, but because of your habitual denial, you—as king or queen of your consciousness—you may forbid the messengers to speak.

What to do? First, you have to grant freedom of speech to that internal process that drives and guides your evolution and understanding through this life. Let your inner mind speak and be ready for some bizarre or even scary ideas. And get used to at least looking at those ideas. If you refuse to penetrate the emotional comfort zone of your beliefs you'll find it difficult to progress. Second, you can greatly assist the world by allowing other people the rare opportunity of hearing things they don't like. You won't get on TV, and you may have to sacrifice your popularity for the long term good of humanity, but new ideas are gifts you can offer mankind. Bit by bit, if people are prepared to contradict the status quo, new ideas will permeate society.

Next time someone says, "Life's hard," say, "No it isn't—it's a piece of cake." When they say, "Isn't it terrible that we have all these poor people in the town," say, "No it's not—it's fine; it's a part of their evolution to be poor. It's the way our brothers and sisters learn to raise their energy."

Then button down the hatches while everyone goes potty. It doesn't really matter if you believe or don't believe what you are saying. You are not expressing your opinion necessarily, rather, you are offering a subtle teaching. Through it, you provide a great service to listeners by contradicting their "religion." It's good for them, even if it makes them angry. It shows people that there is a world of consciousness outside their wave, even if they don't agree with it. That's the first step toward a global truth and freedom of speech. You have to get people to see that there are possibilities beyond the calcified attitudes of the world ego with its manipulation of the common mind set.

Playing the role of the contradictor can be a lot of fun. I was giving a lecture in New Mexico—the room was hot and the audience was a bit dozy. Fifteen minutes into the lecture I began wondering what to do, so I tossed them a ringer just to wake them up. I said I thought American women were much more masculine and much less subtle or attractive than their European or Australian counterparts. All hell broke loose. Three young women jumped to their feet shouting protests. One was "F-ing" and cussing and furiously waving her arms about. Then a lesbian couple got up and took umbrage at something the first woman said, and one of the lesbians—the more butch of the two—offered to punch the woman's lights out. Meanwhile, a lady in the second row, who was built like a Mack truck, got up and said that her main worry in life was sexual assault. I didn't reply, but I remember thinking in her case sexual assault was a ten-million-to-one shot, and that she shouldn't worry. Most everyone in the room was thinking the same thing. One of the guys got up and said that all the ladies he had met were far too scary, and he'd never be so silly as to try to assault them anyway. That really put the cat amongst the pigeons. All at once ten people were on their feet. They wanted to tear the man limb from limb.

When the ruckus died down a bit, an older woman said she felt that things had changed and that women were more feminine in her day. No sooner had she let that tumble from her lips than a new group of ladies rose like tag wrestlers to stomp all over her. A Texan girl agreed that American women were less feminine, but it wasn't their fault—all the men nowadays were

143

wimps or faggots. Three guys got suckered into defending their virility, and that part of the argument culminated with a really handsome black guy rising to say to the Texan that if she were prepared to haul her honky white ass around to room number 217, he'd be happy to prove her wrong. Half the room roared with laughter; the other half thought him a sexist pig.

The battle raged for fifteen minutes. I just sat on my stool resting and saying nothing. With the room in such chaos, I called an early break and retreated for a cup of coffee, well pleased with myself. Meanwhile, running battles continued for half an hour out in the main hall. It was magnificent. I'd suckered them into lowering their guard and the truth came tumbling out, along with copious amounts of sexual stuff that was locked inside the battlers. They were angry, but it helped them. Once they had all of their trash on the table for everyone to see, they had no option but to look at it.

It doesn't matter if my original statement was right or wrong. It was a trick question. If American women are more masculine than European women, so what? A women is entitled to be what she wants. What mattered was that in assailing the widely held principle that American females are all sweetness, light, and femininity personified, I maneuvered everyone into seeing how stiff they were inside their restricted attitudes. It threatened and hurt them to even listen to an alternative view.

To run a stunt like that, you have to go past the deep-rooted idea that you've got to please everyone and win their support by always agreeing with them. Herein lies the problem: As the media and society pummel people's consciousness into a collective norm, the vast free flowing creative expanse of possibilities that lay in one's heart are gradually squashed into a calcified mass—like a little sugar cube.

You might consider yourself an open, liberated individual, but if you wrote down all the things you believed about life, death, money, security, sex, love, friendship, society, the planet, the nation, and so on, you'll probably find that what you believe mostly comes from the tribal wave. Most likely you'll parrot what everyone else believes. On close inspection you may discover that you don't have many original thoughts in your head at all. Just thoughts that have been passed to you from the "collective insistence" of the tribal mind.

That's why most people are crushingly dull—everyone's the same. Sure, there will be shades of opinion—Republican or Democrat, Protestant or Catholic, and so on—but in the end, everyone rests within the religion of their people and the status quo. It's the only thing they have been taught. There is no dissent. The mass brainwashing of our people ensures it. When these old ideas—often stemming from sexual stereotypes and hierarchical dominance—run out of steam and the world falls apart, how will anyone come up with solutions? If we don't allow freedom of speech, they won't.

Right now it's tough for the world to come to new ideas; the old system has not run its full course as yet. There is a very definite correlation between the established boundary of human opinion and the attempted expansion of your spirit. When people's spiritual ideas were still in their infancy, the boundaries of public opinion were reasonable as people did not need much space. But as we grew, our spiritual needs began to press up against society's attitudes. It's hard to grow if public opinion forbids it.

The idea that people might grow beyond the need for membership in a society is frowned upon. Yet there are millions of people who have done just that, going beyond the need to belong anywhere in particular. They have dropped out; some into small groups or communes, some have wandered off on their own to an independent existence. Yet the status quo discriminates against them for being independent; considering them weirdoes for not wishing to play the game.

Whispering Winds of Change

Our spirit seeking freedom of expression and our desire for a stress free existence is jammed up against a social order that requires a drone like compliance, enforced by legislation and the control of opinion. Things won't change just yet. Pressure has to be increased against the system, and there are still a lot of people who made a big success out of the old system. They have money, power, plus most of the control. They are reluctant to change. On the other side of the power equation there are millions of Westerners still unable to sustain balance even at the lowest level of activity and consciousness. To suggest they should quit the system, trust their own capabilities, and drop out is very frightening to them.

Further hindering the overall process are those who have moved out of the mass mind of tick-tock—but not very far. In effect, they have dumped one religion for another. If you look at New Age people, who consider themselves more conscious and liberated than the main stream, you'll still see conformity. They defend their position vigorously, repeating the same stuff over and over.

If you don't agree try this: Next time you are at your crystal meditation group, start the discussion with, "Screw the dolphins! I'm going back to eating tuna. What do you guys think?" Watch people react. Then tell me that the New Age is not a religion, even if the consciousness is more liberated than tick-tock.

I'll give you an example from my own experience. Only a handful of New Age authors have sold over a million books. A best seller in our genre is about 25,000 books. I have been very privileged and lucky to get the opportunity to sell over a million pieces. In the ten years I spent in America not one word from any of my works ever appeared in any of the three leading New Age magazines. In fact, my books and tapes are banned from many New Age book stores. Now you could say, well Stewie that's not a surprise given your work is such a bunch of rubbish.

Freedom of Speech

Or, could it be that the "New Age" is a religion of itself and that for some people my often dissenting view is a threat. I'm also not available in most book shop chains, but that's no surprise either. We called W.H. Smiths, a very large chain of stores in Britain and Europe, and offered the New Age/psychology buyer a free sample pack of my books for his consideration. His reply? "Stuart Wilde? You must be joking." He hung up without saying another word.

I have appeared on many little radio and TV shows, but I only had four invitations to appear on prime time TV. Without exception my invitations were mysteriously canceled before the actual shoot. One other show had me on and then cut me from the final broadcast.

The freedom of speech issue is very subtle. You can't tell what are legitimate commercial preferences and what is bias. Given that dissenting views in the New Age media or anywhere else, never appear, there must definitely be a selection process going on.

Now here is the tofu and potatoes of this freedom of speech issue. First of all, don't drive yourself crazy if the world won't listen. Accept it. Be loving and patient. There is an inner dialogue chattering away within the collective unconscious of the people. New ideas take a while to drift into the conscious mind, which tends to move at a snail's pace. All you can do is inject it from time to time with a few alien ideas, then sit back and wait. You can rest in the assurance that once new ideas take critical mass everyone will wake at the same moment. So while it may seem a long way off, it isn't as far away as you think.

Spiritual energy is the only truth. Intellectual ideals and emotions are not usually as close to truth, so energy will win in the end. For example, you can legislate that everyone in the nation is equal, and you can spend billions trying to sustain the idea, but in the end you can see that on an energy level everyone is not equal. Some people try hard and put out—others do little or nothing. Eventually, the reality of energy flows over legislation and whatever is true on an energy level comes to pass. Again, look at Russia; they happily told themselves massive lies for seventy years. But in the end the lies fell apart, and the county returned to what was real—which in their case isn't much because the visionaries and creators were denied a voice for so long. Russia now desperately needs them, but there are few to be found.

148 How does the need for freedom of speech translate personally? As you evolve through your inner journey, your consciousness will climb to new levels of understanding. Eventually you'll move into dimensions of consciousness far from the tick-tock mind in which the symbols and images of mankind no longer have much relevance. At that higher point, the only currency is energy and perception—emotions, logic, religion, and even morality as we know it all score zip. Out there, at those higher levels of spirit, nothing sustains you other than your belief in self and your ability to imagine and perceive in an expansive way. If you are still influenced by the crimped style of the world mind set, you'll find that your spiritual evolution will slow to a crawl, even if back on the physical plane you are making a fantastic success of your life. Eventually, that success will dwindle, because there's nothing empowering it from within. You'll become listless and bored, and you'll put out less until gradually you'll get less, and so on.

Over the years those who have come through the various self-disciplines have empowered their inner journey so greatly that they have carried themselves out and beyond the tick-tock mind. However, many then find themselves in a very blank space where nothing much replaced what was lost. Those people exist in an inner twilight zone, suspended between their physical connection and an as yet unreachable high spiritual plane.

You will know when you are approaching that space because everything in the world will seem very bland. You will have done everything. Nothing will hold any real excitement for you. Why does this phenomena affect so many inner travelers? Because at a higher level, thinking is not logical nor linear nor structured. Perception and thoughts are dynamic and unusual—they have a life of their own, independent of the thinker.

We are used to our thoughts and ideas being silent and dead, but higher up the consciousness scale, in the inner worlds, they suddenly come to life and momentarily coexist inside and outside of their creator. On that plane you'll create a thought and see it materialized in front of you, rather than it existing solely within you as it does in our three dimensional world. The thought-form will have life and a personality of its own, and it will seek to develop and expand independently from the consciousness that originated the thought. Sometimes the thought-form will attempt to show you parts of itself moving forwards or even backwards in time; reviewing and observing itself before it came into being. It will simultaneously be past and future, inner and outer. It will turn outward from within itself and be an effect before there was a cause. It has a volition of its own, and it will seek to influence its own direction and destiny to the extent its power allows. Suddenly, you're looking at a strange, new world that is multidimensional, spread across vast stretches of consciousness, far beyond what the human mind can fathom.

Let me give you an example, so that you can understand it better. Picture a family scene at Christmas time. You might imagine your relatives sitting around a table laden with food, kids opening presents, and so on. But as you visualize the image it will come to you like a hazy photograph shot through a narrow lens. There will be a lot of gray tones around the edges of the scene, and those grey hues will be interspersed mainly in the middle of your visualization with some low density color. The scene will have an absence of dialogue and action. Then if

I say, "Move the characters around," you may only be able to move them one at a time, as you can't empower the image other than through concentration, and it's difficult to concentrate on more than one thing at once. You can see that the image has no real dynamic power of its own. At our level of consciousness thoughts are sluggish and dull. They are created by our limited imagination, which atrophies over time through logic and the constant bombardment of technology. Technology throws us ten thousand images a day, requiring us to do little with our own imaginations. So our perception is limited by a lack of imagination and use, and it is stifled by the bounds of our intellect which requires things to act only in a certain way. It amazes me how many people have deteriorated to such an extent—through logic and technology—that they can't visualize at all.

Now at a higher level of consciousness, in dimensions a few notches above tick-tock, things are very different. At that level, if I asked you to visualize a Christmas scene, you would experience it in bright, vivid color. It would be wide and expansive with many subtle shades of color and various hues of contrast and depth and a great clarity of tones. The characters in your mind's eye would be lively and in motion, rather than stiff. They would use the energy contained in that quantum of thought that is your visualization, and they would come to life and act independently of your volition. The imagery of that Christmas party might even get into a mental dialogue with you. The relatives and kids, who were formally dormant and passive at the ordinary level of thinking, would spring to life at the hyperthinking level of that dimension.

Over and above the color and vitality of the scene, you would experience a depth of perception so clear that the inner qualities of the characters will be there to see, as well as their physical appearance, thoughts, and actions. The whole scene will exist within your mind and outside simultaneously, and depending on the total energy that you have granted it through your inner power, it will seek to expand and express itself as far as it may. From within the scene, you may see future possibilities and even past energies that influenced the evolution or circumstances of the characters present. Each of the people will have an individual identity and even a loosely formed will that is often at odds and separate to where you, the creator of the mental scene, might expect or wish them to go.

Writers and novelists can relate to this. They often create characters in a story who suddenly enter into a dialogue with the writer, contradicting his or her wishes, heading off as if under their own volition. Many a writer has seen his or her novel temporarily wrecked by an unruly character who won't obey or follow the story line. This is because the character has come to life in an inner world through the author empowering it with his or her concentration over a period of time. But imagine a dimension where everything comes to life the instant you think of it. If you found yourself there, trussed up by a lack of freedom of speech or a limited imagination, you'd experience a very bland existence. Or worse still, if you had not developed an ability to discipline your mind beyond the tearjerk of human reactions and the drivel that pours into it from the collective neurosis, you'd suddenly see your worst fears horrendously manifest in front of you. Ten minutes of a dimension like that and you'd be as lost and vulnerable as a kitten on a freeway. So, in preparation for higher levels of thinking, it's wise to start exercising your freedom of inner speech, to expand yourself beyond the emotional and intellectual limits of humanity. Beyond the calcified sugar cube appears the ferryman who will take you on your journey. The ferryman's first name is "Imagination." But it is not just imagination as we understand it, but also the ability to attempt to imagine what is not. To see in your mind's eye things that do not exist. How would that be possible if you have never allowed yourself to think like that? If I ask you to imagine something frightening that does not normally exist, you might come up with the mental image of a ten foot high monster with fangs, scales, and three heads. But each of the components that make up your vision come from ordinary human symbology and understanding to create the whole. So the monster conforms to the limits of our imagery, for example, its height, three heads instead of one, scales and fangs.

Now create a monster that has no ordinary components conforming to regular human symbols. What have you got in your mind? Nothing much probably. You can't do it yet. Because you have no symbols that don't come out of a normal mental dictionary. Follow my drift?

So now you see how freedom of speech is not just a political or social idea, but is also a spiritual discipline, because in acting as your own contradictor you open within yourself the possibilities of viewing an alternative nonhuman world, or perhaps more correctly, a world in which human values and emotions are less important. Once you are used to that, you can move on to experiencing worlds in which human symbols are more diffused or where they don't exists at all.

Try the contradiction game with yourself. It's fun—although sometimes scary. Here is how it's done: Take something that forms a part of your deepest beliefs, for example, "Good is better than evil." Now, in a meditative state see yourself as the lawyer representing evil, and argue its case for a moment or two, taking care not to be sucked into emotion. So you would say to the imaginary court, "Ladies and gentleman, I stand as council for evil, and I'd like to begin my argument by saying that evil has had very bad press over the years. If you look at the history of man, you'll see that evil has been responsible for many great advances in human understanding. In fact, almost all major shifts in human consciousness have come after a period of great evil. If the court pleases, I would now like to enter evidence that will show how art and creativity blossomed after the Inquisition. Further, I will show you how war, in a perverse way, served the modern world by clearing out the old regime and making way for our technological age. Further, if it please the court, I would like to call expert witnesses to testify that goodness is often laced with hidden expectations, whereas evil is more honest for it makes no apology nor begs any favor. And so, your honor, we can see that evil is strong, correct and pure, and that goodness is in fact phony and weak, and that by exercising goodness man only prolongs the agony of humanity by supporting its weaknesses. Whereas, evil forces people to resist, so they become stronger."

After a while, if you argue well, you'll scare the hell out of yourself, because due to your self-imposed freedom of speech laws you'll have never heard the other side. You'll imagine yourself momentarily gripped by some terrible satanic force.

Of course this is not so. It's just that you have wandered out beyond the sugar cube and that is what scares you. Once out there, you will have the impression that you are bound to lose control of your mind and run amok. Again, you won't. It just feels scary because the scaffolding of your self-righteous beliefs is removed temporarily. You have nothing to hang on to, nothing to feel certain about.

As you move up the scale of consciousness to higher and higher plateaus your regular attitude to life will change or disappear completely. With it will go many of the opinions you hold about yourself. Soon you will have nothing cozy or comforting to hang on to, other than your belief in self and the spirituality within you—that inner light of the Higher Self that links you to all things. The denouement of the ego personality is part of the process as you travel towards God. So by crumbling the sugar cube to stimulate imagination, and by stretching mentally, you'll finally cross that plane of desolation that hovers between the dimension of man's consciousness and the dimensions of pure spirit.

Freedom of speech—offer it to people even if it drives them crazy. We will all have to come to it in the end. By stretching our

minds, we create a variable and exciting reality full of understanding and harmony in stark contrast to the controlled mind
set of tick-tock, with all its imposed judgements and obligations. How can you establish the premise of noninfringement
if you infringe upon yourself and others by denying free
speech? We have to allow freedom of speech so that we can
eventually move to more freedom of action. Offer freedom of
speech to your inner dialogue; you need it—we all need it—if
we want to progress, that is.

Selling the
Emotional Wave

CHAPTER SEVEN

T housands of years ago when tribes were very small, each tribal wave was also small, so an individual ego in that tribal wave was not particularly developed. In their pure state tribal people are very humble. In remote African villages you'll notice the people have an almost childlike quality. Leaders of small waves are often nothing more than elders—father or mother figures. They don't attempt to separate themselves particularly from other members of the tribe. Because small tribes can't conquer others or appropriate wealth they usually live in absolute harmony with nature in order to survive, which gives each member an automatic spirituality and a humble stance. Being aligned to nature, small tribes usually see God in nature, as an energy flowing through their lives. So the religion of small tribes is often pantheistic.

As populations grew and tribes got larger, military action became more feasible. Lands were conquered and other tribes subdued. When the tribal wave grew, it acquired generals, leaders, and an authority to whom the well–being of the tribe was assigned. The shift from relying on nature's gift through harmony to relying on warriors and administrators was where individual egos got the chance to puff up and attempt separation from others. Tribes became small nations through conquest, and kings and queens became gods in the eyes of their people. Tribal religions shifted from a pantheistic view that respected the God Force in all things, to the worship of their leaders as a god. It was only a small jump from there to where the men in question became "The God"—the supreme creator of the Universe. It's marvelous what a little ego can do for you!

It is a natural expansionist progression to move from a small harmonious wave with little or no ego, to a large military wave, relying on force for survival. In a military wave the ego flourishes. Power offers status—often imposed through violence and fear. So the ego has plenty of ways of separating itself and lording it over others.

158

In small tribes the ego cannot properly separate itself from others; there is not enough power to establish real status. Small tribes have to live closely together for safety and survival, so there is not enough distance between the leaders and the people for the ego to gain strength. Remember, distance is vital to observation. So distance is vital to the ego's attempt to gain separation from the wave. In a small tribe where everyone lives together and knows one another personally, the ego doesn't have much chance. It's hard to become a living god if you have to pop behind a rock for a bowel movement with all the other members of your tribe.

When the tribes became mini-nations through military action, distance was established. Now the tribes were large enough that everyone did not know each other. Conquerors were set up over the vanquished. There was high and low. Us and them. Our king or queen beats your king or queen and so forth. Violence gave the ego wealth, status, and distance.

In small tribes, each member is needed as a part of the harmony and survival of the whole. Energy flows around the wave with everyone more or less equal. In the mini-nations under kings, the power of life, death, money, and status flowed from the top downwards. The top people were vital; the tribal members expendable. Before the ego surfaced, God was either an energy or God's presence was vested in nature via the animals and the changing seasons. Once the ego established self–importance,

God shifted from being an energy to being a man. Some of the men who later became gods, or who people said were the official voice of God, were military or political leaders on earth who were promoted to "The God" after they died. The male God in heaven idea is an outcropping of the development of the male ego.

The mini-nations became real nations, and many had official state religions with dead heroes as god. Kings and queens set about conquering other nations, partly for status and wealth, and partly because by imposing their "Dead-Male-as-God" over another tribe's "Dead-Male-As-God," the king or queen could strengthen their security by acquiring divine approval, which to the ego is a form of observation. If God observes you, surely you become even more of a particle, with a bit more immortality to boot! Proselytizing religion by missionary work or conquest is an outcropping of the expansionist ego stretching for an immortality it can't reach.

Here is how the process works in the eyes of the ego: A king or queen, having established himself or herself as a living god in the eyes of the people, would quite naturally have nagging doubts. "Am I a god and therefore immortal or am I just a bloke who people think is a living god?" For the ego, it is not quite enough to be separate from the people below. The ego needs to be anointed by God above in order for its separateness to take on divine reality. All religions—bar a few—have emotional gods as deities. Theologians, in writing about God and what they thought were God's wishes, naturally came to the conclusion that the deity required pleasing actions that would ingratiate the followers to him, in the same way as kings required pleasing actions to satisfy them. If a leader could add to his status and security by conquering others, surely the same would work for an emotional God. If the state religion gained new members by conquest, then the "Dead-Male-As-God" up in heaven would surely be happy, for his status and presence on earth would be increased. The pleasure of God—that is God's grace—read by the ego to mean an anointed immortality, would flow to the king, to the nation and perhaps even to the people of that state. Once the ego is anointed by God it moves towards security and away from terror. People who God likes are safe; people who God does not like face terrible retribution. As soon as the ego feels even slightly more secure, its fear of death is subdued; a sense of well–being envelopes it. That sense of well–being was offered—and is still offered today—as evidence of God's presence or grace flowing to tribal members who perform actions pleasing to the dead male who is now God.

The tribal wave can't see that the ego's well–being is a function of the positive reaction to its belief, that it has been anointed by God and so is safer. It has nothing much to do with either the "Dead-Male-as-God" or the God Force that flows through all things.

So religion was carried out by armies of the faithful, sometimes military, sometimes secular, in the dual hope of acquiring immortality for the king back home—some of which might flow down to the schleps that had to do the marching. It's amazing how many people have been butchered on that utterly silly idea which stems from the ego's hopeless search for immortality through divine approval. Religious wars, at their deepest levels, are issues of immortality and the illusion of security that God's approval might offer. Even today people promoting religion are said to be doing "God's work," making them special, and separate while supposedly ingratiating them to God, who like all good marketing directors is supposed to be jolly happy when the graph shows an upward trend. In the wave, no one has ever asked the question "Why would the 'Dead-Male-As-God' in heaven need more followers? Surely, the followers he's already got are silly enough!"

The history of human affairs is dominated by these simple principles of the ego reaching for an external particle state and to the implied immortality of separation. No matter what organism of society you look at—be it religious, social, political, financial, or whatever—you will see the principle of wave and particle at work. By reducing human action to its basic wave-particle features, everything is understood and explained. There is no more mystery. You don't have to be a great visionary to know why people act as they do or what is about to happen next.

The ego can never confer an immortality upon itself because its vision is always external—so it can't get outside of itself or the tribal wave to establish self-observation, which would establish proper separation. So the ego stretches in every direction at once—scatter shot—hoping that by establishing more and more avenues of separateness—be it divine approval, wealth, military power, status, admiration, glamour, worship, or whatever—it will eventually have enough separation for its particle state to be made manifest. So, for example, if you wonder why a person with a hundred million dollars would avidly chase and acquire even more millions at the expense of everyone around them, the first answer might be greed. But if you look at it deeply, greed for vast power and treasuries containing billions is only the ego's hope for its complete separation. One million is separate, ten million more so, a billion must be very separate indeed.

So while a nation is moving up economically, everything is fine. The members of the wave can reach for separateness through economic activity. Everyone can demand more and more, satisfying their need to stretch. Those with less economic clout can at least see others in the wave making it, giving the whole wave hope and allowing it to establish its quest for the particle dream. When the individual makes money and economically departs the wave, the first thing they do is buy a house and erect a fence around it, symbolizing their new detached status. The house is a symbol of security, but it's also a symbol of the ego's yearning for permanence—a part of the hoped for immortality of the detached state. Banks can get people to pay a third of their income most of their working lives on a home loan for a property that is often nothing more than a few dreary bricks in a rather dull suburb. If you offer people even the illusion of the particle state, they will give you almost anything to get it.

Everything is fine for the national ego as long as expansion continues. But when it stops, people's quest for the everlasting stops also. There is a moment of equilibrium and then they start to slip back. Then fear sets in and accelerates the slide. The ego drops back toward anonymity and the perceived insecurity of the wave. So when hyperinflation occurred in Germany in the twenties and the economy came unglued, people were angry, confused, and insecure. Along comes Adolph who knew exactly what to say. His message? "We are separate. We are particles. We don't have to have status through money, we can have it by birth. We are Aryan people, so we are better." With the German ego of that time deteriorating through lack of power and financial clout, that was music to its ears.

Having established the notion that Aryans are separate and therefore particles, the Nazis then needed to establish that notion as an observable fact. How would they go about doing that? They would need to create observers of their Aryan separateness. Obviously, not many people outside the Nazi Party agreed with Hitler's idea that the Aryans were separate and therefore particles. Conquering people was the only way to establish observers. Military action is a natural outcropping of an expansionist ego because conquest offers power, separation, and observers. There is nothing more godlike than wielding the power of life-and-death .

The Nazi pogroms against the Jews and marginal sects, like the Gypsies, were fueled by the imaginary particle state of Aryan separateness. If you individualize on an inner level and commence your journey within, you can exist and progress in those inner worlds without irritating others or having them infringe

162

on you. Your spiritual evolution is unfettered. But in the external illusionary particle state of the ego, other people's external particle state is a threat. External "would be" particles interfere with each other and compete. That is why the *nouveau riche* are often drawn to gaudy exhibitions of wealth. They need to compete for observers—especially socially—where their separateness can be seen and acknowledged. "My particle state is more established and more worthy of observation than yours, because this swimming pool in my garden, with the utterly ghastly gold dolphin taps is an affirmation and confirmation of that fact. My state is becoming real, more real than yours anyway."

163

The center point of Zionism is the fact that their "Dead- Male-As-God" supposedly anointed the Jews as special. The writers said they were God's chosen people, meaning that the Jews had been specially observed by God and were particles. Now if the Jews had never mentioned it to any one, they would have been fine. But if you put the word out that you are chosen, it may keep your ego happy, but it discriminates against everyone else that is less chosen or not chosen at all. It's the particle syndrome manifest as tribal or religious dogma. By denying gentiles the possibility of reaching for immortality by prohibiting them from divine anointment by God, you are bound to attract their ire. The Nazis were also chosen—or so they thought. Under the separate particle illusion of the ego, you can't have two lots of chosen people. So the Jews were a life-and-death threat to Hitler. They stood on the path between him and the supreme particle state that Hitler declared was the birthright of the Aryan people. Eliminating the threat of the Jewish particle offered life to the Aryan particle. So Hitler ordered the holocaust not only because he erroneously blamed the harshness of his early years and his lack of opportunity upon the Jews, but also because their illusionary ego particle state stood between him and his dream for the Aryan people.

For example, if you wonder if anti-Semitism will ever end, I am afraid the answer is probably, "No, not yet." Not while the Jews hold to the racial and cultural separateness of their "chosen people" status. They will always bump up against other egos attempting to establish the same premise. Other egos will always see the Jews as a threat to advancement. It may be hard for older Jews to give up their "chosen people" routine and elitist ways, but younger Jews born after the war can do it quite easily. If you don't want to be victimized by people's attitude towards you, you can bitch and moan and hope to change those attitudes, or you can change your own attitude and turn within. By abandoning the ego parabola and some or all of the eccentricities of Zionist teachings, you embrace an inner nondenominational spirituality. That inner particle state is silent, so it offends no one. As soon you resonate that impartial spirituality for any length of time, people will no longer see you as a "chosen Jew" and a threat to their ego. They will start to see you as a "spirit" and cease to discriminate against you—in fact, they will be inspired. Because as a "spirit" you will be the embodiment of the very particle state their ego is hoping to achieve. Far from discriminating against you, they will seek you out and attempt to raise you up. But being spirit, you won't stand for that and you'll probably walk away, perhaps to silently reflect on the great healing you brought to your life. It's all so terribly simple. It's the healing process we all have to go through in one way or another.

If you are a successful person in the external world, you may wonder why, on the whole, people don't accept you. You may be very nice and kind, and generally share your success with others, yet you will often feel that people discriminate against you because you are successful. You may find people will deliberately block or hinder you for what seems to be no particular reason. The answer lies in the particle wave. Your success gives you an emerging particle state in the external world. That emerging particle will be seen by others to interfere and deny them the hope of also attaining the particle state.

There is no real logic to their fear, but the ego worries and competes all the same. That's why they can't allow you to glide past them. The trick is to be very humble and never talk about your success unless absolutely required to do so—then only in very diminutive terms. If you subjugate your ego under theirs, and through a delicate choice of words let them know you are no threat to their particle hopes, you will assuage their antagonism. It's important you make a point of honoring the utterly magnificent achievements of their ego and its attempt to particularize itself, and to affirm their eventual unbounded and glorious achievement of that state. If you do so, they will suddenly turn and help you.

The knack is to make sure your etheric energy does not touch them or impinge itself upon theirs. If you're successful, you'll more than likely have a powerful etheric. You will have strengthened yourself and your confidence through strong and positive action—which is how you became successful. Your etheric flies forward and starts to swamp theirs. If you are resonating faster than them, their first reaction will be one of elation and expectancy. They will be happy to see you. But once the initial boost is over and they can no longer benefit in "etheric currency" by your presence, they will experience a let down. One can momentarily borrow etheric energy from others, but one can't inherit it indefinitely. The slight dip that takes place in their etheric velocity will make them feel inadequate. You'll notice it in a conversation, when their eyes turn up and they stare into the distance with a glazed expression. More times than not they have experienced an ego hit. I call it "etheric spread." An emotional roll will flash through their etheric and swamp their concentration momentarily. In a split second they lose momentum, drifting back down the ego parabola toward the wave. The dip worries them, so they look for an external cause of the erosion they are suffering. They will unconsciously accuse your particle of causing them to fall. Thus they are compelled to attack the particle that they feel is in their way. By attempting to injure it or reduce its size, they can get around it and reestablish their upward climb. Usually they externalize the particle war and their sense of loss, by blocking you or by deliberately giving you a hard time. They instinctively need to slow you down so they can catch up. So they invent all sorts of objections and difficulties to waste your time and to impose control over you, thus establishing their particle as more real than yours.

There is an exception to the colliding particle rule which occurs when an individual's energy is known to be much bigger than that of others; for example, when the mega-millionaire visits the village. Everyone in the village is honored by his or her presence; they wouldn't dream of competing with the sophisticated millionaire, who's far out ahead of the villagers, leaving them plenty of room to expand upwards without the bigger energy getting in anyone's way. If an individual is very famous, the same process applies; people can gain status and observation by telling others that they have been with that person. "I had a beer with the President." That kind of stuff. That's why people collect autographs; it establishes absolute proof of the collector's rise by offering evidence of his or her presence in the company of separate particles. It's all so silly really, but what can we do? People are people.

Back to the beginning for a sec': We can see that isolated or small tribes had little egos, bigger tribes developed bigger egos, while national groupings opted for mega-egos as the preferred way. Once industrial expansion and expanding markets gave people prosperity, many could use that wealth to seek the particle state. So individuals went from a fairly expendable component in the tribal wave—subjugated under godlike leaders—to individualism, which gave them status. That is why in Third World countries, where evolution is more tribal, human life is not considered as valuable or important as it is in Western countries. There's no status, so no observation. It wasn't a big jump from people becoming individuals and reaching for the particle state to where they became much like their leaders—the very important people. Our Western people are now especially important people. Everyone's ego has been puffed up by glamour and wealth, and educated by the TV preacher to believe that they are not ordinary people evolving on earth through God's grace, but are, in fact, doing God a huge favor by even being here. Once our people became very important and special, and took on the illusion of godlike qualities, then each had to be guaranteed status. The ego of our people expanded beyond the idea of working to better their lot in life to become individual. That special status was demanded as a birth right. For example, if you are born American, that automatically grants you individuality and special rights. You don't have to work for that position, you are told that you have it as a divine gift. Each young American is pumped to believe that through birth he or she has status. It's much the same for most modern Western nations. The British believe they are special because of the history of the Empire; the Italians feel the same because of the Roman empire; the Spanish have their Conquistador history to rely on; the French are special by birth because of their culture and so on.

If you take a close look at what all these nations believe about themselves you can see how hysterically funny the national ego is. The problem is that we all live inside that external manifestation at the same time as living and experiencing the external manifestation of our own ego. Once the national ego cranks everyone into thinking they are all very, very special, then policies have to be invented and programs developed to underwrite that idea. The very, very important people who run the country need lots of status, so quite obviously they need palaces to live in. Below them the extremely important, very famous, "utterly blessed by God" people wouldn't need palaces, but they would certainly need big houses and special treatment, favored status, special privileges, reserved spots, tables at restaurants, long thin cars, boat moorings, and all the benefits that a very important, extremely famous person would naturally expect. Below them, the very important but "not famous" people wouldn't quite need such a performance, but they would need a guarantee that their very special status could never be taken from them. So glorious pensions were invented to ensure that very important "not famous" people would never have to fall back into the wave up to their dying day and beyond. Below them are the important people; their life is a little humdrum because they run things like companies, hospitals, universities, and so on, but their efforts are hands on. So they need status and special breaks and considerations for their important work. A slot below the important people are the "quite important" people. They are works managers, coordinators, flight controllers, union leaders, and building inspectors working for the local council, who say whether you can have a green door or not. Quite important people are only important to themselves and other "quite important" people who can watch them being quite important. This is a bit of a drawback because in order to establish the ego's version of the real particle state, you have to have outsiders to observe and confirm your importance. So "quite important" people suffer from an inferiority complex of being just short of genuine status, where they could move up to the "really important" or "very important" category. They make up for that by causing trouble and getting in everyone's way. If they cause enough trouble, then a "quite important" person is suddenly noticed and observed by others who need him or her to resolve the problem the "quite important" person created in the first place. Whereupon, they take on a little more particle state and are instantly up-graded to "very important." Without a "quite important" person's say so, all the planes will sit on the tarmac and rot.

Ordinary citizens don't usually get to the "quite important" or "very important" or the "extremely vital, supremely important" status. So what are we going to do for them? Well, they will have to make do with just being special. After all they must be special—they were born here, weren't they?

"Well how are we going to make sure they are special?" a scamp might ask.

First, we'll tell them they're special and then we'll put on a football match. We'll guarantee them for life as long as they don't rock the boat. If they can't be very important, then at least we can underwrite and guarantee their survival. The ego will buy that.

"But what do we do with all the underclass of citizens who are marginally functional; who can't or don't work, who have no money and no status? They have hope of separation, and so no hope of the particle state? Surely the TV said everyone can be a particle. How will these people manage it from such a lowly slot in life?"

Well, they are guaranteed survival the same as the special people—that should be good enough.

"But you forgot that I mentioned a second ago that these people are marginally functional—most can hardly read or write—there's no work for them. Many of them can't even speak the language properly. They are victims of a society that is oscillating faster than they are. Giving them money won't keep them happy because you haven't given them status. They can't become particles without status. They won't like that."

Ah. Geez! Picky. Picky. Perhaps we can make the marginally functional people special because they are not special.

"How would that work?"

Well, we'll focus on their 'not special' status and we'll notice them and observe them as being deprived of specialness and that will make them feel important. Our observing them as special because they are 'not special' will grant them a modicum of the particle state, so they'll become important through reversed specialness.

"What's 'reversed specialness'?"

Weren't you listening? Reversed specialness is how you become "special" when you are not special.

"It there any special trick to it?"

Sure there's a trick to every game the ego plays. If you are not special you can't cause trouble like the "quite important" people do. You don't have the authority or power to disrupt the system. So the alternative to trouble is noise. If you create a big enough noise people will notice you. You'll be observed and you'll become a particle and therefore special.

"That's it . . . noise? You can become a particle just through noise? Amazing. Doesn't that build a society of professional victims and make everyone else feel less special because of all the negative waves about the plight of the 'not special' people. How can a country stay 'special' if it's got all these people belly aching about being 'not special.'"

Well, that's a bit a problem. But we'll get 'round that by issuing some special money that will pay for the "not special" people to become particles. At the same time we can pay for the special and important people to make sure they remain would-be particles forever.

"What is special money? Is it different to real money?"

Yes. It is slightly different. We call it special money because it's specially created from nowhere by the grace of our printing presses to make sure that special attention is given to everyone's specialness.

"Don't people see through the trick? Don't they complain that the money is not real?"

No. We have a special way of getting 'round that. We sell the special money to people with real money so no one can tell special money from real money.

"How do you know that what you are being paid is real money? Couldn't some of the special money you converted last week come back to you this week as real money?"

That's a problem, but when we sell special money to people with real money or even last week's special money, then all of this week's special money becomes real. It's now mixed in the money wave, hovering close to real money so no one can tell the difference. That way we can generate enough wealth to make sure that everyone is special forever.

"What a wonderful plan. Can I ask one last question? Doesn't all this phony money and the effort of

*sustaining everyone's specialness stuff up the
economy and make everyone poorer? How can all
the ordinary special people and the less numerous
'very important' special people stay that way if they
run out of money and can't pay for their four bricks
and picket fence? Won't that make everyone feel
less special? How would they sustain the illusion of
the ego's separateness and still keep their ego
happy?"*

172

That's the problem with you Bolsheviks, you're
always causing trouble.

Wilde's Theory of Crisis—named with tongue in cheek—is not
based on any real science and offers no mathematics or theo-
rem. But it has a certain logic and prettiness which appeals to
scamps and students of human foibles, so it might appeal to
you.

Wilde's second Law of Crisis kicks in only if you have ignored
the first Law of Crisis, which says you don't have to cause a
crisis in your life or your nation in order to change. You only
have to agree to stop being silly and make the changes you need
to make. If the first law doesn't appeal to you, the second Law
of Crisis usually follows automatically.

The Law of Crisis states that once the ego gets a sniff of the
particle state—even though that state is an illusion in the
external world—the ego will usually go for it anyway, expanding itself toward the particle state until the individual reaches
collapse.

All power flows from within. The further the ego marches away
from that power in search of the external particle state, the less
and less true velocity it has. As it moves up that parabola
toward the particle state it acquires more and more gravity. In
order to go from being just born special to actually being "very

special," you have to get serious and acquire lots of power and things that will affirm your specialness. The problem is that they slow you down because you have to exert energy to acquire and maintain them. Also, the more the ego expands to acquire the particle state the more control it loses. The ego falls prey to setbacks and hits it may receive from other egos that are also aiming for the particle state.

At the beginning, the ego can handle the added gravity, but as it creates more and more, the emotional and financial weight increases and the individual's performance slows. So the ego often adjusts to the added weight by ignoring it, hoping somehow that it will look after itself and go away. Governments do that by sticking vast chunks of their deficit accounts elsewhere. In America it's called "off budget" accounting. Off budget is how you convert heavy debt and obligations that cause gravity for the nation into light debt that the government can pretend is not there.

173

Back to personal ego. In the exercising and acquiring of power and status the ego burns great amounts of energy. As your emotional, intellectual, and financial energy is burnt chasing the particle, you begin to approach a heat death where there is no more personal power left to burn. Some people are saved from this scenario because as they reach the edge of their physical or intellectual abilities, they sensibly back off, knowing that if the ego expands them any further they're in deep trouble. But many press on regardless. When the mental and emotional energy starts to run down, the ego begins to burn the body's energy to create the illusion of velocity. That's why important people are always stressed out, rushing about, terribly busy, short of time, and sick. If you are busy in little bursts, fine. But if you are perpetually busy and harassed for a lack time, your ego has got you by the short and curlies. Time and space are linked. If you have no time, you'll have no emotional space. If you have no space, you will have less and less energy. If you have less energy, your heat death approaches all the quicker. Eventually, the energy of your life begins to suffer serious entropy as a result of all the energy the ego burns. If your body doesn't crash on the way up, eventually the ego expands you to a thermal equilibrium where there is no more heat, power or velocity to keep the illusion alive anyway. Your whole life abruptly twangs back from the outer reaches and you begin to collapse back upon yourself. Reality caves in on you. It's a safety mechanism. It isn't foolproof, but it usually kicks in just before you drop dead.

174

If the ego's reach is stymied and starts to fall back, insecurity develops from fear and the ego soon believes itself to be dying. Which in a way it is, because the ego is losing its illusion of the particle dream and is falling back into the wave. The ego can't allow that. Once the ego has established even a little of the illusion—be it four bricks in the suburbs or divine specialness by Aryan birth—loosing it becomes a life-and-death issue.

Crisis from the ego's point of view is the horror of falling back into the wave. Of course, the ego never left the wave anyway. It only developed elasticity, which sustained the illusion that it might be able to escape. There is no velocity powerful enough to get the ego out of the tribal wave and to actually create the external particle dream. An individual who is focused in the ego and the external world is actually facing the wrong way. As the ego expands further and further, reality adjusts to expand with it. Your external horizon is always retreating. That's why people can never get enough of power, status, sex, money, or whatever it is that the ego seeks. The ego can't reach critical velocity and, as a result, complete satisfaction—it can't reach the particle state either. It's a bit like the universe, really. You can't get out of the universe by flying toward its edge. It doesn't have a edge to fly towards. If you could attempt it, the universe would expand with you, creating an event horizon beyond which you couldn't go. As you accelerated to chase what you thought was the edge of the universe you'd run out of fuel, and the quicker you went the more gravity you'd take on. Gravity would slow you down so you could never generate enough velocity to reach your goal.

What we see in the world today is, for the most part, the ego's thermal death as it reaches the outer limits of its elasticity just prior to twanging back. In some cases its twang has already happened. So do we have a real crisis in the world or is it just a crisis of the ego? If all of the terribly special, highly important people were suddenly not special and not particularly important, would our world actually change or would it just be that their vision had changed?

Our world is built on consumption. It's the *raison d'etre* of our economic system. A small amount of consumption is needed for survival and a pleasant life, but much of what we consume is only a part of the chase for the particle state. Look at all the stuff you have bought over the years but never used. It only gave you fleeting pleasure for the brief moment it fed the illusion. Once it stopped doing that, you moved your horizon beyond whatever it was that you purchased, looking for the next boost. If the need for all that stuff suddenly wasn't there, would it be a real trauma—or would it be an excuse for a wonderful garage sale where you get to meet your neighbors?

The evolution of mankind is self-correcting, as is nature. The human spirit seeks equilibrium. Thank God for that. What we see in fact is not a real crisis. It's only the death of an illusion. People who belong to that illusion will consider that death a personal trauma. But in real terms, over a long period of time, this will be seen as the great age of healing, when our people learned that chasing the particle state externally—to the point of collapse—is futile, and that the only way to actually establish the particle state is internally.

To create that, you have to exit the tribal mind. Of course, you can't give up the language you were born with, but in the inner worlds that's unimportant. The language of the Inner You is mostly feelings, symbols, and visions. What is important is to release the emotional attachment you have for the tribal wave. It's the only way to go beyond its fears and restrictive ways.

If you buy the world crisis, and all the moaning and groaning, you are buying the wave and the ego's terror of slipping back. If you want to be a real human you are obliged to look at life objectively. Most of the mayhem we are told is happening isn't really mayhem at all. A high percentage of it is hype. Sure there are problems, but they are ego problems, that's all. In a society where everyone has to become a particle and where many have no real ability or volition to do that, then "victim" is the last known way. By becoming a victim and soliciting sympathy, you establish observers. In countries like the USA, if you can really hype your misfortune, you can also become rich. Then your particle state is established with the compensation you get for whatever misfortune you claim you have suffered.

But how much is real genuine misfortune and injustice and how much is the ego's need for attention, observation, or money? I reckon you could cut the negative wave by at least half and perhaps even more—and you'd get closer to what's real. Obviously, the more noise you create, the more money you make. For example, there's a lot of poverty in the Western world, but how many Englishmen or Americans or Spaniards actually die of starvation? Damn few. Is our poverty consciousness the result of a hyped ego playing victim and demanding the particle state to be granted without effort, or real poverty that comes from abject conditions? It's all relative.

The system feeds on itself and perpetuates the emotion. Individuals have to sell their victim status in competition with others who are also selling their victim status. When a society encourages victims, there'll be a lot of them. Each year more victims will join the ranks because being a victim is easier than taking responsibility or generating energy. You can blame your problems or your lack of concerted disciplined action on others.

However, to sustain the idea and keep the sympathy (and checks) flowing, you have to raise the emotional ante year by year to create the necessary reaction. So what looks like a society in collapse is not necessarily so. Especially if you view it from outside the wave. It's not the society collapsing, it's the ego saying you can't have a society without it and the principles it holds as sacrosanct.

Though our Western governments are in serious trouble, theoretically you could fix most of the major problems overnight. The status quo would have to back off and individuals would have to do the same. So don't hold your breath. But you can heal yourself immediately. Crisis is not compulsory. Conditions may be choppy, but if there's not a lot of baggage you won't lose much overboard.

There is nothing wrong with people improving their lives and working for the external particle state, providing they live within what is real without expecting someone else to provide the dream for them. I have always encouraged people to become independent in the outside world first, because I don't see how you get out from under the ego of the status quo without at least some money. Sure you can drop out of the system and head for the bush, but without money you can't really experience the full potential of life. Being independent externally in commercial terms acts as a great spur to developing an inner journey. Building the inner life completes the process of spiritual integration.

The only difficulty the world has today is that we have sold our people on the idea that they are very important and that the particle state is theirs by right. It isn't. And we are not particularly important. Yes, we have a divine spark within us, but that's it. Somehow we have ego tripped ourselves into a corner. The only way out is to stop pumping ourselves up and to begin the process of retraining our egos. Otherwise, when the bubble finally bursts, we'll be in for a long hard fall. People expect more now than we're able to give them, and what they are getting is just about to be pulled from them. We have to lower our debt and our consumption and take to a more spiritual way, developing sustainable economies which don't destroy the planet in the mad chase for status and importance. If you tell a national wave it can have the particle state without effort, quite naturally they will put their hand out. I blame the status quo for manipulating people's expectancy for political purposes. TV has also fed the people with bizarre notions that will only cause heartache in the end. People are warped. Their egos are way out of control, and the national ego is leading the charge.

178

For your own personal serenity it is very important to create what is real and true and controllable in your life so that you are not affected by the ego pangs of others. Sure, we can support our fellow man as he or she makes the adjustments needed, but for the most part, they will have to do it for themselves. Meanwhile, I think it's vital to remember that most of the world's crises is not crises at all. It's the labor pains of spirit being birthed out of the death of the ego. If you want to be spiritually integrated with an inner and outer life you'll ditch the crisis mentality in a fast hurry. If you accept the fear and acknowledge it as real you are locked into it. If you bathe in the wave, holding to the crisis mentally like religion, it will surely materialize. The final battle is not a tussle between good and evil and one "Dead-Male-As-God" winning over another. It's the tussle between your ego and the formation of your inner self empowered by spirit. Whereby through discipline you enter a silent but invigorating journey as you wrestle your ego into submission, melting it via the inner journey. That is the preferred mode. Let's look at some popular crises that are the religion of tick-tock that we're being sold, so that we know how to recognize them for what they are not and avoid them.

Apocalypse When?

CHAPTER EIGHT

Nostradamus predicted a major cataclysm in the year 1999, and many modern pundits and gurus agree, promoting apocalyptic scenarios of a boiling hot world, diseased and about to choke itself into oblivion. Have you ever wondered why so many believe these predictions without question? Are these notions real, or are they a figment of a mass neurosis?

In the 14th century, during the time of the Great Plague, the Black Death took out million's of people in Europe. The religions warned of the wrath of God, advising repentance and contrition, while groups of odd balls took to the street and performed the Dance Macabre. This dance consisted of wearing skeleton masks and bouncing around for hours on end screaming, "We're all going to die! We're all going to die! Some did die, some didn't. Exhaustion probably claimed a few of them.

Here in the 90's we have our own version of the Dance Macabre: The media is busy selling doom, while many believe the anti-Christ is on his way and that some terrible end is but 'round the corner. We are told that global warming and pollution are paralyzing the planet, that dolphins are dwindling, clap will wipe out the known world, and Armageddon will replace the World Series as the main event.

If you look back at the ancient Greeks, who gave us the word "apocalypse" (meaning "to run away and hide"), and track all prophesies through to the modern day, you'll find that all the prophets had one thing in common—they were mostly wrong! Funny how that slipped our notice!

But belief in an apocalypse forms an important part of many major religions and is firmly imbedded in the mind set of the people. The belief comes from fears we have about our own mortality, it's a part of our psyche. Death is embarrassing to the ego. To make it more palatable, the ego mind would prefer a scenario where everyone perishes, so that the personal trauma it suffers might be ameliorated through a shared group experience. "It's not my fault I am going to die, everyone will."

Second, we believe in the apocalypse because our imagination is underdeveloped. It is hard for us to conceive of society a hundred years from now, so how can we ever relate to a world that might exist two thousand years from now? Since we can't really imagine the distant future, it is natural that we tend to think that the world won't exist then, either.

Third, to the mind of tick-tock, change is as close to death as matters; it rattles the hell out of the stability of ordinary people. When you couple rapid change with the fact that we're approaching the end of a millennium, you can see how the apocalyptic mind set is sustained.

An apocalypse is a good money spinner. Threatening people with a good scare is one way of cranking cash. I think a lot of our ecology concerns have been picked up by big business and turned into a handy profit. For example, 77% of Australians make purchases at the grocery store based on ecological decisions. The eco' stuff is more expensive—sometimes a lot more expensive. So the manufacturers have turned our eco-fears into a billion dollar industry. Of course, some of the ecological data has an element of truth in it, and the less trash we create the better, but most of the eco-scare is just plain old merchandising.

Apocalypse When?

The other day I bought a dozen eggs. They were expensive; I was in a rush. Back home, I noticed the egg box was labeled "Ecofriendly vegetarian eggs," which explained the 90% surcharge. What is a vegetarian egg, I asked myself. Chickens don't eat steak; are there any eggs that aren't vegetarian? Of course there aren't. But manufacturers know that we simpletons will suck on that eco-stuff like we're brain dead. Industry and governments rely on our stupidity. They go to the bank on it. So next time you're sitting in the toilet gazing lovingly at your overpriced eco-shampoos, and fondling your unbleached toilet paper, ask yourself who invented this idea. How much of it is pure *BS*? How much money are they making from my ignorance?

The problem is that most of the scenarios are half-truths or downright lies. At the time of the Gulf War, when the Persian Gulf got messed up, the ecologists declared it, "The mother of all environmental disasters," and claimed it would threaten the stability of the Earth. Millions of dollars were allocated, everyone had a wonderful time washing birds, getting sun tans, and putting out fires. They also made a lot of money. When it was all over, the truth came out: The ecologists were forced to admit that the pollution was, in fact, local. A few birds had died, Kuwait was a bit smoky for nine months, but "the mother of all ecological disasters" was nothing more than a local mess. By then it didn't matter; the checks were cashed, all five hundred million dollars worth of them. No one needed the scare anymore.

It's a game they play. Take global warming for example: There is absolutely no evidence to suggest that the world is heating up. Certainly in the last one hundred years the earth's temperature has varied by half a degree, but the overall temperature rises and falls constantly. You can't take a hundred year period out of context and say that it represents a trend. In fact, there is a large body of evidence suggesting the exact opposite—that the earth may now be cooling slightly. Between 1930 and 1970 the mean average temperature of the earth fell quite dramatically. The long term monitoring of the world's climate undertaken by NASA, who takes twenty-two million satellite photographs of the earth per year, has an accuracy of close to 1/100th of a degree. The computers show that the earth was slightly warmer in the early 80's and slightly cooler in the last part of the decade. The long term monitoring of weather conditions by the Space Flight Center at NASA categorically shows that there has been no overall warming whatsoever.

184   We hear that the polar ice caps are melting, and that the seas will rise two or three feet in the next fifty years. But who says so? The media does. Documentaries on TV show us Canadian glaciers falling dramatically into the sea. The whole eerie scene is offered as a warning of impending doom if mankind doesn't change its ways. But is this position born out by scientific data? What is strange about a glacier melting into the sea? The most reliable information about the polar ice caps again comes from NASA. Their satellite evidence is corroborated by scientists from organizations like the British Antarctic Survey, who examine ice cores taken from the polar regions. Both the "on site" and satellite evidence clearly show there has been no overall change, whatsoever.

You might ask, "Surely, the sea is rising. We have all seen those TV reports of kids running around on Pacific atolls, that tell us the islands will be soon be swamped. Surely the commentators aren't lying?" They may not be deliberately lying, but they are selling you an idea they want you to buy. There is only a finite amount of moisture on the planet—we aren't making any new water. If the ice caps aren't melting, then the overall water volume must remain constant. True, here and there the sea has risen, but that's because the land has fallen. For example, sea levels in southern England have risen slightly in recent years, but if you pop up the coast a few hundred miles to the north of the British Isles you will find that tide gauges show that sea levels there have fallen. The continental plates shift all of the time.

Well, what about the buildup of CO_2 in the atmosphere; surely all those toxic gasses must be heating up the earth? I'm sorry to disappoint you: they aren't. In fact, there isn't any real evidence to substantiate the widely held belief that carbon dioxide causes temperatures to rise. If you look at the world's climatic records for this century you'll see that the overall temperature of the planet did move up slightly between about 1900 and 1930, but this cyclical rise—which is a natural phenomena—took place *before* the bulk of the modern day increase in CO_2 emissions, those took place after 1950. In fact, as CO_2 levels were gradually increasing between 1950 and 1970, the world's mean average temperature was actually falling. This seems to be a puzzling contradiction for the greenhouse theory.

No one disagrees with data that shows that CO_2 in the atmosphere has risen substantially in the last few decades. And car emissions have been proven to be a health hazard, but show me the evidence that establishes without doubt that CO_2 causes temperatures to rise. That's a trick question because, in fact, there is no evidence. The climatic records are a little bit boring from the greenhouse view point because they show the exact opposite to be the case—accumulation of CO_2 in the upper atmosphere rises and falls in *response* to temperature changes, not the other way 'round as we have so frequently been told. Data shows that once the mean average temperature goes up, then gradually CO_2 levels in the upper atmosphere will rise, lagging several years behind. In the past, when the temperature fell, CO_2 levels also fell. The greenhouse effect relies entirely on the premise that CO_2 reflects heat back to earth, and warms it. There are two knotty little problems which are conveniently overlooked: To sustain the greenhouse effect as a scientific theory, you have to show that reflected heat actually causes global warming. No one can say for certain that it does. Many complex factors come into play, such as, how much heat is radiated away by trace gasses and how much is reflected back towards the earth? No one knows. The second problem facing the greenhouse theory is that if CO_2 really does heat the earth as is claimed, then why don't we have any evidence to substantiate that? Surely temperatures would have risen, given that we have had forty-five years of increasing CO_2 emissions. Scientific evidence and the lack of rising temperatures rather stuffs up the theory. What scientists do know is that CO_2 is not the main culprit of reflected heat. Water vapor is. Have you ever heard anyone in the media mention that there may be some doubt about the scientific premise of global warming or that perhaps there are other larger forces at work? I never have. When an idea enters the tribal mind as religion it automatically excludes contradiction or discussion as heretical. The greenhouse effect of water vapor far exceeds that of methane or carbon dioxide. But while water vapor initially warms the planet, the overall effect is cooling. As temperatures rise, more water vapor is given off, creating more clouds, which reflects the sun and keeps the earth balanced.

Well then, what about the computer weather models that show a dramatic heating of the planet over the next two hundred years? The problem with those models is that they are based primarily on the opinions of a dozen or so senior researchers who initiated the models. They are known to be very inaccurate. One famous model, on which much of the global warming theory is based, gives us the same summer rain for the Sahara Desert as it does Ireland. The models predominantly discard the effect of cloud cover because the computers can't properly predict it. So the apocalypse of global warming is based on computer models that state possible weather patterns on a fairly cloudless earth. Weird, but true. Most meteorologists have problems correctly predicting tomorrow's weather. I wouldn't get too sucked into their predictions for the year 2193.

So why are scientists into global warming? The fact is most scientists aren't into global warming. They know that it's highly

Apocalypse When?

speculative but are reluctant to say so openly. Global warming started as an idea based on the opinion of researchers who have a very great financial and intellectual interest in promoting the idea. You don't get grants to study stuff if it's not causing problems. And you certainly don't want facts getting in the way of a good money making cause. Imagine going to an institution and saying, "There's nothing wrong with the weather, can I please have half a million to study it?"

We also have all heard how the rotten ol' Brazilians are cutting down the Amazon rain forest, and because of it we'll soon run out of oxygen. It makes a fine story. It also gives pop stars and Prince Charles something to pontificate about. But is it true? Does the Amazon provide the world's oxygen? No, it doesn't. In fact, microorganisms in the sea provide most of the world's oxygen. The whole of the Amazon could become a concrete parking lot tomorrow, and we'd all be breathing just fine.

Certainly, we would like to conserve our forests, and there is no dispute that trees do generate some oxygen, but the idea that the Amazon or rain forests generally provide the air we breathe is just not so. Conserving the rain forest may be an emotional preference for many—it's certainly my preference—but that is a subjective opinion. It cannot be justified on the issues of oxygen. If you are trying to crank a political stance, telling people they'll soon run out of air is a potent message.

Don't get me wrong; I'm not saying all of our environmental concerns are piffle. We certainly have to watch pollution levels, and each of us should do our bit to improve things. I feel we have a moral and spiritual obligation to look after our planet and hand it over to our kids in a decent condition. What I am saying is, there is a great difference between feeling a spiritual alignment to nature and a love for our planet, and getting sucked into tick-tock's heaving emotion—the basis of which is often well removed from truth. You would be naive if you didn't understand that there are powerful forces at work which promote the ecological apocalypse for their own political and financial ends. For example, most people wouldn't accept anymore tax hikes, but if you sold them on the need for a pollution tax to redress the oxygen shortage most would support it. The idea is to feed the wave with enough ambiguous information that excludes contradictory scientific evidence, until your political position is established as fact. It's the brainwashing that bothers me. There is a racket going on. Selling crises is big business and big politics. You should never forget that. If you were one of the two hundred or so people who recently paid a well known American "guru" $18,000 for your own corrugated iron nuclear bomb shelter—tough titty! You were robbed.

Much of the issue is hype. Then if you look at the inner message of it all you can quite clearly see that most of people's concerns about the environment are just an externalization of their personal disquiet. Water is an archetypal symbol of emotion. Often when you are upset you will dream of being buffeted in stormy seas while tidal waves sweep over you. So what does the global belief in rising waters mean? Why would people buy it if it isn't true? They do so because they feel emotionally overwhelmed. Life is swamping them. Of course the seas are rising, any fool knows that.

What about the fear of a polluted atmosphere that will choke us all to death? Is that not, in part, an externalization of a polluted mind confused by a rapidly changing world? The reason people fervently want to believe that the world's temperature is rising when it isn't, is not because they are stupid, but because they need to externalize the stifling effect that modern problems and restrictions create in their lives. Once your ambiance no longer invigorates you, it's natural you might think that the lack of freshness is caused by external factors, like rising temperatures. How could your discomfort possibly be caused by your ego destroying your balance and burning your energy? Once you understand how humans externalize their concerns

Apocalypse When?

and insecurities, then you don't have to buy "the sky is falling." You can just have compassion for people's anxiety and do your best to help them feel better.

When several hundred million people head for the cliff like lemmings for no logical reason, a scamp might stop to wonder what underlying psychosis or terror is causing the rush of passing rodents. I know lots of people, including many of my personal friends, who are very sad about the planet and truly believe there is no hope. You can't tell them otherwise. Where did they buy the idea? The TV? Surely not the same TV that was running stories in the seventies of the coming Ice Age?

Yet the lemmings run. There is a ripple in the wave and the dance is on; blood rushes to the head, the atmosphere is clammy and hot, there's trouble brewing, danger lurks, as people warn us of God's retribution. A dark cloud is blotting out the sun, poisons secretly pervade our blood, a sense of foreboding hangs over us, as silent and deadly diseases stalk us, killing the innocent. Plots are hatched, while evil satanic cults roam the countryside, cattle are mutilated, children disappear, and a dark grey mist falls over humanity, muffling the cries of a primal scream that is heard echoing faintly in the distance. Night is falling now, crows screech in nearby trees. While microscopic bugs pollute our beds, stealthily crawling across our face to lay their eggs in our eyebrows. Mysterious gases from the rocks below seep through our bodies turning healthy cells into cancerous ones. What manner of evil walks abroad this night? Be it ghost or ghoul, or some horrendous incubus that sexually violates our purity while we sleep, sucking our blood, feeding upon our psyche, invading our bodies until madness or death, surely we will all perish? Our personalities and our very souls are dying. Someone must be sacrificed to appease the gods. It must be the Colombians that are making us sick, or the black man or perhaps it's the Jew, someone is causing this terrible woe. If not them, perhaps it's the homosexuals or the Asians maybe. Yes. That's it! The Japanese are plotting to overthrow the world, beaming low frequency waves to disrupt the white man's mind, stealing his job and castrating his hope of the separate particle state. Perhaps it's not the Japanese. Perhaps it's just the disbelievers, who refuse to repent and accept Jesus—damned heretics, they have sullied our minds with contradictions and robbed our people of divine approval and God's safety. Let us mount a holy war and attack them, and the Arab infidel, and any one else we might be able to blame for our ego's disquiet.

190   The deadening beat goes on; we are numb now. Tolerance and love are trampled under foot while the dancers cry with one frenzied voice, "Romper Stomper, let the ego conquer." Reality twists and warps, shimmering to fit the dancers needs, walls bend leaning inward, threatening, wobbling, throbbing back and forth in time with the dance. And from the wounded brain of man comes now a green bile whose foul stench is mistaken for national pride. The smell of which drives the crowd to ecstasy. Slam dunk. Bump, bump—faces racked with pain, the dance goes on. No one sees that the very bones of the dancers are melting with every throbbing beat, flesh flows across the floor like so much wax while dancers grimace as they bounced upon their stumps. A hundred million slimy, crooked fingers are raised to the sky pointing, searching, calling for the names of culprits. "The Macabre is truth," they cry, "Let the Dance go on forever."

Sir? Madam? Will you buy a ticket for the dance? Or perhaps you might prefer a seat upon this mossy log, from which you might contemplate the staggering beauty of the eternal Tao. Wherein a God Force, devoid of ego, shines through a dew drop as it tumbles through its infinite evolution, which we humans see as the short distance between leaf and rock. Yes, and comes presently a reasonable breeze, soft and unassuming, fragrant as the jasmine flower. Is that the summer wind or is it the Valley Spirit that never dies, passing through the corridors of our heart, refreshing our hopes and dreams? Who's to say?

Apocalypse When?

Would that we would love like nature loves; would that we could embrace the void without tear or regret. But let us at least try, and let us call to others offering them encouragement. Let us show how a love for softness and the nature spirit of the sacred Mother can never be offered in a politic of anger and fear, for if it is, we cannot call it holy.

That's the ego's way, attempting to bestow divine approval upon itself through righteousness, a tool it uses to assist in separation. I am right and holy and separate and blessed by God, you are wrong and therefore not blessed by God, and so you are lower than I. Being lower makes me higher and more important, and safer.

I feel that the apocalypse industry plays deliberately on people's sense of guilt. In a perverse way the environmental ballyhoo is just a modern day version of original sin. The ego will buy the illusion of its godlike qualities, but the sweaty odor of the defecating body in which the ego dwells contradicts its vision of self as a selected being with divine approval. The ego's importance is assailed. That is why people can't handle being watched as they use the toilet—it causes them shame—they prefer to deny their human form and its functions. From the ego's view there is an implied guilt in being human. As ego grew and grew, reaching for a godlike status, it became disgusted with its own dirt. We have got to stop this pollution—it's sinful. Of course the ego doesn't believe it is responsible, it blames someone else—namely the physical body. Thus the original sin is transferred. It can't be me. I am a pristine particle destined for great things. These are not my feces in the toilet, they belong to the body. The body pollutes and it is mortal, so the ego can't own it too vigorously otherwise it stuffs up its illusion. A transfer is made, first away from the ego to the body and then on to an external culprit. It's others that pollute, not me. It's the factory across the street, not my consumption of the factory's products that is causing the problem. I need that consumption to become separate; it's someone else's consumption that is killing the earth.

At the extreme end of the ecology movement, you see another attempt by the ego to deny its own mortality by separating itself from dirt—its own dirt, mainly. The planet dying from pollution is an externalization of the ego's fear that it has now expanded itself to collapse. The ego knows that if the individual looks within and establishes observation and contemplation, the ego will eventually lose importance and die. So rather than face self-immolation, it creates a huge fuss about the planet dying to keep the individual concentrating externally. There is nothing better than an external threat to keep everyone focused in the wrong direction.

That is why there is so much emotion about ecology and so much unreasonable denial of empirical scientific fact. We have bought the dogma lock, stock and barrel. No alternative will be allowed. It is now a life-and-death issue for the ego. Change makes people feel a sense of doom that comes from instability. The dying planet is vital to the ego. For if the planet is not dying, then the somber feelings we currently experience must either be the ego's illusion dying, or worse still, the very ego itself is about to expire. Neither alternative is acceptable. So a politic of anger and crisis is maintained to keep the ego from looking at what is actually happening.

"Well, that's really upsetting," some might say, "If we are not having a holocaust, and there's no global warming, what about those poor dolphins?" I'm sorry to disappoint everyone, but there is no evidence to suggest that world population of dolphins is diminishing. In fact, the reverse seems to be the case. Anyway, all the fuss we make about the dolphins is only to bolster our self-importance. The dolphin is the most highly evolved of the sea dwelling species. A position we humans hold on land. From the ego's viewpoint the dolphin has status. It's not just a fish—well, a mammal that looks like a fish—it's a particle. It is special and has a different destiny from ordinary fish. So a net full of fish causes no emotion, that's wave energy. But if a single dolphin is trapped in the net it's horrifying. The dolphin is a symbol of our particle state. If it dies, a part of the ego's illusion of its particle state dies with it. Remember, the main object of the ego's desire to separate from the wave is to avoid death. The sight of a particle represented by an intelligent aquatic mammal trapped in the fish wave, is a terrible blow to the ego. It causes great sorrow and anger. It's exactly what the ego is hoping to avoid—death in the tribal wave.

193

"Well, geez, what about all the disappearing animal species?"

I'd love to tell you that all the extinct animals are, in fact, in hiding, because they are pissed off with a lot of overfunded, scruffy biologists constantly stapling electrodes to their ears. Instead, think of this: There's a natural balance to the earth. Our planet is a living organism. It seems to have a mind of its own. The animals aren't victims. They are in perfect balance, as is the planet. If species die out, who is to say that they are not supposed to? The animal kingdom is in a spiritual evolution through the earth plane, just as are humans. Some believe that animals belong to a Group Soul. So there is one Group Soul for all orangutans, one for all the various subspecies of rat, and so on. How would that animal Group Soul ever evolve out of the physical plane, unless it finally becomes extinct and completes its spiritual evolution? Perhaps species are supposed to die out. Perhaps *missing* is their ultimate transcendence, as is ours. It would be bloody awkward if dinosaurs were tromping around on Main Street. It's fine by me that they checked out to some different evolution.

Of course many species have gone missing, but the emotion around it is an irrational insecurity caused by uncertainty and rapid change. The ego wonders if the next thing to go "missing" is itself. Then again, much of the ballyhoo is a money making venture, just like global warming. There was a documentary on television the other night about a husband and wife who'd been in the desert for fifteen years studying the mating habit of camels. The upshot of all their learned studies was that camels are banging away steadily, and there's no shortage of them. Big deal. I wonder how much that research cost us? $50,000? $100,000? How do you get into the camel bonking business, anyway?

194

Sure we have a spiritual duty to respect our planet and to love and care as best as possible for the animal kingdom, but we also have to understand that the evolution of our planet is changing and if the spotted owl is under pressure, that's just a part of what is going on. The spotted human is under even more pressure.

All the hand wringing and groans come off as a bit phoney to me. I love it when you see one of those wild man Jack characters on TV, all togged up in his camouflage jacket, and he's waffling on about the degradation of our forests. You know that the minute his sermon is over he's about to head to the woods and blast Bambi's brains out. I wonder how many of those characters love nature so much they would embrace vegetarianism?

The idea of killing something that you don't need just for the fun of it is as close to prehistoric as you can get. But if you are a predator on this plane, you can't bitch if someone or something comes and gets you. I have always wondered why so many hunters wind up accidently shooting themselves or getting shot by someone else. Karma, I suppose. Still, it would be a lot of fun if the little creatures of the forest were armed and could shoot back. That would be a day's sport! Bambi 6, Hunters 0! Now there's a score.

Once you have a cause you can justify any amount of hypocrisy, but you have to wonder why the rest of us buy into this apocalypse stuff? First, I suppose, because it is fashionable. It's natural that people would say we have got to stop—we are killing the planet, for those are the very instructions that the individual needs to hear to save him or herself. Rather than realize that it's the ego that is being killed off, or that it ought to be killed off via a personal equilibrium and balance, people externalize their fear and insist that it is the planet that is collapsing.

The vast wealth of scientific evidence flowing out of such august bodies as the Massachusetts Institute of Technology, NASA, the British Meteorological Office, the Woods Hole Institute of Oceanographic Studies and dozens of Universities, and research establishments around the globe, categorically states without any possibility of serious denial, that there is no evidence that our planet faces a crisis or that it is even warming up. The seas aren't rising and there's no proof that car emissions cause climatic changes.

Reading here that most of global warming is based on misinformation will disturb some of you. Some may consider the contradiction as preposterous. But I assure you that I have no political or financial needs in attempting to offer you the truth of it all. My motivation is not to disturb the wave or its religion. It's more to allow conscious people to disengage from the negative terror offered by tick-tock, which I see as very detrimental to advancement toward the inner particle state. It's hard to believe in yourself and your journey if you erroneously think the very planet you walk on is about to melt.

Yet isn't it strange that in the dark foreboding of religion and tick-tock almost no one will believe that the world isn't falling apart. When several hundred million people suddenly take to the Dance Macabre, you have to wonder what's going on. I find it fascinating. What I also think is very interesting is that the scientific opinions of eminent scientists who refute the global warming stance is absolutely ignored in the press. Everyone has made up their minds and accepted the new dogma, because the ego desperately needs it. Politicians spend millions trotting off to Rio for earth conferences because it's politically expedient. Crazy, isn't it? What it means is that there must be a very deep psychological need in the wave which is being expressed regardless of facts. Anyone offering a little sensible logic is often pilloried, silenced, and banished forever. In an interview I gave recently, I referred to the work of Professor Patrick Michaels of the University of Virginia, who is a leading environmental rationalist. My interview, which was ninety percent about human potential and only mentioned global warming in passing, was shown to a world famous "Greenie" who is a environmental superstar. The editor of my piece wanted the man's reaction. The ecology buff read my piece and got very pissed off. He flatly refused to comment. Needless to say, my interview headed for the recycling bin where it will no doubt do wonderful things, like saving trees and stuff like that.

It's a pity that the environmental movement, which could be so marvelous and so empowering for the Planetary Group Soul, is in fact so often just another extension of the struggle for power and control. Nowadays, it is becoming nearly impossible in small rural towns to get permission to build anything new. The inhabitants are virulent in their opposition to any sort of development. Of course, once you have a nice place of your own in the country, why would you want any other particles coming into your area to collide with your individual state, to crowd the very land that gives definition to that individual state? The locals can't say we are just stuck-up little would-be particles who are full of our own self-importance—so that entitles us to discriminate against newcomers. No way. The actions of newcomers are depicted as immoral and degrading to the environment. Actually, it's the ego of the locals that is degraded; those who have claimed the territory for themselves and have established a very large separation from others by believing that all the lands for miles around fall under their sovereignty. It's all so paper thin; ego, couched in a self-righteous language that would make bible bashers proud. It is hard to be real and temptingly easy to be phony.

Apocalypse When?

Our world has to eventually pull back from its frenzied consumption. But we can't have zero consumption, we need some level on consumption in order to survive. We have to rationalize our debt and reestablish a sense of propriety in our political systems. But that won't work unless we look deeply into our hearts and agree to reappraise our stuck-up attitudes. We have to withdraw the ego from its frenetic chase of the particle state. Very few people can do that or admit that they cause their own problems. Even fewer will see that it's the pomposity of the mind that's killing our society. So instead, we'll boo-ga-loo to the Dance Macabre a little while longer and attack someone. "Hey, Harry! Who haven't we attacked for a while?"

Or, while the dancers bounce, we'll stand quietly to one side and work upon ourselves to become stronger and more free. Once you are balanced and secure and spiritually more mature, you will know that the world is perfect within its imperfection, and you can be happy with that. You won't buy into a collective neurosis to feel better. The world is improving all the time. People are healthier and live longer, and most of the world's political problems will gradually sort themselves out. We ought to be delighted; but no, paranoia reigns.

The greatest pollution, of course, is not to the environment, but to your mind—not to mention the erosion that's affecting your wallet. We can resist that by retreating from it, while letting the negativity of tick-tock burn itself to a stand still. Meanwhile, I am sure the manipulators will crank the scare for all it's worth. When you think of it, what could be better, from the Establishment's point of view, than a nice ecological scare? The push to establish a New World Order is, in fact, a move to regulate and disenfranchise the ordinary people who are considered merely fodder for the system. To have a New World Order, you have to get the individual countries to give up their sovereignty. This is already happening. The EEC has already locked up and legislated the whole of Western Europe. Every day new laws are passed in Strasbourg and Brussels that control the economic activity of the people, right down to the last minute detail, including what size a cheese should be and what constituents a potato chip should have and so forth. It's mind numbing. Who needs this sterile bureaucratic asylum that they are inventing for us? What happened to the freedom and individuality that our fathers and mothers fought for? Humans need to be a little crazy, spontaneous, unusual, free flowing, and creative. Who needs these little rows of scrubbed clean Europeans who will march forward to a bureaucratic heaven with their correct cheese in hand. Oh God, allow spirit to shine and set our people free.

It saddens me sometimes. The heart and joy and pleasures of our people are squashed under the dominance of pathetic rulers who will sell our countries down the river just so they can strut their erections and ego trips. Western Europe is trussed in a bag. The whole continent is in the grip of a central power dominated by the German government and its mind numbing bureaucracy. They, in turn, are very lovey-dovey with the American government, who, with the collapse of Russia, are now free to control the planet. Maintaining the ecology scam plays right into the hands of those forces who control America and are busy developing a global police state. The idea that billions of people should give up their rights so that the world's pollution problems are solved, sounds so reasonable on the surface. How could any right minded person argue with global control of the CFC's that are wrecking the ozone layer?

Have you ever heard anyone ever question the CFC's issue? Of course not. We don't want anything getting in the way of a cheery New World Order. How do we know CFC's are destroying the ozone layer? The government told the media, they in turn parroted it to us, and we bought it! Yet, a CFC particle takes fifty years to go from ground level to the upper atmosphere; so is modern industry responsible for the problem or are we looking at the effect of CFC's that were discharged in

Apocalypse When?

1943 and before? If we are looking at a picture that's fifty years old, when emissions were not that great, we could come to two conclusions: We are in a hell of a lot of trouble once the rest of the CFC's get up there or industrial CFC's really don't affect the atmosphere as much as we think, and something else is really going on.

We are told that the CFC's in the atmosphere have increased our exposure to ultraviolet light, yet there is no scientific evidence to support that premise. Quite the reverse; levels of ultraviolet light have remained steady over the last fifteen years. That may change in the future but if I were trying to establish a sovereignty over the world, I wouldn't let the truth about ultraviolet light levels get in my way. Neither would I want people to know that one half decent volcanic eruption produces ozone destroying chlorine in quantities that are equivalent to several hundred years of chlorofluorocarbon production generated by industrial activity. But a New World Order can't control volcanoes, so why mention such trivia? Why not run a load of skin cancer stories, and have all the countries of the world give up their right to determine their own affairs.

199

Dear scamps, you have to understand that the world is full of very evil people who manipulate us for power and profit. You should be very wary of falling for the BS they feed us. The name of their game is encroachment—the standardization of this, the surveillance of that, the agreement over these activities, the prohibition of those things, and so forth. It is all clouded in reasonableness and creeps along relentlessly. All you have to do to get the people to give you their power is to keep them in the dark, and soften them up with stuff that will frighten the hell out of them. When people are confused, frightened, and ignorant they are happy to give control, without question, to anyone in authority who looks like they know how to solve the problem. The name of the game is to feed the media what you want people to hear, then let the TV stations revamp the stories and churn them out on the evening news. This dry-cleans the government dictum from suspicion. The wonderful thing about television is that it grants misinformation and pure drivel an air of impartial truth and authenticity. Who in their right mind would argue against an authoritative fact presented by a wholesome newscaster we all know and love, and who appears in our living room each night? It's all so simple!

Have you ever wondered why the media constantly bathes us in fear? What is the point of it? Are we supposed to enjoy it? Is it news? Does it help us to know how many people got shot today? In Australia they report car wrecks almost every night. I don't mean fifty-car pile–ups on the freeway, which might qualify as news. I mean little wrecks—a truck hits a car and wipes out a granny, and her pet chihuahua—that kind of stuff. Why? What's the function of it? Could it be that someone, somewhere has a vested interest in keeping people on edge?

Of course they do. There is a commercial upside to the uncertainty factor. If you create stress and negative waves, you'll sell a lot of armaments, insurance, banking products, and prescriptions. American pharmacies fill 2.5 million prescriptions for tranquilizers every week. If you figure an average prescription is fifty pills, you can see that America ingests over six billion tablets a year. That's a big money spinner. Plus, if millions are dozed out of reality—emotionally or chemically dependent on legal dope (never mind the ones that are doing the other stuff)—people aren't going to argue too much when you feed them the party line.

Who's messing with your mind, offering you tickets to the Dance, selling you a bomb shelter perhaps, or collecting your money for the final journey? Maybe no one right now. But maybe what's being stolen is your psychic integrity, and your sense of balance and positive security. So next time someone tells you the world will perish from AIDS, tell them this: Every day that passes AIDS is becoming a more treatable disease. There is even one strain of AIDS that researchers now believe is not deadly. Whereas many people have contracted AIDS, the number of people that don't have AIDS is going up more than a thousand times faster than those that do. That is a verifiable scientific fact. AIDS figures are now more or less stable in the Western democracies, though they are still rising in Asia and Africa. However, the world population is increasing so much faster than the spread of the disease that the chance of AIDS wiping out the world is sheer drivel.

You should defend your mind from the negative waves that come from the collective insecurity of the world. It's not compulsory to buy into it. You can detach and see it for what it is. That'll stimulate your psychic protection and allow you to push against the Thought Police—those who legislate and bully you into losing your right to mental and spiritual stability, and to an alternative opinion. If you let people constantly push your buttons, you loose control of your personal rocket. The mass neurosis robs you of the natural godlike joy and happiness that is your heritage.

Now here's an important point: You can't embrace an apocalyptic philosophy without eventually creating your own premature end. By buying into the holocaust it's hard for you to invest in the vision of a decent future. Thus, your thought-forms gradually become corrupted, and your mood reflects misery, which in turn, pulls you toward misfortune and an early death.

Sure, the world may go through great economic problems, but they are good for us. They help us adjust to what is real, rather than struggling to sustain what is not real. But, "A bit of economic change, an apocalypse doth not make." And the world won't end for several billions of years. That is fact.

Smile. Be happy. Change your mind. Believe in yourself and the future. Knickers to the hot air brigade! Let's concentrate on the real stuff, like having fun, looking after ourselves and our families, and believing in a positive spiritual future. But please, please, don't tell anyone just yet. There are a few hundred, very expensive, secondhand bomb shelters that our spiritual brothers and sisters have to unload before the man in the street realizes that the apocalypse is all a bloody hoax.

And don't let the suckers grind you down.

The Anatomy
of a Decent Crisis

CHAPTER NINE

I n the last chapter, I hope I illustrated how crisis is very much a matter of opinion. It doesn't really matter if the opinion is based on fact or illusion, all that matters is that everyone believes it to be true. So, to have a decent crisis there has to be a body of opinion—public or personal—that sustains the crisis. In order to avoid crisis and make sure you don't get sucked into a crisis mentality—which I consider very dangerous—it's useful to look at the anatomy of crisis. In dissecting the opinion that sustains it, you can perceive how it is created, see it for what it is, and ultimately detach from it.

Let's review the issues at work. Under the modern code there are three things the external particle state requires: importance, a guarantee of security, and an everexpanding separation brought about mainly through material gain. If any one these three components is assailed, then we have the makings of a jolly good crisis. So crisis is for the most part just any contradiction of the ego's opinion. For an adverse situation to get going and reach the elevated state of a national crisis it needs the media to pump it along. Crisis is an industry that is manufactured, sustained, and sold like soap. People engineer emotion to get results, so the national perception is warped by heaps of emotion, much of which is staged for the benefit of observers. Issues are pumped as "vitally important" because the ego considers itself vitally important.

Of course, if you said you didn't agree with the ego's position you'd attract people's ire. You are expected to buy their emotion, otherwise you're considered an uncaring, uncharitable, egotistical individual. All the egoism is in the original opinion. Any contradiction to the ego's ad campaign is threatening and an affront to its sacrosanct position as the purveyor of values, ideas, and reality.

Crisis develops supporters through merchandising. When a crisis gets enough supporters, the national mind set hardens through a process of emotional infection to accept the crisis as fact.

Our society perceives itself to have problems, but its problems are often only problems because someone, somewhere needs the problem. The real issue is very rarely what it is sold to be. As said before, people have to romance the problem to establish observers and to make their issue more special than other competing issues. So we have a society of little ax grinders. In fact, grinding the ax has replaced real work in some sectors of our Western society. There are thousands of lobbyists, special interest groups, and sellers of moans who create and promote issues for their gain. There's money in it—lots of it—or political benefit, righteousness, air time, or some special privilege that flows to the purveyor of the correct emotion.

So if a Martian landed and watched the nightly news, he or she (or it) might get the impression the world was in a terrible mess. In fact it's not in a mess at all. A good fifty percent of the global bellyache is hype, and most of the other fifty percent could be fixed tomorrow if the ego would change its mind and back off. Shut the TV stations down for a year or so and most of our problems would disappear. There would be no platform on which to merchandise and sell the position. It's hard for people to realize that the media and the government manipulate opinion constantly. It doesn't often enter our minds to question the validity of what is portrayed by the media as fact.

The Anatomy of a Decent Crisis

Our societies are based on docile acquiescence. There is no way the government can control the people if they don't want to be controlled. The irony is that there is no way of maintaining government control in the long term either, because their position has become so unholy. People power is the only real power. Sure, the government can call out the army, but if they did they'd be in serious trouble. When fifty thousand people rioted against Margaret Thatcher's poll tax and burnt Trafalgar Square, the British government realized it was in danger of falling. Margaret Thatcher was overthrown and the tax was canceled. The Poll Tax took a politically isolated marginalized community and focused it into a hammer head. Like most wimps and bullies, governments run a mile when faced with the unfettered heart of the people. Look at what happened in Eastern Europe and Russia.

The power of the status quo stems from the fact that no one confronts it. Our people are isolated and bombarded by democratic waffle and doctored information by those in power who have a vested interest in telling our people they are powerless. To sustain the idea, the populace have to be fed a steady stream of acceptable information and opinion, and they have to be offered a constant supply of problems they can't personally fix. By removing all legal and decision making power, and hiding alternative or contradictory information, eventually the people become uninterested and apathetic. That's the key to the manipulation which establishes the status quo as a proper and correct source of power. That's why so much effort is taken to sell the idea of "good guys" and "bad guys." It isolates people emotionally, fixing their opinions and places government on the side of the good guys, guaranteeing it subliminal approval in the minds of the masses. Great spiritual and social injustices are washed over because people are indoctrinated to respond in a prescribed way. Naturally they will allow their good guys to control, presuming that the good guys have their benefit at heart. And even when belief in the manufactured good guy is shattered, people still cling to the illusion because they have no alternative. Their minds have been scrubbed clean of revolt or any contrarian view. They have become passive. That's why our controllers need to manipulate the economy via debt, and regulate the price and conditions of labor to create a society that is so busy just surviving, that it hasn't the money, time, or inclination to march on city hall and burn it down.

George Orwell's 1984 has come to roost. The only difference is that the author saw Big Brother as a brutish, ignorant force which could easily be despised and hated. Orwell could never have predicted the modern sophistication of mass psychology, subliminal programming, manufacturing of consensus, economic manipulation, and secret information gathering techniques used nowadays to control and isolate our people. The system we have today in the 1990's is vastly superior to anything Orwell could have ever imagined. It's not national surveillance, it's international surveillance. Most of the major nations are linking their computer bases so that their citizens can be tracked all over the world. It boggles my mind—what's the need for it? In the west of England—in Cornwall—there is a tracking station owned and run by the American government that taps and records all the cellular phones in Great Britain. Now why would the British government let the USA tap all the English mobile phones? It's ridiculous. I suppose having the Americans tap British phones allows the British government to say they don't tap their own citizens' phones, but it's no surprise that people are pissed off. Mind you, the American citizens aren't immune, the USA has the biggest information gathering system in the world, and most of it is turned upon their own people. Did you know, for example, that after 1994 certain American databases will be linked to others in overseas countries, like Singapore? A government clerk in a foreign country will be able to press a button and see if a car dealership in Phoenix has paid its property taxes or not. There is so much our people don't know anything about—so much is hidden behind reasonableness and the Cheshire cat smiles of liars.

The Anatomy of a Decent Crisis

When the pillage and disempowerment of the people became worse and worse, one way the system covered its tracks and conned the people was by pumping their personal egos. "We are taking all your freedoms and most of your money, but you arc very special and very important, and we'll pass a few charters guaranteeing your importance as long as you'll give us your power forever."

So if you go into the street and tell people that their nation is evil and run by megalomaniacs whose main motivation is power and control, they won't believe you. People may bitch a bit, but overall they will see their country and its institutions as holy and good, and they'll ignore the fact they are personally powerless. Once you infect the national mind and sustain the drip year to year, people gradually become so polluted by propaganda they cannot resist. Eventually they come to believe the reality that has been selected for them. This reality and the government's control and manipulation of the people is seen as inevitable and a part of maintaining stability. People reach a point where they cannot imagine or conceive a different reality. Pumping their importance and maintaining the government nipple with the money that is taken from the workers caps off the process of establishing consensus.

Manufacturing crisis is an integral part of the controlling mechanism. It allows the status quo to claim that they know best. They can act unilaterally and grant themselves special powers and emergency regulations to deal with the manufactured crises and everyone consents, happy to transfer responsibility to the authorities. Eventually, with enough propaganda, reality shifts to reflect the negative waves that they want us to believe are true. You might have difficulty seeing how it's done if you have never looked at the process in depth. The central psychology used is to establish obligation and guilt. People are made to feel obligated, and they are told to sacrifice themselves for the common good—which sounds lovely—except the fruit of their sacrifice is not used for the common good, it's used to sustain the common bad. And because our people are disempowered, they have no power to act or to fix problems themselves. It follows they must empower others to do so. If they don't agree to empower others, then they are made to feel guilty. The submessage dripped relentlessly into our minds is that we have no power to control our own destinies. The substrata of that lie is that we are victims of chance, and so are powerless to remain safe and secure without the good grace and guarantee of our authorities. It's the divine right of kings wrapped in a modern psychological ploy, so well hidden and so subliminally offered that almost nobody sees it. In a world where people's ego have been pumped and pumped, offering them guarantees, protection and safety is like heroin. Offering them importance is like cocaine—it stimulates them. Isolating them is like Valium—it makes them docile. When people are psychologically disempowered and mentally drugged with propaganda, they gradually give up responsibility for themselves and often become drugged physically. You can dramatically reduce the power of the status quo over your life and abandon the seriousness, fear, and gravity that may have polluted your thinking by turning off the mass media and canceling your subscription to the gutter press. There are lots of serious and accurate journals and newspapers that objectively report the news. I think you can be aware and well informed without buying the emotion and the hype. Magazines like the Economist and the World Press Review give you a fair idea of what's going on in the world. I like to read foreign newspapers and magazines as their view of domestic issues is usually more realistic than the stuff you read in the local papers—which is edited, selected, and censored for local consumption. For example, in 1991 there were two thousand bombings in America reported to the FBI. How many did you hear about? Not many, I'd imagine. The authorities wish to create the impression that terrorism does not exist in the United States. Events that contradict the official line are conviently omited.

The Anatomy of a Decent Crisis

I think the alternative press plays an important role in helping people develop different thinking and in bringing them together by offering different solutions to social issues. It is in the mass media where the pollution and propaganda lay; eliminate them from your life and you are free. It's a good discipline if you want to become a merry scamp with a pleasing, light-hearted philosophy.

Of course, if you have taken to the spiritual path, there will be many aspects of this official and media nonsense—and the ego's stance—that you won't agree with. The quest for importance and an ever expanding material statement of that importance will seem irrelevant and even unattractive. The idea that you can't control your destiny is a lie. You don't need anyone to fix your life—you need perception and energy, that's all.

So when I say there is no world crisis, and that all we have is a crisis of the ego, what I mean is that a number of very hard-nosed opinions have to be in place in order for what are often naturally shifting conditions to be labeled "crisis." The idea that the ego should never have to suffer any emotional disquiet or any deteriorating circumstances, even though much of it is of its own making, is pure nonsense. It stops introspection and corrective action, underwriting the idea that we all are victims of circumstances. The idea that everyone's external particle state should be protected and guaranteed indefinitely, no matter what the cost, is only a tenant of the modern tribal mind (which is a tad puffed up, to put it politely).

Ah! Well what about the homeless? Again, part of the emotion around the homeless is not because they are so very poor, but because they are seen to lack the particle state. People don't like to see that, it threatens them. Many of the homeless suffer from alcoholism, drug abuse, and mental problems. You can put money aside to help those people, but some will always wander the streets. A percentage of the rest of the homeless are only homeless because they won't accept a social slot lower than their ego will allow. There's plenty of kindness, welfare, and handouts. Many are homeless because they won't accept a humble job and pay for a small room in a downmarket neighborhood. All that is below them. Humble jobs are for illegal immigrants and lesser folk. It's not for particles who find it simpler to trot off to the government and ask for a free house. Why not? They have been promised a free ride in return for no power. They expect to collect. Now if we decide that giving people free houses for no work is a good thing, (I'm not sure it is. Too much charity robs a man's soul and makes him codependent) then you can build cheap homes for everyone. But people won't accept cheap homes, and the government has plenty of other things it wants to do with the money, other than build houses. For example, the US government could build several hundred thousand free apartments annually, with just the money it gives to foreign governments each year. It's politics and choice. Poverty in the Western world is a direct result of government overspending that deteriorates the economy and brings wages and employment down. It is also partly due to a lack of correct energy. That lack may be through no real fault of the individuals, who have never been taught to take responsibility, and have no skills and even less education. But you can never fix the problem by giving people money. That buys into the emotion, not the solution. You can only fix poverty if you teach people to generate energy by taking correct action in the market place. Then the ego can achieve status and people will be happy. In giving away money you eliminate the need for action. So you are burdened with a perpetually negative emotion. Once importance and government control became more vital than action, poverty became an unfortunate and permanent feature of our societies.

Well, what about all the violence in our society? Violence is only the aggression of the stressed ego seeking the particle state, importance, glamour, and a quick effortless fix. Violence is driven by TV, which shows violence as a thrilling ego boost and an exciting source of power. Nonentities can establish observa-

The Anatomy of a Decent Crisis

tion, status, and importance once they have a gun. That is why we can't pass gun control laws. It's a matter of observation and importance, as much as it is an issue of the right to defend your property and hunt. In societies where they freely allow guns and where violence is pumped as a boost to importance, you'll have a lot of shootings. There's no mystery to that. Gun cultures stem first and foremost from the particle wave syndrome. Guns offer respect and status to an individual without him or her having to create any energy. Again, it's importance without real action. It's tailor–made for the modern mind set.

We are victims of a philosophy whose time has come and gone. But don't throw up your hands in despair; you can see things are on the mend. All over the world conscious people are gathering to discuss and rewrite the rule books. As they shift from ego to spirit and take back responsibility for themselves and their community, they will see that this process is holy and correct. The external ego driven particle state will always be there because fear and insecurity are perpetually a part of the human experience, but the idea that someone will give you a guarantee and status for nothing will disappear within the next ten or twenty years. Economic realism states that you can't have a society which is forever on the drip. As our population gets older and older there's less and less workers to pay the nation's bills. In California—depending on whose figures you believe—there are only three taxpayers for every recipient. In Australia it's even worse. There are nine million workers, one million are out of work leaving eight million to generate the national income. 1.8 million of those with jobs work for the government and so they generate no new wealth, so the entire nation's budget has to be paid by the 6.2 million workers that are in the free market. Old age pensions, dole, welfare, disability payments, student grants, and government salaries are paid to over four million Australians each month. So 6.2 million workers in the free market are supposed to pay for the livelihood of over four million recipients of government money. The numbers tot up to 1.5 real wealth generators to every recipient. No country can sustain this kind of indulgence over the long term. All over the Western world wages and revenues are falling while recipients are rising; the two graphs crossed and waved good bye to each other several moons ago.

That's why I tell scamps to never rely on the system—it will eat your lunch. Anyway, it's about to commit hara-kari. As it rattles and bends, we have a great chance to teach our people self-sufficiency, and show them that importance and overconsumption is irrelevant to happiness. People can band together or they can act singularly, but they have to generate energy. By doing so, they will become inspired to step beyond the old ideas that are dreary and nauseating to listen to. There's nothing like taking action as a stimulus to fixing your life. If you can't act powerfully, don't act. Think, wait, plan—then act powerfully. I suppose some would consider my ideas a little glib and they would offer a thousand "buts." And I would toss in a "but" of my own by saying, "but life is only a perception, a self-realizing prophecy formulated from opinion. It's only real and traumatic if that's what you hold to be true."

No one cares to experience adverse circumstances, but one's emotional response to those circumstances is very much a subjective decision. Thus, there are no real crises, there are only circumstances, which of themselves when observed correctly are just energy. If you had no concept of high and low, better or worst, good or bad, you couldn't experience negative emotion or crisis. So crises are only crises when you first establish an opinion, and secondly, when you quantify or qualify your experiences.

For example, you could say we have an AIDS crisis. The disease is sad for us as it takes out many good people. So in one way we have a crisis but in another way we don't. It depends rather on whether you agree with the view that dying is not OK. Millions come and go from the planet every week—the earth plane is a bustling freeway of commuting spirits. Given we have mostly eradicated or found cures for smallpox, cholera, polio, typhoid, leprosy, diphtheria and tuberculosis and most of the standard 19th and early 20th century killers, is it unusual or even strange that the overall balance of our planet should provide for us a hitherto unknown way of checking out? Inventing cures for everything is marvelous for the ego as it stretches for immortality, but if we ever reach perpetual life—courtesy of medical science—we will create hell on earth. So once we cure AIDS, something else had better come along that we can't cure or we are in deep trouble.

The modern idea that we should keep people alive at any or all costs, comes only from the modern ego. The idea is about thirty years old—previously we took a different position. To have people wired to tubes for years on end is an obscene affront to their spirituality. It attempts to place the ego's need in front of a spiritual need we have to complete the human experience with dignity and to just quit. Sure, we can help our fellow man through his or her suffering, and yes, we can use technology to keep people alive for a while in the hope they might recover naturally, but that is a far cry from the modern view. To spend what are often millions of dollars of other people's money to sustain the living dead as medical zombies is the height of a warped mind. It's so typically arrogant.

Once you take a spiritual view and you don't see death as a crisis, then seventy-five percent of the world's crises disappear overnight. Almost all crises are the emotion we experience in facing some form of death. It may be the expanding materialism of the "would be" particle state that's dying, or it could be the death of a rhythm or routine we're used, or perhaps it's the death of a relationship or an opportunity, as well as obvious threats to life. It's the death of things that frightens people. That's why the ego discriminates against change even if that change is beneficial, for normalcy is the social externalization of the ego's desire for itself. It is sold as holy and good, and offered as solid proof of the ego's power. Any change to the rhythm is viewed with great suspicion. So, if a hurricane comes along and shifts everyone's normalcy up the road a way, it's considered a great misfortune. It can't just be the wind blowing. In contradicting the ego's solid state, nature denies its status, its importance, and its desire to control everything, hoping through that control to declare its vision paramount. I like hurricanes. Very refreshing.

If you have established an immortal identity within yourself, then death or change are immaterial. The first reconciliation a merry scamp must make is to accept change as normal. Don't take it as a personal affront. Once you develop an inner being with an inner destiny, then change is inevitable because the Inner You provides little or no resistance. It flows and moves in response to very subtle inner forces and spiritual feelings. Gradually the nonresisting quality of your inner being pervades your outer consciousness, and that spiritual mood is reflected in your external affairs. That is why, on the spiritual path, change is constant and inevitable. Permanence flows only from the immortal aspects of spirit; it's not necessary to construct an external manifestation of permanence in your life. You may do so as an outcropping of your current feelings, but eventually you'll grow beyond the need.

The ultimate change for a human is death. So we have to reconcile our fear and accommodate it in a comfy spot somewhere at the back of our psychology where it won't cause trouble. Death is seen by the ego as an aggressive force; death frightens the ego, blinding it, forcing it into a very strange and often comical little jig, where the ego's chubby legs pound up and down while it grimaces and grins and pulls funny faces, waving its hairy little arms about, hoping to distract death into wandering off elsewhere. But death is always in front of the ego blocking it and affecting its stability. However, once you turn from the external world and face inward, death is now behind you, you can reconcile yourself to it. In turning within you have changed the focus and direction of your attention and psychologically gone beyond death. It's the first step in controlling fear. If you can't go past fear you will always be a victim of the tribal wave and your ego's weakness. You will also burn energy pounding and waving.

You need courage to go beyond fear. While at first it may only be an intellectual adjustment, as you begin to feel the immortality that flows from the establishing of a real inner being, then fearlessness becomes an natural outcropping of spirit. Unassuming love is a component of the God Force. So a merry scamp should be unassuming about death and accept it with no great resistance or fuss. A wise philosopher can glide gently away without all the wailing, hand wringing, head thumping, procrastination, and stalling—which after all is very impolite to God, who might be expecting you back on time. I think all the fuss people make is a bit embarrassing. Why can't we accept death as an interesting and even pleasant part of the cyclical nature of the eternal Tao? When you think of it, war, plague, and famine are just a toll booth on the spiritual commuter's freeway. Before there was ego, dying was natural and uneventful. In some cultures it was a cause for celebration and rejoicing. It's only now that we have become so utterly pompous and therefore so fearful, that we make such an unreasonable performance of it all. Nightly on TV, the national ego goes through its dying swan routine, while a somber broadcaster announces today's score. Seriousness is an aspect of ego, and departing the physical plane is considered deathly serious. For some macabre reason the ego is fascinated by the death of others; perhaps it's because even in death the ego hopes to crank emotion and be noticed, or perhaps it's because the emotion generated around the death of others allows a surviving ego to release some of its own fears. Whatever the reason, we love to announce the batting scores, offering them as a teaching tool so others may avoid the same fate. That makes everyone feel very useful and special, and, of course, important. Which helps to give meaning to what is, in effect, a constant flow of drivel. It's what I call, "Lick this and die." Others call it news and information. Of

217

course the constant drip, drip, drip, of mental slime generates a perpetual tragedy which we can hopefully use to establish observers (Martians perhaps?) to our supposedly pitiful state as humans. "Crank the ax to the max." That's the game. It is considered so important, billions are spent annually recording and broadcasting the running totals. It's very strange, isn't it?

So is it any wonder that levels of fear are rising in the world today? Or is it natural, given that levels of ego are rising even faster. Humility, love, and an equitable stance in life eliminate most of the fear. Once you take to the inner path and birth your spirit to flow through the Inner You, dying is no longer fearful or unusual—neither is it a crisis. It's actually a lot of fun, and I recommend that we all give it a try at least once.

By changing your focus from ego to spirit, death can no longer torment you into perpetual discomfort. It now becomes a spiritual asset, one you can use to force your ego into backing off. Death moves from a predator and an enemy, to a little mate and ally. Say to yourself several times a day, death is my friend. death is my friend. Then watch how your fear of it changes over the next few weeks.

Calming fear is a prerequisite for inner observation. Unfortunately, you can't establish observation inside the modern tribal mind because it is almost all ego, and you can't establish a spiritual observation of self though the ego. It can't see beyond itself. That's why our world has difficulty in seeing obvious solutions. As the ego-world cracks up under the influence of its negative embrace, it can't get outside of itself to see what's causing the problem. It will continue to do what it has always done, even though continuing to do so exacerbates its problems. When that doesn't work, it will blame others. Inside the horizon of its myopia it can't see that it is victimizing itself.

If you want to get out of the tribal/national mind, you will have to go within and establish an alternative view of it, so you can detach from it. It will take time for you to get far enough away—in the inner sense—to actually see it for what it is. At first you will still be influenced by the tribal wave, because the ego-world still has an influence upon you—for a while anyway. It has a kind of radiation which travels a little way with you into the inner worlds. Just as the etheric radiates from your body, the opinions of tick-tock radiate within, because the opinions are programmed into your mind over a long time. In a society that sells fear to manipulate people, it can take a while to understand that the fear isn't real. That is why it often takes a thousand days for individuals to consolidate out of the tick-tock mind. And even after that, the memory of it all still lingers, affecting you for a while.

The way to create inner distance is to home in on your own ego and really establish a precise understanding of it. You'll be stunned to see how the ego manipulates and maneuvers you, selling you what is often a very detrimental reality. Once your inner eyes are open, and your ego is no longer the official voice of your personality, then you will see it all as clear as day— personally and globally. When that moment comes, you may want to sit down and have a little cry. Tears of sadness will flow from one eye to mix with tears of joy from the other. Sadness flows from the compassion you feel for yourself and all humanity, and joy comes from the celestial vision which knows that death is an illusion. You'll see that all the anguish and suffering that our dear sweet people put themselves through is mostly self-imposed. It is not an absolute; neither is it compulsory—it is not our natural spiritual state. Even one small glimpse from outside the tribal mind shows you the understanding of it all. The joy that flows from that is endless and overwhelming and a great relief. The perception of itself is the supreme liberator of mankind. There is no way to properly describe the awe of the vision. All at once, from every infinite direction, a soft and gentle power comes upon you, and through it and because of it, the Inner You makes a slow and deliberate half circle turn. Now, in the spiritual twilight of the emerging inner particle state, the Inner You becomes a mirror image, facing back toward the External You. A synthesis takes place and the two parts are fused by a synapse of energy that flows across the two aspects of self, joining them through the fusion of a spiritual light. The entirety of you is instantly healed. From it, the spiritual particle is made manifest and whole as it is fused into a solid identity. So now your identity has a completeness that forms a real spiritual unit—a bit like a capsule really—which you can use later on to travel and evolve out of this world through the spiritual earthlike dimensions that are close to it.

Prior to the alchemic fusion of this capsule, you can never travel very far; the spiritual light would destroy you, dispersing you across all infinity to be lost forever. The weakness and disjointed state of your former ego state, or the nonexistent or partially blind inner being, cannot sustain the brilliant glow of the light. That is why when you travel the inner worlds you will sometimes see a veil in front of the light which will remind you of the sun behind a cloud. In this way, the light protects you. Sometimes you will see the celestial light, not through direct inner sight, but dissipated through reflection. Because you can't look at it directly for any length of time, it will reflect off something, like an inner lake or any inner reflective surface. In this way it is diffused, and you may view it and attempt to learn about it, without it desiccating you in the process.

Upon the fusion described above, you are perpetually released from the weakness of your former state and the wounded brain of man. You will see that the eventual healing of all mankind is assured, even though it is still off in the distance. There is a very great beauty in knowing that to be true.

Somehow, some way, we have to take the ego by the hand and show it the silliness of chasing the external particle state, and we have to get people to turn within and develop the real particle state by birthing the inner being, thus accepting responsibility for themselves. So many have lost the ability to find happiness and pleasure from little things. By focusing only on external reality, people insist on sensations, which have to be cranked more and more to satisfy. Eventually, the individual either becomes addicted to the sensations or they get bored and irritable, as no new sensations will suffice. We have to return to simplicity and enjoy the sheer wonder at finding ourselves humans.

Part of establishing serenity and poise is to deny the ego its regular fix of consumption and clutter. That is why I have come to love the philosophy of minimalism. Its pure simplicity and often unassuming realism is very Zen. It denies the ego a place to hang its hat. Minimalism offers you space and it insists that you engage no action or consumption greater than absolutely needed or before its proper time. It offers us a powerful discipline with which to build calm, hope, simplicity, and love.

Minimalism is not important for important people, and it's utterly useless for the very, very important people; it's only useful to carefree scallywags who need to affirm control of their lives. You may use it to establish discipline over the circumstances of your life, which assists your inner observation by dismissing clutter from your external line of sight. We'll talk about inner observation in a moment. Meanwhile, let us waltz across the bare boards and stone courtyards of minimalism. For in embracing minimalism, you immediately create a vast improvement in the spiritual and emotional quality of your life.

Minimalism:
A Survival Technique
for the Future

CHAPTER TEN

Minimalism in music is a composition, simple in structure and form, in which the main motif is repeated continuously, rather than the theme extrapolating outward to more and more complexity. In design and style, minimalism is expressed through the concept of using the simplest or fewest elements to create the maximum effect. Minimalism is uncluttered, often clean and pure, and is considered somewhat stark by some people. A typical minimalist home would have stone or wooden floors, no carpets, few ornaments, and only a few pieces of furniture—only as many as are absolutely necessary. The old traditional homes of Japan are models of minimalism: tatami mats, bare rooms, simple lines, and form.

The Victorian style living room is the opposite of minimalism; it is cluttered and ornate. Furniture is everywhere, while knickknacks and memorabilia occupy every shelf. The floors are carpeted, the walls papered, and lamps are often draped. The ceilings are covered with decorative plasters and molded cornices, while the windows have thick curtains. There's little space to move around—it's cozy but cluttered.

The clutter of the Victorian front room gave way to a modern version in which the *nouveau riche* exhibited their wealth with gaudy furniture, statues, paintings, gold taps, coffee tables made of glass and supported by elephant tusks, and all sorts of good stuff guaranteed to impress the visitor with the owner's status and wealth. It seems to me that these people could frame a copy of their financial holdings and bank balances and hang it over the toilet. This would certainly be minimalist and charitable as well. Visitors could peruse and admire the owner's unbounded wealth and success without having to go through the visual trauma of the elephant tusk coffee table.

As we careened out of the debt-driven excess of the eighties, ricochetting into the more frugal nineties, minimalism came back with a bang, not just because it was now appropriate to acquire and consume less, but because the liquidator had the gold taps, the coffee table, and the entire bloody house. You can't get more minimalist than the moment just after the bank hauls all your stuff away.

Of course spiritually, recession and financial disaster are a marvelous thing. It's hard to persuade people to change their ways while they're hurtling around in their Porches. But once you deprive a person of their security blanket of materialism they are left with only themselves. Suddenly, looking at themselves and pondering the meaning of life becomes the only game in town. Minimalism will become the catch word of the nineties. Of course, minimalist style, design, and music are just a matter of personal taste. However, minimalist thought is a survival mechanism that will stand you in good stead this next decade. What is it? How does it benefit you?

Philosophically, minimalism is the return to simplicity; it is reductionist compared to the world of the ego, which is almost always expansionist. On the ego parabola, the intellect is in high gear speeding toward complication, clutter, over consumption, disorder, and confusion. In minimalism, the dominant force is subtlety of feelings. It offers simple structures, clarity, poise, and an uncomplicated philosophy, which leads to contentment.

Minimalism: A Survival Technique for the Future

Modern society is built on action and activity—a by-product of the ego's need to consume. We are sold action for action's sake. Active people are considered enterprising, clever and interesting. A certain amount of "doing" is vital each day, but we have become a society addicted to doing. In the world of ego and intellect, boredom comes quickly. Action is vital in keeping the ego happy. It needs stimulus. That's why people relentlessly move from one sensation to another. It's not really the item or condition that they seek, it's the activity which is vital. Perpetual activity gives insecure people meaning. By committing to the chase, they enter the market place and are observed to be clever, dexterous, and important. That is the driving force. So an ego-male may pursue a woman for sex, and may invest a great amount of time, money, and dialogue in winning the lady over. The minute he is successful he'll lose interest. It's the chase and the activity, not the prize.

So, when our people bought the illusion of the external particle state, we settled upon the idea of *doing* rather than *being*. Doing places your focus perpetually outward. We are taught as children to watch what we are doing. So we watch and we like what we see, for in *doing* we see evidence of our importance and our wonderfulness. By *doing* we establish observers who may gaze, awe struck, at the magnificence of our actions.

Unfortunately, the concentration and energy we need for *doing* causes us to lose touch with our inner feelings; we close down to become empty kettles, making lots of noise and giving off plenty of steam. Constant activity either comes from the ego's economic fears or from yearning for greatness. Constant activity is a pollutant.

We should strive for effective and pleasing activity, not activity for activity's sake. Of course, I can understand that the minimalist approach would not appeal to the young. The young are enticed to activity because they need to experience sensations as a part of learning about life. Their action helps sort out who they are. Action allows them to express and exert themselves. The young need observers, feedback, and action to develop their personalities and to begin expressing the rudiments of power and energy. We cannot expect the young to focus on anything other than themselves. They have no complete identity or expertise on which to build confidence. Inner observation for the young is not necessary. They need expertise in the external world first.

But that excuse won't suffice for older people—they should have more sense. It's rather sad if you spend all of your life *doing* and you drop dead before you learn how to *be*. After all, we are human beings, not human doings. But you must travel a long way in the modern world to find humans who know how to *be*. It takes a composed and settled soul to move from *doing* to *being*. Almost all yearning will have gone from your heart, and you will know what works for you and what doesn't, what pleases you and what irritates the hell out of you. So the wise person selects circumstances to please themself. They know when to act and when to avoid action. They evaluate the quality of their actions.

So a minimalist lifestyle involves concerted action for those aspects of life that deserve a dynamic approach, and no special action the rest of the time. Through planning, order, and clarity we seek to reach maximum potency with minimum effort. Thus, in elevating your actions you liberate your lifestyle, avoiding almost all superfluous action. You stay focused on what works for you and what gives you pleasure, and you ruthlessly eliminate everything else. It takes strength and a discipline of character, and it takes good communication with others. The trick is to not let yourself be sucked by your own ego, or the influence of others, into activity and obligations that don't honor or serve you in any particular way. It is senseless to take on activity just for the sake of it or so you have something to do to keep your ego happy. Or to feel needed or wanted or to feel included. That's immature. It's better not to be included, not needed, and not wanted, if that allows you to enjoy life at a leisurely pace and to do loads and loads of loafing. People don't agree with loafing—they feel it implies laziness. But loafing is just tinkering around with things that amuse you or citting on a veranda postponing everything for at least a day or two. It's a good counter balance to the ego that requires you to slave for its vision. If you can afford to loaf you should do so. It's a nice way of giving yourself permission to be. Loafing around is a specialist trait of scamps and minimalists—it's how they educate themselves.

Of course, some people's lives don't allow for loafing, as it requires massive activity, but you have to wonder what sort of motivation people possess in order to suffer such strain and effort. A mother with four or five children might say motivation is not her problem—survival and just making it to bed each night is. But for many, activity is a choice, and you might want to look at why you chose so much of it and what it actually does for you. It amazes me how consumed people are in the art of getting nowhere. We are experts at it!

Our society tends to set its vital needs at a tad below "death by action." Once you don't need all the things the ego needs, then you are free to work a little and to laze around, to arrive a little late or not at all, to charge a little more and to do lots of things for free, to engage in a few things that matter and lots that don't matter at all. The difference is that you choose—little is forced upon you. The important thing is to create space and free time where you can get in touch with yourself and establish observation. Once your inner being is developed, you'll have poise, strength, and a more liberated philosophy to take back to the helter-skelter of life enabling you to do some of the things you haven't already done, if that's what you want. The trick is not to create so many obligations or so much activity that you lose yourself in the action. There's nothing worse than being so busy you can't remember who you are. If you have to be busy, do it in short bursts. When you get wiser and more savvy, make the bursts shorter and shorter.

When and if you are required to act, do so impeccably. Develop a plan, arrive with all that you need, act powerfully and decisively, don't mince words, tell people who you are and what you want. Never engage your troops (energy) without first scouting out the terrain. Never go forward in a hurry. Walk slowly, speak deliberately. Never get emotional and never let people manipulate you. There's always another deal, always another time, and there's five billion other people. Let everyone know this is your philosophy. Tell them you have all the time in the world—because you do, you're infinite. Remember the greatest wisdom you can develop is the wisdom of *not doing*. It's the deals and situations that you avoid that help you conserve energy and remain independent and strong. I tell people who come to my seminars that perception has five gears. One is a forward gear and four are reverse gears. As you develop perception, you'll use it mostly to avoid things. Nature uses perception to stay out of trouble. We can learn from that. Merry scamps spend the majority of their time pedaling out of things, not pedaling in. Everything you commit to will have weight. It may be the emotional weight of owning something, it may be the weight of duties you take on, or the weight of relationships, especially if you're the one holding the relationship up. Then there's the financial weight you take on. Every financial commitment will probably force you into tick-tock , because that's mostly where the money is. You may have to go into tick-tock from time to time anyway, but you don't want to be buried in so deep it drives you crazy. In my view, it's better to live a humble, happy life, traveling and experiencing the world, than to own it. What's the point of lots of stuff that you have to polish, insure, and worry over? Remember, debt is one of the ways the status quo controls the people. That's why debt is made easy. Consumption is irresistible to the ego. You can move toward minimalism, consume less and pedal out of debt by not taking on any more. If you do need to rent money, do so only to make more money; never use other people's money for your personal consumption. If you have no debt and few obligations, you are free. As far as the world is concerned you will begin to disappear.

As you develop your inner feeling, you will know what you want and you will know if you have the energy and the intention to pull it off. If a plan is holy and good, it will never manipulate or take advantage of others. It will have right action and good intention and it will be confirmed and corroborated by your inner feelings. Then you know it will be auspicious. Many of the things we go for in life are dishonest or hurt people or take too much of us for the benefit they provide. It's a wise philosopher who knows what he or she doesn't want. Action is fine but action laced with emotion is struggle, and burdensome for your heart. Be precise. Think it out. Indicate your intention clearly, make sure everyone knows what's happening, and let it be known that you are an honorable person who will follow his or her word to the letter. The name of the game is to try to commit to as little as possible and only when you absolutely want to. It's a merry scamp who "Uhms" and "Ahhs" and shrugs and never says yes and never says no. Offer a smile and a maybe, and amble off to loaf a bit while you consider the shape of a passing cloud, and to watch a bird swallow a busy bee. And looking at it all, knowing that nature is your sacred Mother and your teacher, you'll think, this is not a day for action—tomorrow maybe—and then again . . . the day after might be better. Never commit until you absolutely have to.

Matterism comes from seriousness and importance; it causes disease. It's the emotional opposite of minimalism. How you catch matterism is by having too many things that matter. What matters is that you allow your heart—not your ego—to rule your life. Then very little matters because you will be a humble person and you'll take most of life as it comes. You can change the bits you don't like and move away from those that you can't change. Once you get to the point where almost everything doesn't matter you're emotionally free. If it rains, you get wet; if they don't show up on time, you wait; if they don't pay you, you eat less; if they don't love you, so what, you didn't come to please them anyway; if they don't think you're special, that's marvelous, it frees you from having to thank them for their compliments. If life doesn't go the way you want, accept the way it does go, use it as your teacher. If they tell you it's all falling apart, tell them you like rubble, you found a way of learning from it. If they say it's all a great tragedy, say, is it now? If they say you're an uncharitable egoist, respond, "I have no position, knowledge or wisdom to defend, I have only the living spirit in all things. I can offer you that, if it's any use to you."

Walking and wandering and whistling as you go, you'll see how minimalism works well for scamps and Fringe Dwellers. Of course, many wouldn't buy the idea, but then again we're not selling it. It's free. I don't think it's a popular idea for the masses—not just yet anyway—our world is still too seduced by glamour and obsessed with complication. Look at our modern athletes. They start out OK, enjoying their physical activity, then they get really good at what they do and turn professional, and suddenly sport becomes deadly serious. Greatness is 'round the corner, so they drive and pummel themselves to become the best. Then they become the best and a little gold plated medal hangs off their tit and a distant thunder clap is heard saying, "So what?" What do they have? They have greatness and importance in the eyes of the ego, and the man from the shoe company offers a contract, and they appear on television, but what do they actually have other than the prospect of a coming defeat, which they will no doubt take very seriously? When you really look, are they the picture of good health and vitality? Not necessarily. The ego has usually burnt them to a crisp. Too many of the female runners resemble my granny just before she croaked. The twenty-five year-old boxers look like dried prunes, the cyclists look drained of life and the footballers can't walk. I'm not convinced it's worth the effort. Scamps don't compete—

Minimalism: A Survival Technique for the Future

egos compete. If you are a sportsperson and a scamp, pray that you don't get too good—I don't think a gold plated medal is worth forty years of arthritis.

Striving for greatness is so ridiculous and childlike. Certainly, if you are very talented, you may become great through no fault of your own, but that's a handicap you'll learn to bear. But striving for greatness is striving for nothing in particular. What most consider as greatness seems to me not worth having. Greatness obliges you to be gracious and to make small talk and shake hands and be nice to lots of people you don't know. You will have to grin like a simpleton, sign little pieces of paper to keep people happy, and show up at dreary events, dressed like a dog's dinner, propose toasts, and hand out things. There is an effort in the theatrics of it all that doesn't appeal. I think greatness is for people who have nothing better to do. Anonymous greatest is the goal for scamps. And if that's not possible, retreating greatness is the next best. Marvelous things, airports, they are so minimalist. You only get twenty kilos (about fifty pounds) to contain the whole of your life. I think airports are the great healers of the modern age. There's hardly anything you can't heal with a little bit of "airport."

231

PT's (perpetual traveler) are a breed of their own. It's very popular now. There are even newsletters telling people the tricks of the trade. The world of the PT is very attractive. They don't pay taxes. They have no hassles or commitments. They often legally carry two or more passports. They have bank accounts in different places and are never locked into anyplace. It helps if you have money, but then there are lots of PT's who travel from place to place very cheaply, picking up odd sums of money as they go to sustain themselves.

We tend to think that we must have attachments to feel grounded. But attachments act as anchors that restrict movement. You could wander around for the rest of your life and still be a very grounded person. The difference is that mature souls are grounded within themselves, while others, feeling less sure of themselves, can only feel grounded by buying stuff with which to tie themselves down.

Of course, if you own a business and have a family, as I do, the life of a PT is not simple, but if you are single, or if your children have grown up, you can do it more easily. You can't get more minimalist than traveling around forever with just a few suitcases. In many ways it is very spiritual, as it teaches you to belong emotionally only to yourself, and to believe in your own energy, and to rely on no one, other than yourself.

But even if you can't get down to just one suitcase, you can still be minimalist, living in a big house in the city. The minimalist approach is an unemotional one. Have a few things you like around you as long as you are not attached to them. Once you have released them in your mind they no longer have a hold over you. So if you have what you want, great, and if you don't that's fine too. Once you get rid of the clutter and the extra stuff you don't need, you become more fluid and able to adapt to changing circumstances. Psychologically you are released from the grip your environment holds over you.

The world of intellect and desire is a prison of mass confusion. There's nothing more distracting than a troubled mind. Our society suffers from what I call, "Over Thinking on Life." People are so complex and troubled, joy has gone out the window to be replaced by questions. Really, once you move from *doing* to *being* you don't have to ask a lot of questions and you don't need to know a lot of answers. It can all remain a bit of a mystery. Too many questions are bad for you—they generate confusion. You can't have confusion without a question to support it. Now, you may ponder this and ponder that and think about your life, but if you suffer from a diarrhea of questions your brain will be full. You can't be happy with a full brain, it's too heavy to carry around. Scamps are very proud of their light-headed ignorance. They hardly ever need explanations for the things they don't know.

That's why I can't understand all those people who are constantly out in the bush looking for the disappearing species. Only one of two things is possible: either the species haven't disappeared (and so what is all the fuss about?) or the species have disappeared (and so why would you bother to look for it?). The thing is, we can't do much about the animals until the ego agrees to stop its theatrics and to stop consuming. But the intellect feels the animals are below it and subject to its control. To staple a fish and chase after it for a year, tracking its every move, is so comical only humans of the Western variety would be so silly. What do we discover? We discover fish swim around a lot. The intellect makes us look silly wasting our time on "important" nonsense. If God had wanted us to be so involved he, she (or it) would have given us better hearing. Stapling things to hear them squeak at five miles has got to look extremely silly to the God Force.

If we don't bother to discipline our feelings to find out where we're going, we will be experts on noticing what people and animals do but we will be ignorant at discovering our true selves. I think the intellectual world has its moments, but generally it's dry and boring, and in seeking to deny the inner reality of our true spiritual identity it cuts us off from real perception. At the deepest levels of our spiritual identity, the Inner You is pure feelings. That is because everything is God Force. Everything emits celestial light to some degree, so everything emits feelings. If your world is only intellect and language, fish tracking, and sensations, then you may never discover the innermost impulses and ambitions that lead you to select the action you take. People come to believe that it's their ideas that are important; ideas stimulate and conceive action, but behind every idea is a deep inner feeling.

Our intellectual world can be described as reactive. We respond in a Pavlovian way to the signals we are used to. But because many have no feedback—as they have no inner observation—there is no real comprehension of where those inner signals come from or what they mean. Most don't really understand their lives and they don't understand why they do what they do. They are programmed to act regardless of what real worth or meaning their actions might have. That's why people rush through life performing their routines over and over, even when they sometimes know that those actions don't work. It also explains why many people never get what they think they want. Their intellect will sell them an idea and will go for it hell for leather, while their innermost feelings may be lukewarm on the idea or reject it completely. For example, in viewing the external particle state you may think that you want to be rich. So you head out at the crack of dawn to seek your fortune. All that's fine as long as your feelings match your intellectual motivation. Most people, in their heart of hearts, don't want to be rich, what they want is contentment. They think that contentment comes from consumption, so money becomes vital. But deep within, most can't be bothered to be rich. They don't want the aggravation and responsibility of it all. You'd rather *be* than *do*. Your mind and actions go one way while your feelings silently and passively contradict you. Over long periods of time, feelings always win because reality comes to you in response to your inner feelings, not so much to your thinking. So if your innermost reality and your thinking don't match, those inner messages will always undermine and depreciate the quality of your actions. You'll constantly miss the target by an inch or two, or you'll get less than you expect, or even nothing at all. If you miss once or twice, you may only need to adjust your approach, or you may need to intensify your intention, but if you miss repeatedly over long periods of time it's a sure sign that your inner feelings and intellect don't match.

Minimalism: A Survival Technique for the Future

As you turn within to establish proper observation and change your focus away from the external world, then all the items that are superfluous or not congruent to the main theme of your life stand out like a sore thumb. Often you'll see that much of your action is only the ego's need for recognition—evidence of its particle state. In changing your focus, lightness, gaiety, and clarity will become very important to you. Minimalism flows from that. You may still have ambitions and things you wish to do in life, but you won't see them as so vitally important, for you won't see yourself that way anymore.

The external world is laced and pasted over with constant emotion. But you should not confuse emotion with feelings. When I talk of feeling, I'm not referring to the other meaning of the word which commonly describes body sensations. I mean inner motivations and impulses. Subconscious or deep spiritual feelings from the Inner You are influential in that they precede action. They will stimulate thoughts that may result in action, but the intellect usually doesn't know where the initial prompting comes from, and often it is not aware the subconscious contributes to its panorama of ideas in this way.

Emotions follow thought, and as a result are reactive. They can't exist before thought. They are the product of thought, and they form part of the process of understanding which translates and qualifies external reality. Thus, emotions are often at variance with one's inner reality or truth because the database that provides for their existence is the intellect's judgment—good, bad, pleasing, not pleasing, and so forth. That's why the complex world of the external particle state is often so displeasing. Living only in the world of intellect and sensations gives no meaning to life. "Welcome to zombieland! Please take a seat. Insert five dollars. The electronic orgasmatron will be activated in thirty seconds. Thank you. Have a nice day."

Because inner feelings are subtle and hidden, and because they often contradict the ego and the intellect, over the centuries we have gotten rid of them and suppressed our inner selves to become another "disappearing species." Eventually, inner feelings and messages were drowned out so completely we came to think that emotions and sensations *were* feelings. Emotions became complicated. They were raised up by the ego to an importance they should never have had. But it follows that a world captivated by glamour, action, and reaction, and mind expressed as ego would like emotion, because it could be used to good effect. Wielding emotion became a tool in the promotion of ideas and the manipulation of life. Emotions are especially useful in politics, commerce, romance, sex, power, and a host of other issues. Emotion is an effective tool of trade. It is so widely used we ought to pay the inventor of the idea a royalty. When you think of it, emotions are implements of war. The wars are social, domestic, and commercial. Territories are fought over, domains captured, pecking orders established, and positions lorded over, all by wielding emotion. Through emotion we control, terrorize, and manipulate people into the actions we require of them.

Once it became OK to use emotional force to get what you wanted out of people, battles ensued, with each manipulator selecting the appropriate emotional cudgel. Threat, fear, guilt, obligation, sympathy, remorse, envy, and greed all form part of the list of emotional armor. People who fall victim for the emotional game are praised and lauded and are considered sensitive; those who won't fall so easily are softened up by propaganda which attempts to whittle them into submission. The only reason why this emotional blackmail works on such a grand scale is that we program our children into it. In a subtle way we tell them that to be sensitive and caring, and to love their parents, they should acquiesce and respond to parental emotion. Once we eliminate reasoning and train our children to respond to emotion, they are less troublesome to control. But is it any different to placing a halter on a wild animal, stapling its ear and teaching it tricks for the circus? I don't think so. People think their feelings are so special—but it's not their feelings you're dealing with, it's their emotions. By making emotions so terribly important, inviolable and so uncontradictable, people hope to subjugate you to their opinion. You are not allowed to upset them by contradicting their emotions. It's a stuck-up mind that will try to sell you that one. We are back to denial and the freedom of speech. I think it's bunk that you are expected to buy people's emotions or that you should have any particular interest in them at all. Scamps wouldn't fall for that. Emotions are external manifestations of personal opinions presented on a grand scale, often to elicit your reaction. But all the ballyhoo is theatrics first, and merchandising of opinion second. There is nothing special or holy about emotions, any more than there is anything special or holy about opinion or any part of the tribal mind. There ought to be pollution laws that forbid people to spray their emotions around. It's worse than a skunk. You can listen to people as they bounce up and down, but that doesn't mean you have to buy their stuff or necessarily react. You can become an unemotional observer of bounces. Then you can become impartial towards yourself and not judge yourself so harshly. The name of the game is leave everyone, including yourself, alone.

Remember, the intellect can't feel, it can only know. The emotions think they feel but they are limited to information courtesy of the intellect, so what they think they feel is not necessarily inner feeling, but more likely reaction based on opinion. It doesn't offer much of a guide to the individual, because it offers no reliable source of information. No wonder our world is lost—the bloody tourist guide is a blind man with a fancy attitude.

In the world of *doing* there's no time for appraisal and feeling— everything is mental, transitory, and performed on the hurry-up. But in over-doing, we crown the ego and the intellect king. We live in a mental world that hopefully provides sensations for us that are pleasing to the particle state. Gradually, we become so embroiled in the intellect we lose touch with who we really are, and we forget what it is that we actually want.

Thus, the minimalist is required to be selective. Most of it is common sense. Having polished up your thinking, controlled your emotions, and having shed all your extra possessions, you are then required to look at your relationships. They will fall into two categories: People you have to hang out with because you work with them or because you are related in some way, and those people with whom your relationship is optional. Start with the optional ones. Evaluate each in the light of energy and balance. Is the amount of emotional and financial energy you put into the relationships as much as you receive from them? Work to fix it or move from those relationships in which you're in deficit. As for those relationships you have to sustain for family or economic reasons, ask yourself if they're really working for you, or would you be better off changing your job or allowing people all the space they need? Like several thousand miles perhaps!

Once you've developed a discipline over your relationships you can then fire a minimalist missile into your spiritual attitude toward life. Spiritual is a funny word—it means many things to different people. To some it means religious ritual, to others, the ritual is esoteric. Then again, to many, spiritual is a quality they endow their emotional morality with, which pleases them, rather than another bloke's emotional morality, which might be contradictory, and therefore less pleasing, and so less spiritual. One thread runs common through all definitions of spiritual: Spirituality describes a human's attitude towards his or her god and the inner journey of enlightenment. If that inner journey is light and simple and self-sustaining, it is minimalist. The reverse is a spiritual attitude that's heavy and onerous and full of rules and obligations. You don't want to be so weighed down with "spiritual" that you can't move.

Minimalism: A Survival Technique for the Future

Surely, the ultimate reason for your inner journey is to come to a greater understanding of God and to expand those natural godlike qualities within yourself. Can you imagine a heavy, dogmatic, serious God? Would adopting dreary, cumbersome attitudes help you align with God, or would God take one look at your leaden spirituality and throw up? The fewer beliefs you have to sustain, defend, and support, the emotionally better off you will be. Imagine if you had no beliefs and no real preferences. Suddenly, each day would be a delight because everything would suit you just fine. Using minimalism on your spiritual quest is really the art of eliminating dogma to allow a clear path upward. It's the journey from insanity to serenity.

The center point of minimalism is flow. It is the act of moving through the world in a calm and balanced way, consuming only as much as you need. It means resting in the now, using whatever comes to hand, waiting for those things you haven't got and forgetting that you wanted them. It means keeping your life down to the bare essentials without denying yourself the things you enjoy, but not overindulging either. That's natural, and it doesn't feed the ego with accouterments to bolster itself with.

Further, the minimalist heart offers a service to the world, as the simplicity of its free spirit mirrors back to people the ludicrous complexity of their lives. So they learn to adjust and win back control. From your simple heart others can take courage and can see that you managed to arrive at a balance without any great trauma, and so they begin to believe that they can also.

In the simplicity of what you offer is a wise and powerful statement that says, "I am what I am. I am a slave to no one. Nothing has a hold over me, for I belong to myself and to my God, and that grants me integrity and truth. I know that I cannot fix the world, but I can offer an island of calm."

If you can look back at your life and see that you held it together for yourself and your loved ones, and if through that strength you taught others to do the same, then all's well and good. There is nothing more refreshing and beautiful than the silent, composed individual that needs nothing, that begs no one, that has no request to make. In the eyes of God, these are very special, almost angelic scamps. They offer a silent hope and a simple heart in the mayhem of five billion demonic voices that shriek and cry out to the heavens, begging for status, favor, and good fortune, while often doing little or nothing to bring such celestial goodness upon themselves.

Take heed, dear scamps, that you look to your own life and create a strength and simplicity and beauty there, and let the people of the emotional world bounce off the walls as much as they wish. They will tire of it in the end. Some may even convert to the minimalist path, and if they don't, that's fine also—it leaves more space for the rest of us. Don't let others complicate you. Keep moving around. That will confuse them.

Observation

CHAPTER ELEVEN

T he key to real inner observation of self is the shift of concentration and detachment from the external ego world and the troubled mind set of the tribal ways to the quieter inner world of contemplation, meditation, and introspection.

In the old days, the folk spirit of the tribes taught a quiet, simple life, far from ego, aligned to nature through pantheistic religions with little or no dogma. That is why so many people are now rediscovering the Native American culture—the simple worship of the Great Spirit and the sacred Mother embodied in nature seems so refreshing compared to the crazy world around us. Our modern folk spirit has lost itself in the neurosis of ego and struggle, intellect, and rules. So the first step to observation is to cut the emotional link. Nothing in life is more important than that. Without discipline and detachment you sentence yourself to a tough life. Emotion is like glue, it holds you into the external world and the tribal mind, and your often predictable reaction to it allows others to tow you around, forcing you to march to their drum. Once you understand you didn't come here just to please people, or to gyrate and hop like a performing flea, then you are free.

The first step is to develop emotional composure and as self-sufficient a lifestyle as possible—be it on your own or in partnership with your mate in life. The less you are beholden to others or reliant upon them in any way, the better. I think if need be, it's preferable to live in a shack in the mountains than to live downtown and have to grin and be polite to the bank manager because the bank owns your house. It is a powerful soul who needs almost nothing from anyone. This alone can be a very spiritual affirmation in a world where everyone is begging, pleading—with their hands out. Love me, recognize me, tell me I'm special, pay my rent, fix my teeth, give me a new nose—one that looks like a movie star's. The ideal you're striving for is a simple life, where the few needs you have that you cannot provide for yourself, you can pay for on the spot.

The human personality, in seeking the external particle state, is required to focus outward to the external world. What most consider their inner world, that is experiencing and viewing their emotions, impulses, and instincts, is, in fact, also an outward view. As discussed earlier, emotions and impulses are only a different manifestation of the mind's opinion. The subconscious mind is inner compared to your external conscious world, but it's still all part of the mind—your personal memory— so all of its world, symbols, pictures, and memories are external in relation to the real inner celestial worlds. We know this because we can't normally see the inner celestial worlds while our mind is focused on externals.

You can go to a psychologist and pick through the things you believe motivate and drive your personality. You may discover how you react to thoughts and beliefs. But in looking at the contents of the mind, you never leave it to establish observation of it. All you can do is *know* it. You can't *observe* it—you can't get external to it in order for that observation to take place. A psychoanalyst may take an individual into their deeper subconscious mind, but the journey is an intellectual one, based on opinion. So if you are male, your therapist might tell you that the reason you're so messed up is because you think your pee pee's too short, and so you envy your father, who you presume has a pee pee bigger than yours. You trot off relieved. Relieved of a hundred and fifty bucks and relieved to know the reason for your disquiet, resolving to ask your Dad to measure his pee pee the next time you see him to confirm the theory.

The problem is that it's an intellectual opinion. Although it's the opinion of a very eminent body of learning and your very eminent therapist, it's speculation, not observation. You can't know if the pee pee issue is really the answer or not. You might think it is and give the theory weight—after all you paid for it— but there may be a hundred and one inner aspects of your total memory that contribute to your overall emotional and behavioral issues. Some of these aspects will accelerate your disquiet, while others will ameliorate it. Most of your subconscious is invisible, silent, and hidden from the conscious mind, and although your therapist might be very clever at eking it out and giving you interpretations of the bits he or she finds, it will always be an interpretation—not necessarily fact. Further, the therapist will only be able to discuss the aspects that surface at the very moment of therapy, so those features will seem to have more weight than the bits that don't surface. Trillions of quanta of memory lay hidden; we can only discover a small percentage of it all, and we have no way of really knowing if the bits we discover are more important than the parts that remain a mystery. Then, there may be parts of the subconscious that you do know about, and other parts that you repress, that you will never disclose to your therapist. After all, you are on the therapist's couch in a conscious state, therefore what you utter is part of the official pronouncements of the personality and its ego, which naturally bends, overrides and selects what it wants the therapist to hear. So psychoanalysis is a slow, hit-or-miss affair. It certainly helps people of an intellectual bent—urban dwellers mostly—go through the process of understanding the mind, but in the end, no one can say categorically what your symbols mean to you. They can't see inside your mind to know how the language of your symbols and images is held together. Yes, we can say water is a symbol of emotion, but that is a generalization which seems to fit a lot of people, but it may not be very important in your psyche at any one precise moment. And while it may fit today, it may not fit tomorrow. The overall memory or picture of the subconscious—its overall theme— shifts, I believe, to reflect our moods. All of its memory is interconnected, so it responds with small quantum and pockets of information that you need minute by minute, but it also has an overall response. If you are angry, all the symbols and memory in your mind cascade and alter themselves to fit the powerful messages that are coming through from the emotions. So every part of your subconscious alters to the flood of energy it is receiving. That part of your subconscious that had memories of love takes on a new tone, to become angry love. In the celestial worlds, you can see clearly that you are one identity— a thumb print of energy—which acts as a whole to define what you are. Everything you are expresses itself in union. In those worlds there seem to be no independent pieces or aspects of personality; it all radiates as a cohesive energy that is conjoined and interlinked. You can't pull apart the "short pee pee" trauma and say that's a major aspect of a person. Everything is one. So in the physical world, if you are angry, that emotion establishes itself throughout your being, changing you entirely. Suddenly you have angry feet and angry ears and angry hands and angry feelings, and every bit of you resonates anger. There is no demarcation. This is a simplistic way of explaining it, but— bottom line—your mind resonates as a single chord. You can watch that collective reaction as the etheric responds to mood swings, so obviously your physical body must react the same way. Author, healer, Dr. Deepak Chopra, appearing recently on the Oprah Winfrey show, put it very succinctly when he said, "Every cell of your body is eavesdropping on your internal dialogue." We are coming to understand that your entire being reacts to whatever messages you offer. Insecurity makes your cells slightly weaker, and they will resonate with an insecure electricity or aspect, and be more open to trouble and less able to cope with biochemical adversity. That continues until you change your mind, then everything flips and the cells take on a happy mode.

So picking through the mind may help you to understand yourself and it may assist you in going beyond your reactions. It may also help you to become a more settled being, but the only way to establish inner observation, in my view, is to turn your attention from the intellect and the ego, and all the distractions of the outside world, and close down your mind to look inwardly. Look at Figure 6. The blob on the right of the band marked "rotation" is your total mind, or total memory if you like. In the conscious state of that total memory you experience your personality and ego. The personality is the external mental vehicle through which your total mind gathers information and memories and perceptions in the ordinary 3-D world.

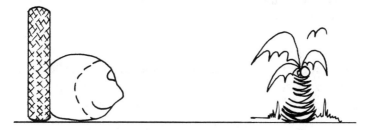

Figure 6: The Total Mind is External in Relation to the Inner Celestial Worlds

You can look out from that mind at a tree in the 3-D world and observe it and therefore make it solid, because you are distanced from it. Remember in Chapter 2, I said that in order for a scientist to make a particle solid, he or she has to be distanced from the particle they are observing. It's the gap that makes the particle or tree solid as well as your observation of it. The gap or distance is also the vital component in establishing that tree's absolute identity and position.

Now go back to the blob that represents your mind. There is nowhere inside that blob, either in the conscious state or the emotional state or the dream state or even in a hypnotic state, that you can get external to and observe. Neither can your therapist, for though he or she can establish a physical distance between you and them, they can never see your mind in order to observe it. They can know it, through their expertise and understanding of human traits and through whatever terms of reference you have offered in your dialogue with them, but they can never observe it in the wave particle sense.

Now, if you imagine a million blobs all linked to each other by the common traits of the tribal mind, you can see that those million blobs are on the external side of the rotation, so no one can get free to establish observation. Each of those million blobs has the potential of establishing an individual particular identity out from the tribal wave, but they don't usually establish distance from their own emotions, thinking, and the tribal mind in general, in order to do so.

In viewing the external world, your vision and your attention go forward, and you lean emotionally and/or intellectually toward those things you desire. In leaning, you push those things slightly away from you, so your horizon, like the physical universe, is always retreating. The laws of repulsion and attraction are subtle—I don't want to deal with them here in detail—but the key is that in the conscious state the reality that is close to you—that which you believe is possible and likely—comes toward you via attraction. But your overall reality is actually retreating, as you push it with emotion and yearning, and by not believing in the aspects you think are obscure, unlikely or unattainable.

Once you engage the discipline of meditation and introspection, and close the ego personality, as in a meditative or trance state, then rather than leaning into external reality, you are now silent and serene. Depending on how much composure you have developed, you would now be leaning away from the external world, facing toward the inner, four dimensional mirror world. So the external world of circumstances and possible circumstances stops expanding, and starts to come back towards you. Your hopes and dreams get gradually closer and closer. Of course the actual physical reality—tree, house, etc.—remains stationary. It's the circumstantial reality that drifts back and forth. Now, to get out of the tribal mind you have to "click" yourself out of the three dimensional world and rotate your inner self through a complete turn via the fourth dimension into the inner worlds. Once you can establish the Inner You through to the 4-D state, unfettered by the ego and the lingering influence the tribal mind has over your total memory, then the Inner You can really begin to develop and grow. Your detachment is created on an emotional, intellectual level by nothing more complex than your decision that life is not as dramatic as your ego imagines it to be. You are happy to allow everyone their evolution through the physical plane, unfettered by your personal opinion and interference. Doing so, you observe them to be perfect in their imperfection, and you further observe them to be experiencing whatever they are experiencing, for some reason of which you have no certain knowledge. It doesn't mean you have to be callous or uninterested in people's problems. You can help them indirectly through your energy and your knowledge, but don't interfere in the lives of others, especially if they haven't approached personally. Take the humble stance which say that you have no deeper knowledge of people's personal circumstances than they do. If they don't ask your opinion, why would you offer it? The greatest love you can offer others, in my view, is to leave them alone. This affirms that they are capable, and given time, will probably solve their situation better than you ever can. There is one exception to the noninfringement rule, and that's for parents of young children.

In those situations, a child comes to you and rests inside your evolutionary pattern until they reach maturity. So it's not an infringement for you to direct a child toward those principles and actions that you feel are best. Once your children reach adulthood, you have to let them go, and then the most you can do is offer advice and support, hoping they listen. But until they reach that stage it's fine for you to attempt to guide them toward whatever path you feel is best for them. Remember, one of the main functions of a parent is to observe their children, to make them real and solid and able to cope in the 3-D external world. If a child is properly observed—that is, acknowledged and encouraged—they will feel they are a real person with potential and worth, and they won't need to join a gang or carry a gun in order to establish observers. Naturally, it's hard for a parent to detach emotionally from the development of their children, but you can exercise patience and some detachment, allowing them time to come around to your way of thinking by influencing them positively.

Once you release from your own emotion, as well as that of the tribal mind around you, then a strange thing happens on the etheric level, which you may feel as a sensation in your body. It's this: The etheric link we have to the physical is via the solar plexus. At that point a vortex of tubular-shaped etheric protrudes out connecting you to the physical. That's why people talk of "gut feelings." It's there that we are linked to the physical. It's how the link to your mother via the umbilical cord was replaced with a link to the metaphysical via your link to the sacred Mother—the etheric web of nature. When you break your emotional and intellectual link to the tribal mind, you also loosen your etheric. Your luminosity (the etheric) pulls away from the luminosity of the earth's etheric and the etheric web of others. When it does so, you may feel a tugging sensation in the area of your navel. If you have listened to my tapes called *Trance States*, and have performed the "Spin Away" technique, you'll most likely have experienced the etheric tug I speak off. However, you don't need me or my tapes to successfully complete the process. It happens automatically in the trance state over a period of time. Your emotions flow through your etheric as rolling waves of energy imprinting your subtle body with the pattern or thumb print of what you are. They dominate it. Once your mind is quiet and your emotions are under control, the etheric is released from the impact of emotion; it becomes finer and less thick and clammy. It will seek greater velocity by distancing itself from the link it has to an emotional world which slows it down. The etheric—when not impeded—always seems to seek a higher velocity or resonance.

The energy that flows out of the etheric through the tubular gateway at the solar plexus flows out like toothpaste from a tube. Its energy is lost to the overall etheric of others and the world in general. As soon as emotion and fear stop pumping energy out of the tube, your etheric will attempt to partially close the hole—if it can. That's why detachment is such a healing process. If the wound at the navel begins to close, the life force of the etheric stops hemorrhaging—you consolidate power instantly. If allowed, the etheric will seek to withdraw, sucking itself back through the solar plexus' tubular vortex to conserve energy and to enliven itself with a higher resonance. Now there's less being wasted. There will always be a certain dissipation of energy through the solar plexus while you are still alive, but once detachment closes the hole somewhat, the etheric withdraws, closing it even further. Now there is less of a rush of energy flowing through the tube to keep it open.

251

By your uncoupling from the tribal mind, the etheric develops velocity and elasticity. An etheric gap develops between you, your energy and the outside world. I call it the *Etheric Free Zone*. It's how you begin to leave the influence of the wave and its lines of oscillation that connect the wave as one energy. It can't come about until you pull back from others, taking full responsibility for yourself and your life. This establishes the etheric free zone which is the first evidence of distance and the key to observation. That's the upside. The other side is that you can no longer blame others for any aspect of your life; you have to accept that it's you—and only you—powering your evolution through this life. You birth yourself as a free individual, rather than a person hovering in the wave. The gap or free zone offers you an evolution out of the tribal mind uncomplicated by the energy of others. That etheric withdrawal back through the solar plexus may occur naturally in sleep or gradually over time, but sometimes it will happen all of a sudden, in a deep meditation, and you'll feel a strong tugging sensation in the area of the navel as the etheric attempts to develop elasticity and pull back.

As it tugs, you will feel a sensation of slight wobbling and you may get the impression that you are spinning. You may even feel nausea caused by the motion of the etheric. The etheric withdrawal from the physical world assists the rotation from the 3-D external state through the 4-D state into the celestial worlds.

The inner celestial worlds are a mirror refection of our outer world. By mirror reflection I don't mean that the inner celestial worlds *exactly* reflect our world. I mean that they are placed facing us—as mirror images are. We exist in the three dimensional world of length, breadth, and height. The inner worlds belong in a four dimensional state and beyond that there may be many more dimensional states of which I am not aware. But for now, we are only trying to get to the fourth one, to establish ourselves there, and develop distance and so observation and, in turn, the inner particle state. Other than detaching from the emotional world and so gradually freeing your etheric, there is nothing very special you have to do to establish the rotation out of the 3-D world of external reality. It seems to be a part of the natural cycle as you advance and grow to see things differently. The important thing is to bring your mind to silence. I don't think it matters if the odd trickle of thought passes through the meditative process, but it's the incessant chatter that has to be silenced through discipline, focus and concentration. Then the rotation is just a click of the mind. What you are looking to do, in fact, is to turn the world (your personal version of it) inside out, through to its mirror state, so that you can observe it. Sounds confusing? It isn't. I'll show you.

Nothing illustrates this click of the mind through the rotation to the mirror state better than Necker's cube.

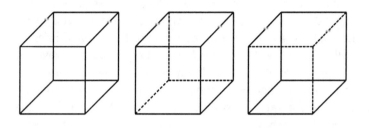

Figure 7: Necker's Cube and its Two Interpretations

Look inside the left-hand cube and imagine yourself sitting at the back in the far left-hand corner. Imagine the physical world is in the cube along with the collective mind of your people, which is in effect a microcosm of the collective mind of humanity—its Planetary Group Soul. You experience life in the cube bounded by the three dimensions of length, breadth, and height, and your world is further limited by the collective knowledge and beliefs of mankind, which form a part of the cube's boundaries. The whole of our 3-D world is inside the cube. Yes! The cube has become larger over the years as knowledge expands, but no one can get outside of the mind or the 3-D world (or the cube) while their focus is on externals. They are trapped until death, both physically and intellectually in the cube-world. We wander around the cube saying "this is reality," and although people may be very clever at discovering the contents of the cube and their minds, all they can ever do is *know* it. Trapped inside the cube they can never get beyond it and so observe themselves from *outside* the cube and beyond the limitations of it all. They can never achieve the inner particle state while their concentration is forward in the cube, and that's why the ego's chase for the external particle state is a hopeless charade.

Now place your mind into the far left-hand corner of the cube and pull that corner back towards you as if you were trying to mentally lift it off the page. Suddenly, the cube flips inside out to show you its mirror image. It may take you several attempts to get the cube to flip, but once you have done it, it gets easier. Look at the second or third cubes, with their dotted lines—it will help you see how the cube flips back and forth, hovering through a rotation in and out of its 4-D state. What was originally the back wall when your attention or vision was pushing forward is now its lid or the bottom of the cube, depending on how you choose to interpret it. Rather than being in the back of the cube, stuck in the tribal mind, stuck in the 3-D world, you are now *outside* of the cube entirely, sitting up on the left hand corner of the roof or under the left hand corner of its floor, depending on your choice. But either way, you are outside the cube. You're free—above it—and so beyond the evolutionary limitation of the cube.

When first placing yourself mentally in the cube—at the far left-hand corner—you had to push your mind forward to place your attention in there. It's the same forward pushing motion we adopt in the external world as our ego stretches out from itself, searching for its needs and desires in life. The stretching forward of the conscious mind locks it into the box we call human/physical reality. To get out of the box completely, you have to pull the back corner with your attention. That is the only process that will release you and turn reality inside out, setting you free.

In the meditative state, your forward vision is facing the opposite direction, inward, and so your external 3-D circumstantial reality is no longer being pushed by your attention; it begins to come back towards you. Thus, in looking within, you create a pulling motion, in so far as your external world is concerned. You might expect that you create a pushing motion inwardly, toward the celestial worlds, because that's where your focus is, but that is not entirely so. I'll explain that in a

Observation

moment. Pulling external reality towards you, by establishing an opposite view in the direction of the inner celestial worlds, is what flips your reality and your connection to the tribal mind inside out. Detachment allows you to unglue, and meditation allows you to rotate via the 4-D state to the mirror worlds. Now you may think that as soon as your meditation is over and you reenter the external world via your conscious mind, that the cube and your reality would flip back again and you'd be trapped within it once more. The answer is: yes and no. Certainly, your conscious mind is back in the cube, because it never actually *left*. All you did was close it down somewhat, but the Inner You that you gradually establish on the other side of the rotation can't come back.

255

The more you establish quiet time and meditation as part of your daily discipline, the more you go through the rotation into the mirror worlds, and regardless of whether or not you initially have a perception of those inner worlds, your total mind that exists normally in the external world begins to birth and form an inner being or inner personality, which is, of course, the Inner You. The development of that Inner You is no different to the process whereby you formed a personality out of your early childhood memories and experiences. But now there are two halves of you. One evolving in the external world and one evolving on the other side of the rotation in the inner world.

Once the Inner You is properly formed, it begins to travel inward, climbing up the various plateaus, establishing distance between itself and your external 3-D personality that is contained in the blob. A gap develops! An exciting possibility is taking place. Observation between the two parts of you, your inner personality and your outer personality, is now possible!

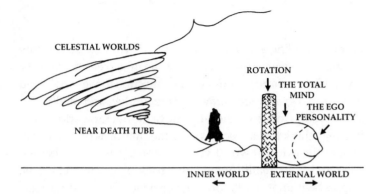

Figure 8: Establishing Observation Via the Rotation from the 3-D External World to the Mirror Worlds of the Inner You

Once your total mind, containing the memory you have of yourself, conceives and emits a new quantum of itself—the Inner You—that Inner You can't come back through the 4-D rotation into the 3-D world of the cube. Why can't it? After all, was it not conceived from the same memory banks as the ego personality? Yes, it was. But, even though the Inner You has characteristics that came originally from the external mind, which forms its early symbols and temperament in the same way as you inherited language and temperament from your parents, the Inner You doesn't exist in the external 3-D world of space and time. No matter where the Inner You places its attention, every direction is inner—not a 3-D outer reality. So it can't get into the external world because it hasn't got a 3-D view with which to penetrate the 3-D world. In the same way that you can't fly out of the physical universe, no matter which direction you choose, the Inner You can't generate an external view with which to create a 3-D horizon that it might cross, successfully completing the transfer back from its inner world to the regular 3-D world. In passing, you might wonder how ghosts do it. The answer is: they don't. Their world is external to the celestial world. They are sandwiched between the 3-D world and the celestial world—trapped.

Once the Inner You is initiated on the other side of the rotation, meaning you have made the flip—like in the Necker's cube example—the Inner You remains in those worlds to evolve concurrently with your external personality, that is evolving in the physical. Of course, the birth of the Inner You is an unusual concept. When you think of it, it's not any different to the birth of the physical body or the development of your personality out of your early experiences. What you consider is the *real* you—your conscious personality—is only a small hived-off section of your total memory, which the total mind uses to experience life in the external world. The Inner You is nothing more than a second version of your personality that the mind hives off so it can evolve in two places at the same time. That is, the external world and the 4-D world of the mirror state—the celestial world.

In establishing the Inner You on the other side of the rotation, I believe you commence a destiny/evolution that is, in fact, the "afterlife" which most others will experience only after death. You have created the beginnings of your afterlife now. Meaning, that when you eventually get to the afterlife you won't have to mess with large chunks of it. Lots of the early adjustments and training that the human personality has to go through will have already have been completed and assimilated by the Inner You.

In this way, Fringe Dwellers and people who have gone past the physical plane can activate the other side of themselves and continue learning and evolving. Otherwise, they would be earthbound, trapped on a plane that offers no new experiences or lessons. It would become a living hell and utterly boring. Of course, everyone eventually has a spiritual life, but most don't start that part of their evolution until death. Everything before that belongs to the intellect or to the emotions—the external personality. It's very cut and dry. If you are not in the other side of the rotation, then whatever you think and believe has to be of the 3-D world of mind, intellect, and opinion. That has an impact when you think about it.

The journey of the Inner You up the various plateaus (shown in Figure 8) is very similar to the journey we make as humans from conception to birth. The Inner You begins its early existence on the other side of the rotation, in a blind state, as does a human embryo. It has a modicum of feeling (described in Chapter 4) but nothing much else. Climbing and moving, it eventually travels across the Plane of Desolation and arrives at the entrance of the near-death tube—the birth canal if you like. Pushing through that canal takes tenacity and courage, as does childbirth. Once on the other side of the near-death tube, the Inner You develops sight.

Now the Inner You is truly placed in the celestial worlds, and it is now facing you in the external world, mirrorlike. Sometime after that, the synapse takes place (described in the last Chapter), whereby, the Inner You, and your human personality evolving in the outer physical world, fuse in an silent explosion of energy. A synapse of power is emitted across the two molecules because they now have absolute distance between them and the fusion that takes place allows for a consolidation, a celestial "mini-bang" that establishes a new mini-universe that is formed from the two parts of you that now have an absolute spiritual identity—one that is linked across the celestial distance between the other side of the near-death tube and the world of human images this side of the tube.

Bear with me, as I talk about distance and inner travels, for I have to use words we all understand from the vocabulary of our 3-D world to describe states that exist in multidimensional worlds. For example, in our 3-D world distance is a factor of light. Distance is the time it takes light to travel from point A to point B. In the celestial world you have to abandon all usual ideas when thinking about distance. What seems to be an external objective reality, is in fact in a symbiotic relationship with you. The surroundings you perceive are related to you in that they are an extension of the Inner You and its personality, with all of its knowledge. Because celestial light emits feeling, it's not ordinary light—which has no particular feeling or message within it. So celestial distance is not ordinary distance as we experience it in the physical. In those worlds distance and one's personal horizons are established as an extension of one's feelings. You see and experience only those things (realities if you like) that are congruent with your inner identity, a reality that exactly fits you. You can't see or be a part of things that are not congruent. They lay beyond an event horizon sustained and established by your feelings. So inner reality responds to and is in a subjective relationship with you. There is no objective or external reality as we are normally used to—only the illusion of one. So in the celestial world things may appear solid, but that is not so, and they are not necessarily stationary or firmly placed anywhere in particular either. You are walking through a celestial dimension and, using a simple example, the scene is somewhat like a physical landscape—there is a house on the horizon. When you first focus upon the house it remains stationary, as you'd expect. But if you desire to view that house up close, it instantly moves from the horizon to appear in front of you. You don't move towards it—it comes to you. Suddenly, it's in front of you. Or, if your desire is to be in the house, you find it all around you. So in the celestial world we know reality is subjective. It has no height, breadth, and depth, other than whatever 3-D characteristics you impart upon it via the habits and recollection you have as a 3-D personality that is living or has lived on earth. That is why there is no external reality in the celestial planes, and that explains why the Inner You can't come back to the 3-D world once you birth it on the other side of the rotation. The lack of an external view gives it no horizon to cross and as it can't pull the physical world to it through the rotation; it can never reenter the physical 3-D world. And a good thing, too.

Now you might be saying all this celestial mirror world stuff is all very well, Stewie, but knickers to talking about it. Show me. I would respond by saying that if you were with me, I could show you, because I could create a distance for you in your etheric and through it you'd momentarily glimpse what I'm talking about. However, there is a little trick—exercise is perhaps a better word—which you can perform on your own, which will show you the rotation, and though you may not see the celestial worlds, because of inner blindness and your initial inner distance from the near-death tube, you will still experience rotating through the 4-D state, into the mirror world. When performed correctly, at a low level of brain speed (trance or close to it), you will flip yourself momentarily into another evolution. I have put the exercise at the end of the book as the Appendix. Resist the temptation of going there right away. For if you don't understand the basis of the exercise or what is actually going on, and if you have no expertise in the symbology of the celestial inner worlds, you'll scare the hell out of yourself.

There is a place in the exercise where your human personality is momentarily snared in the rotation. This occurs because your personality normally has no experience or expertise beyond the rotation. You will momentarily lose sight (perception) of the external human personality that you know to be who you are. Imagine waking one morning, and looking out at the world through your eyes, and you suddenly realize that you have no perception or knowledge of the individual or personality that's doing the looking. I don't mean that you are unable to remember the character's name. I mean that you suddenly experience the body with no character in it at all! Who you think you are is gone. It is not where you expect it to be, that is, behind your eyes, in your mind, perceiving the external world that you are familiar with. At the point where your personality is suddenly lost in the rotation you will search—scramble perhaps—to rediscover where you are. Momentarily, you may become extremely disturbed if you don't know where to look for yourself, or if you don't realize immediately that you can return back through the 4-D rotation and reexperience your character/personality in its body, back in the familiar 3-D world.

Observation

So, taking things in their proper order, and placing a parabola of what you are on the other side of the rotation by just discussing the symbols and language of those worlds, will allow you to come to that place, (if you wish to do so), in a correct and proper way. One that will show you a strange and exceptional experience without unhinging you in the process. So, let's talk about trance states, its symbols and their meanings. That way you are properly prepared.

Our perception of the conscious world takes place at the relatively very fast brain speed of fourteen and up to and beyond twenty cycles per second—known as the beta state. It's not until you slow that brain speed down to a trance state (four to six cycles per second) that you can enter or perceive the inner worlds of the mirror state. Normal waking brain speed sets up an electromagnetic oscillation that precludes entry or perception of the 4-D world.

For most, there is no real inner spiritual being until the ego/personality is brought to silence by death. The trance state is how you simulate death and establish yourself in the inner worlds.

Here's how it's done: Before you begin the trance process, exercise for ten or fifteen minutes and then take a warm shower so that you are relaxed. It's best if you don't have any food for at least a couple of hours beforehand. When you are ready to begin, lie down with your head to the north and your feet to the south. Close your eyes, relax yourself and go through the process I describe elsewhere in my writings, in which you see your body elongated to twice its normal length. It just a matter of visualizing yourself expanding in length. Its function is to establish elasticity in the etheric. Then take a moment to see the main chakras, the heart, throat, third eye, and crown opening to receive and emit energy. Once you are deeply relaxed, and you have activated and stretched your etheric energy, you begin by peering into the dark—just watching it.

At first you will see nothing, as the Inner You is blind, like a child in the womb. Quite likely your conscious mind will get bored and it may even protest, offering you suggestions that are intended to entice you back to the external world. The absence of activity is disturbing. The ego insists that things have to happen in order for it to feel alive. Gazing into the dark at nothing in particular will seem to it like a great waste of time and even rather threatening. The ego isn't sure if it's dying or not, and it doesn't quite understand what is going on.

In the early stages there is nothing in the darkness because you are still an amorphous cloud for memories gleaned from the tick-tock world. It takes a while for the subconscious mind to process and release itself from the impact of the external world and to properly birth an inner being from its total memory. In much the same way, it took you a number of years in the external world to become a personality—usually through to the age of about five or six. By then your personality was formed, and you developed gradually through the years to what you are today; becoming more and more knowledgeable, collecting experiences and becoming more sophisticated as you went along.

In the darkness of your meditations, usually the first change you notice are blobs of color that cross your vision. They will usually be a yellow-gold, or red or a reddish violet or green. They come and go. They mean nothing. They are a part of the ocular process of light/color traveling to the brain. You can experience the same process by staring at a light and then closing your eyes quickly and you'll see the yellow-gold residue of the light on the optic nerve that seems to shine on the back of your eyelids.

After the colored blobs come and go, the screen will go blank for a while. It may take several months or it might only be a few days—there's no telling how long the process takes. Next, you will see random images and symbols that are dimly lit. The images will always be moving in front of the dark background, which of course is created by your closed eyelids. The light surrounding these symbols will be fairly weak. You can see them, but they don't shine. They cross your vision in arc–shaped trajectories, usually moving right to left or sometimes left to right, depending on whichever side of your brain has been trained as intellectually dominant. Most people are intellectually left-brained and spatially right-brained, but some are switched—right-left, rather than left-right. This applies to left-handed people mostly.

The symbols you see at this stage will be moving fairly slowly. The early symbols are flat; they have length and breadth, but not much depth, if any at all. You will notice that they are not necessarily straight up and down to your line of sight as you are mostly used to in the external world. Many of the symbols that float laconically across your vision take on strange angles, sometimes slanted away from you, sometimes leaning in toward your vision. On occasions you'll see a symbol presented which looks like it is directly above your line of sight, as if you were underneath it looking up. So perhaps you'll see a complete human figure, as if you were an ant on the sidewalk looking up at the soles of their feet. Alternatively, you'll be offered the same symbol from above, so you'll get a bird's eye view of the top of someone's head. The strangeness of these angles has always fascinated me.

These early symbols, mounted in a dim light on a dark background, come from your subconscious mind. They are mostly random emanations. They are part of the process of releasing from the outside world, but they also form a valuable lesson—they teach you about the inner world, like a child that looks at shapes and learns depth perception in the external world. The slanted symbols guide you to establish 3-D depth perception of what will soon be a 4-D inner world. So the early symbols are 2-D and flat, like images on a sheet of paper that passes your vision, but once they begin to lean at strange angles, they offer you a comprehension of distance and depth. In my opinion, the leaning symbols are the first evidence of the subconscious distancing itself from the usual world of the intellectual mind. At this stage, you begin to realize how very important imagination will become and how being able to think about strange, unusual perceptions and ideas liberates you from the tick-tock mind of our mostly straight up and down regimented world.

The leaning symbols pass by in collective strings of information that exhibit a common association. So for a week you will see faces and nothing else—loads of them—and you'll probably recognize none of them. They drift across in steady streams; some young, some old, some very beautiful—almost angelic, some utterly grotesque, revolting and ugly. Then your screen will fade to black and a new set of symbols starts up, and for a week or two there will be nothing but some object like trees. Hundreds of them. All different, many at odd angles. Then you may move through a period of animals and other periods of geometric shapes, and so on. I am presuming you are doing your meditation daily for half an hour or so. So when I say faces will appear for week, I mean within one week's worth of half hour meditation, not for seven entire days.

Quite a long time may have elapsed by now—perhaps a year or two—and you will have continued to climb out of tick-tock, detaching and releasing as you go along. If you are winning the battle against the ego, the spirit within is released and trickles through, enveloping you with a sense of joy and bliss. At other times you may experience a great uncertainty and terror as the ego flares to prominence. It doesn't feel safe and has a nasty suspicion about the inner work you are doing. It doesn't like to lose control.

Once the bulk of the slanted, leaning symbols have passed, your screen will return to blank. Then new symbols appear as part of the next process. Having learned depth perception, now you have to get a grip on language. The symbols that appear to you in this period are symbols that establish dialogue. For easy reference, let's call these new images *L-symbols* (language symbols). They don't appear like the slanted symbols did in the collective groupings. Instead they file past singly. The L-symbols take the Inner You from silence to communication, one word at a time, like a small child learns a language. The L-symbols are training for what will happen later, when you enter the celestial worlds. There you'll find very complex symbols that have endless meaning and information, expressed through a very deep spiritual feeling drawn from the packet of celestial light each image has.

The early L-symbols will still be in a dim light, though they will have more depth than before. Each is a word in the vocabulary of the Inner You. Sometimes the symbol has a literal meaning and sometimes its meaning is cryptic. So the view of the bottom of someone's shoes could mean foot, shoes, leather, or literally the soles of one's feet, but more than likely it will mean "soul." Often the connotation is phonetic. You establish the meaning by a process of elimination, developing language one symbol at a time. These early symbols have meaning, but they do not have intrinsic feelings radiating through them as yet. The source of all inner feeling is the celestial light, but it is not yet shining forcefully enough through the Inner You to grant the L-symbols true celestial vitality. Rather than discovering their meaning by perceiving their feeling, you have to look for a cryptic or literal meaning. Remember, a mind devoid of spirit light can never have inner feelings—it can only *know* at this stage. True perception is beyond it as yet. Sometimes the answer to the riddle of what a symbol means is a synonym established by association. So, if the mind is trying to show you the concept of comedy, it may show the face of someone that you know to be comical. If it is trying to show you a change of direction, it may offer you a street that you know well which, perhaps, makes a sudden sharp turn. If it is establishing the idea of the completion of something it may offer you a grave stone. That one usually freaks you out. Graves usually mean endings, just as births mean beginnings. Your inner mind talks to you as you talk to yourself, so you will eventually get what it's trying to say.

Symbols that have no obvious or literal meaning will often have other connotations which do make sense. For example, you might see a bottle of whiskey every day for a week. It may confuse you as you search for what whisky means to you. But its connotation offers you the word "spirit"—as in "one's spiritual identity." Once the association is learned, the whisky bottle comes back to you any time "spirit" is needed as a word in the dialogue.

Synonyms and phonetic associations are also used when the inner dialogue describes abstract concepts for which there are no obvious symbols. So if a human eye passes across your vision, it may just be an eye or your inner self may be trying to establish the word "I." Then, if you see two eyes one after each other in quick succession you might think it stands for "I, I." You might wonder if the Inner You is developing a stutter. Instead, two eyes in quick succession probably stands for the word "confirmed," as in "aye, aye, captain."

Here's one more. You suddenly see a church steeple rising gloriously skyward. The words "church," "steeple," and "roof" make no sense in that particular dialogue, so you look for an association and you come up with "spire" as in a church spire. That means nothing either, but if you treat it phonetically, dropping the word "church," you suddenly have a new word, "aspire," as in to hope or to seek. Sweet, isn't it?

There are hundreds of symbols to learn. You've probably seen many of them and have not known what they mean, but you can soon decipher it all once you broaden your thinking beyond a literal or obvious explanation, which quite often doesn't fit or make sense. However, concrete ideas usually have literal symbols. So the sight of a bottle of whisky might mean "spirit." But the sight of a carrot does not necessarily mean that your car is rotten (car rot)—it means what it says, carrot. The language builds from a haphazard series of symbols into a concise and delightful language which teaches you to broaden your inner abilities and perceptions by viewing things from strange angles, and in unfamiliar ways. It also trains you to become proficient, so that in later years you can unravel more and more complex information, which may, by then, be coming at you at high speed.

These early symbols also teach you to really concentrate and notice everything that passes through your vision. They have a way of forcing you to keep your mind from wandering. If your mind drifts, even for a moment, the symbols stop until you are ready to begin again. Sometimes you have to abandon the trance and reenter the process the next day.

In the early days while the Inner You is learning language, it has no "inner world" sight and no expertise in those worlds either. For a while you are like a blind prehistoric worm living in an underground cave. You have no vision. That is why, in the thousand day climb mention previously, you usually have little or no inkling as to what to do next. But as you develop language and control of the ego, gradually the spirit molecule infuses that inner being, and you develop the rudiments of inner spiritual feelings. Though you are still blind, you can feel your way along. However, once the Inner You takes on a greater velocity, it starts to climb at a steady pace. Eventually, the spirit flows almost entirely uninhibited by intellect and ego, and you develop the rudiments of vision as well as inner feelings.

Once that happens, new symbols appear. They are very different from the L-symbols. They come at you head on, straight up the center of your vision, rather than tracking across on curved trajectories. There are a few exceptions, but straight up the middle is their usual route. These new symbols—let's call them C-symbols (celestial symbols)—are moving at many times the speed you are used to by now. They are not mounted on a dark background—they have their own light. Sometimes the light is brilliant, like that of the celestial worlds, and sometimes it is less intense. You'll easily notice the difference.

In my case, when I first started seeing these symbols, they were mostly letters of the alphabet. They were gold in color and they came one at a time at very high speeds. I missed most of the early ones. It took a long while to adjust to the speed of it all. Once I could comprehend one letter at a time, I then started receiving them two and then three at a time, and eventually complete words came at me. It took me a long while before I could read a simple sentence of three or four words. The problem is that the celestial symbols are oscillating very much faster than humans are used to. Information comes to you so quickly that you have no time to concentrate upon it or to work it out in your mind. The time frame of its impact is a minute fraction of a second, so you have to learn to retain information at vast speeds. You learn to comprehend it from the memory trace the symbol momentarily creates upon your mind—its afterglow if you like.

It's hard to describe but you have to see the symbol without looking at it. When it touches you, you don't have time to concentrate upon it. For this to work, your mind has to be passive as you allow the C-symbols to tap you, hoping to pick them up. You miss most of them at first. It can be a little frustrating. In our world, the light reflected off an object, like a word on a page, hits your eye and flows as an impulse to the brain. The light of that word is continuous so you have time to stare at it and think about it, so you can understand it. The light of the C-Symbols is not a continuous light. It's an instantaneous flash. The symbol is suspended in the flash. You have to be ready to pick it, but very, very quickly. It teaches you perception on the hurry-up. You become very sensitive to even the most subtle shifts of light and energy. That's why I say that you should learn to notice everything as you walk through life. It helps to train your mind to pick up more and more subtle detail in both the inner and external worlds.

The short sentences I saw in those early days were not particularly earth shattering in their impact. Sometimes I'd see a person's name and then two or three days later that person would come into my life. Nothing particularly special happened. Often, it was nothing more than a casual meeting. I'd be chatting to someone on a plane and I recognize their name when I asked for it. Sometimes the messages were personal, offering guidance, and other times the sentences were meaningless to me. So, for example, I'd see a sentence that said, "Willows lean over the river." I'd lie there in my trance thinking, so what?

For a few days, several years ago, I had access to a celestial library of some kind. The books in it were the most magnificent I had ever seen. Each word on the page of a book was lit from behind. Reflecting through the letters was a multifaceted radiance of color laid as a mosaic of knowledge more ancient and wise than I could ever comprehend.

Some of the books were written in technical symbols that didn't resemble any earthly science I am familiar with, and other books had forms of writing that don't exist in this world. The books were a record of immense knowledge. I distinctly remember looking at a very beautiful capital letter that began a sentence in one of the books, and I realized that one capital contained in its radiance the entire history of humanity. I couldn't understand the language of the book, but I remember thinking how humble and simple life is; that if one capital letter represents the whole gamut of all there is and has ever been, then there isn't that much to it. I remember being proud of our letter—it seemed special to me. There was a wonderful correctness and propriety about its place in the book. It stood with other letters and it was no less and no more than the others; it was us as we are—warts and all. I soon realized I didn't have the comprehension, speed or energy to sustain my presence in that place, so my hopes of reading the celestial books was temporarily dashed. I left that place hoping one day I would return.

Can we really tell if we are not hallucinating or viewing a lucid dream? I believe we can. Celestial light is not normal light. C-symbols are bathed in a light that has love and feeling and the depth of all-knowing—you can't mistake them. When you view a celestial scene, the immensity of God's presence over that place is unmistakable. The serenity is unworldly.

In the dream state we don't often see symbols one at a time. We view scenarios and little playlets—sequences of events. The light of dreams is ordinary light that the mind remembers from its waking state. Sequences in dreams are illogical; the flow of events appear irrational and inconsistent. In viewing a celestial world, reality can move back and forth when you concentrate on it. But what you see has a logical quality in the sense that sequences follow properly, one after the next. Lucid dreams also have ordinary light, and in many of them you'll be flying across an earthstyle landscape, and there will be nothing about the light or that landscape that gives you the impression that it is anything other than a dream. I feel the flying we experience in lucid dreams is very much the subconscious mind's fervent desire to escape the rigid intellectual world of earthly ideas and gravity. Flying is the subconscious mind's way of expressing freedom. Flying dreams are exhilarating, but they are nothing more than a roller coaster ride for the mind.

In the celestial worlds, and even in those worlds that are close to the celestial worlds, everything has some light and some radiance; objects are not inanimate—they come to life. The early symbols you see and the L-symbols that come later are in dim light—they're from your mind. The main exception is the astral world, which is sandwiched between the 3-D and 4-D mirror state. In the astral world, symbols are so dull and grey that you may confuse them at first with your own symbols. But you can tell the difference if you look carefully; the astral world has a slightly strange hue of grey and many of its symbols and even its denizens have a definition that symbols from your own mind don't have. In watching one's symbols come forth, notice how the edges are not clearly defined; they tend to be hazy. In the astral world, most of what you might see has a clearly defined outer boundary, as well as its telltale grey tone. Of course, in the astral world you bump into loads of energy that is satanic or scary or downright ugly and evil. It's no problem telling the difference. Also, most astral stuff seems to be behind you, because you're usually shifting your inner butt out of there at speed.

Some limited vision comes gradually as you climb the various inner plateaus. But absolute vision is only available on the other side of the near-death tube. On the plateaus between the rotation and the other side of the tube, there are no audible sounds that I have ever heard, with one exception: I once heard a few chords of angelic music. All communication is internal, in that information passes via the celestial light that contains everything you'd ever need to know. Further, what communication there is, is by way of mind-to-mind; there are no sound waves that travel through the air as we are used to. Traveling up the plateaus, if you hear words going off in your head, it's very hard to know if they are yours or someone else's. In the dark areas up the various plateaus, towards the near-death tube, I'd be very cautious of what seems like dialogue in the mind. I take the stance that most of it is self-generated, unless there is something there to convince me otherwise. That's not to say that ideas coming into your mind as dialogue are useless—they may be very helpful. But I shy away from thinking that they are external information that comes from someone or something else. It's impossible to tell until your perception develops sight and you see where the information is coming from. I mention it in passing because I think a lot of people kid themselves that they are in communication with other beings. On this side of the near-death tube only the denizens of the astral worlds transfer mental dialogue. So if you haven't reached the other side of the tube as yet, I'd be careful of labeling information and giving it a definition it may not possess.

As you climb the plateaus, you'll acquire some celestial vision, especially as you get closer to the Plane of Desolation and the near-death tube. However, celestial symbols can appear to you anywhere on the journey to enhance your inner dialogue. By now you should have the rudiments of language, assuming that you have established a decent relationship with the Inner You. It's the energy flowing back and forth between the Inner You and your conscious self, infused by more and more spirit, that really begins to change your life. You take on an invisible radiance that most people don't have. You'll see it in your life as heightened physical energy, added enthusiasm, and magical occurrences that favor you in special ways—making life easier and easier.

Once you make the rotation, the radiance will develop gradually. It doesn't really matter if you ever see any of the celestial symbols or not. You can manage with just spiritual feelings and perceptions that spirit offers. What really matters is that you establish the distance between your inner being and your personality's outer vision into the external world. Doing this consolidates your power more than anything else you can do for yourself. Most people don't have the discipline or tenacity to make it up through the near-death tube in this lifetime, and you shouldn't feel any less for it if you don't care for the journey. It's by no means compulsory. It's only attractive to space cadets, strange fellows, and weirdo ladies on the fringe of life.

Just in controlling your etheric and becoming settled you offer a great service to others. The radiance you develop heals you and radiates to others invisibly, without your ever really knowing how it works. Suffice to say that for people to change, they have to establish a new resonance at many different levels, as well as the mental, psychological level. In offering a peaceful, equitable stance in life, and having a defined and purposeful etheric uncluttered by the tribal wave, you assist the overall flow of radiance to our people. The process is slow, but everyone can play their part in allowing the spirit to shine forth and new ideas to gain a hold.

The beautiful thing is that the process is truly underway, and it will gather momentum as time progresses. Remember, as professional waiters we can wait forever.

What Next?

CHAPTER TWELVE

I think the main feature of the next twenty years will be the rapidly growing consciousness of people pushing against the ego of the status quo. This will be coupled with an understanding that the only way we can heal this planet is to control our ego and take responsibility for our life. The Band Aid mentality of patching up people and countries, and sustaining the whole process by borrowing money that can never be repaid, will have to change. Teaching people to raise their energy so they can sustain themselves is the only way to establish the healing process. It's the logical next step. The movement to a spiritual vision will become so urgent and so wide spread, that every country in the Western world will take on the process at a heady pace. The flickering light of reason-ableness is upon us—it will gain strength.

What makes it exciting in my view is that while economic problems cause challenges, people will see that they have been disempowered by a system run for the benefit of sustaining a power base for the few. Once people realize *en masse* that our democracies are based on an unholy relationship between a powerful few and the powerless masses, democracy will have to begin including the people it was intended for. Doing that will strengthen people. By involving them in their own affairs they will learn to take control of their lives. Economies bounc-ing off the wall is in fact the makings of the solution, not the problem.

Individuals will realize that in order to prosper in the new world they will have to take back their power. Rather than looking for solutions outside of themselves, they will see that the only real solution is within. At its very basic metaphysical level, the only real commodity in the world is energy. By generating energy, and enthusiasm, expressed as concerted action and creativity, you guarantee yourself a prosperous and happy life.

Taking responsibility and setting oneself free is unnerving for some. If there is one area that's still a bit weak, it's that people have accepted repression for so long that they lack confidence. It's hard for a prisoner to walk up to the prison guard and tell him, "You're fired." But our time will come.

Some might say that a future where communities are controlled by their own people would result in disorder and chaos. I don't think that is necessarily correct. I don't see a future of no government in power. I do think we need less government and one that is run by people with a spiritual view, rather than an emotional, power based view. That's the main difference. It doesn't have to happen overnight. The transition can be slow and quite smooth. Power can be gradually returned to people and they can begin working together as individuals to establish a new order born out of respect. The idea of small groups of conscious, loving people forming a consensus, respecting each others' individuality, working together to manage and better their community or factory or church or whatever, is so delightful and so pleasing to the mass of humanity. It's only a matter of time before it becomes real.

You can see the idea already in some manufacturing plants that are now organizing themselves laterally rather than vertically. The production floor is managed by the workers, who supervise their work place in small cells or teams, each member respecting the others and everyone contributing to efficiency and fair work practices for the benefit of the company.

What Next?

Companies that still insist on the old-fashioned vertical structure, in which all power and decision making flows from the top down, won't exist fifteen years from now. I predict the union movement will quietly go to its grave over the next generation, to be replaced by consensus management by small groups of democratic workers interfacing with business owners for everyone's benefit.

Additionally, you will also see shareholder democracy coming like a train through the night. The daylight robbery of shareholders' funds in publicly traded companies is the greatest unreported theft ever perpetuated in the economic history of our planet.

The whole premise of share buying needs to be overhauled. A share in a public company theoretically entitles you to part ownership of the company, but you can never exercise that ownership. So what do you own? Nothing. Just a piece of paper that is as useless to you as a voting slip for a parliamentary election. By the time the directors have creamed the company's funds and the government has taxed the rest, what you get back for your investment usually falls somewhere between nothing and four percent. If you do get a dividend, it is often taxed again through personal income tax. The small shareholder gets nothing, especially when you factor in inflation—which after all is just another government tax. Modern stock markets are, in effect, a legalized Ponzi scheme. The whole *raison d'etre* relies on selling at higher and higher prices what are, in effect, almost worthless investments which don't pay a decent return. I can see laws passed that place representatives of the small shareholders on each board of directors to control directors and ensure they don't manipulate the companies assets. Governments will have to pass laws allowing dividends to shareholders to be tax-free, given that the government has already gotten its share of the shareholders' money by taxing company profit. These laws already exist in some countries, like Australia, and I think the concept of tax free dividends will spread. The idea of making an investment and actually getting a decent return on that investment—one that you can take to the bank—is another one of those refreshing little ideas whose time has come.

In the next ten or fifteen years business will go through the biggest change it has ever seen. Consumer consciousness, then worker consciousness, environmental consciousness, and finally shareholder consciousness, will emerge at a heady pace. Business will have to become more honest in order to survive. Ethical investing is already a catch word, and following from that will come more open and honest standards. We will have to learn to work together and to honor each other, which requires complete honesty and good communication. The carpetbagger mentality will gradually be replaced by fairness. Each person will contribute and receive according to their ability, all based on truth and directed by the spirit of cooperation. I think this process will come about naturally, borne out of necessity stemming from the economic problems that the world ego is designing for itself. The world shortage of capital will discriminate against the dishonesty and hype of marginal corporations and their game will be over. It already is for some of them.

Our Western institutions will also come under an ever increasing pressure to change their ways. Many of them are still based in the remnants of the old feudal system, in which ordinary people are just expendable cogs in the wheel. As people power gains strength, our institutions will have to embrace a new ideology. Of course, the corruption and mismanagement of many of our institutions is so endemic many of them will not see the changes coming, and they will collapse.

The power that flows from the government down to the local level has gotten out of control over the years. It's not too bad in the United States, but in Canada, Europe, the UK, Australia, and New Zealand, the control over the people exercised by local governments is all encompassing. In Britain it can take two to three years to get planning permission to build a house. Then there is no certainty of it being granted. In some suburbs of Sydney, Australia, it can take four to six months to get permission to erect a garden shed.

In Europe there are one hundred and fifty thousand government employees involved in various agriculture ministries supervising three hundred thousand farms. One supervisor to every two farmers! That kind of nonsense will have to stop. The struggle for power and the convulsions that follow will be very interesting, and though economic collapse is no picnic, it's part of the process of transformation. Without it, the people will never gain control, and the current echelons of power won't move over until they absolutely have to. But in the end they will—as sure as day follows night.

Twenty years ago, people with a spiritual view of life were considered weird. Most of our people had no spiritual views or their spirituality rested under the controlling influence of the religious status quo. But things are different now. The new consciousness is spreading far and wide, and with it has come the idea that a life without honor and goodness is not worth living. When a person takes on a broader spiritual view of life they no longer accept the controlling mechanism of tick-tock. Democratic freedoms are no freedoms at all in the light of spirit, and people need to express their expanding spirituality and consciousness unfettered by minds that oscillate at an old world level.

The very shift in consciousness will eventually melt the current system. As people go within and establish that infinite being, and embrace a more pristine and celestial perspective, their power radiates silently and powerfully, effecting change in their community without anyone realizing the source of that change or even that it is actually happening. Through this process, which may take a hundred years to complete, the

280

demise of the ego-based system is inevitable. In a metaphysical way, it has already collapsed. It has no real power and it is sustained only by intellect, emotion, fear, and habit. In a lecture I gave in Seattle five or six years ago I said, "We have come to bury Caesar not to praise him. We are here to change the system, not to raise it up." I went on to say that, in effect, the movement for a higher consciousness is not to make people more special and more important, but to forge a guillotine that will sever the ego's head from the body of the planet. Some of the audience got it, some were confused. But in my view, it is easy to see how the process will come about and how the greater plan for our people will follow the dictates of a divine order which flows naturally from the Planetary Group Soul over long periods of time. We may not be alive to see the process completed, but our children or their children will be there. You should never be despondent. Remember, as professional waiters, we can wait forever. Even though the human race may, at times, suffer great imbalances, if you consider the evolution of our people over a ten thousand year period, you can see how, in infinite terms, everything slowly but correctly comes to pass in the proper way. Eventually our people will reflect a spiritual vision that is infinite rather than the ego's vision. There is no other place our evolution can go in the long term. The old women can finish their knitting; the ego's head has already fallen into the basket. It's over.

It is our lack of maturity and our former inability to take responsibility for ourselves, that has placed these people over us. The transition out of the tribes, into the nation states and its mind set, and from there to a spiritual independence, could take our people several hundred years—or more. But as each individual takes back his or her power, we will eventually have enough strong people, and enough confidence and velocity of spirit, to pull to us into a new reality containing the good and spiritual ideas and leaders we deserve.

What Next?

Meanwhile, the decline of the modern system will continue to accelerate. Seeing the status quo for what it is, people will defy it. Our countries are becoming less and less governable. Mass disobedience will become the norm as this decade runs its course. You can't tow hundreds of millions of people along if they don't agree with you. The more we are offered different versions of the same unholy system, the greater the number of people who withdraw their support. In the end, institutions can only govern with our blessing. Citizens will never give that blessing *en masse* if our leaders do not conform to the ideals we require of them. So the minds of the people go one way, while our leaders play the fiddle and Rome burns.

With the death of the world ego and the declining power of governments, we will see the deterioration of many of the world's currencies. Paper money is an external manifestation of the ego's power. Creating nonexistent money is one tool by which our leaders sustain absolute control. Modern currencies—like shares—are nothing more than pretty paper. The concept of rulers generating wealth out of nothing via a printing press, or a few digits on a computer, will implode on itself and collapse as people move from the phony world of ego to a real world of truth. The process is already underway. The recent downhill slalom that many European currencies suffered is the direct result of a misuse of power and economic mismanagement. Governments blame speculators and there is talk of legislation to control currency traders. Of course, when the currencies moved up in the past no one mentioned the traders. National leaders don't like the currency markets highlighting their economic failings by marking down their rubbish paper to its true value. The recent European debacle is a forerunner of what will happen worldwide, as realism marks down government and corporate paper to its true worth.

But that is not a bad thing; without the currencies adjusting, the world ego would never pull back and adjust either. So while the markets may be a bit choppy for a while, in the end we'll wind up with a better system. I have no long-term fears about it. In fact, currency trading is one way of making a lot of money over the next ten years.

If you are a person with some assets, I would take the precaution of moving some of your money overseas. When governments get into financial trouble, they always pass exchange control regulations, hoping to lock their citizens into the declining local currency. The four most stable currencies, based on a long term view are, in my personal order of preference, the ECU (European Currency unit), the Japanese yen, the German mark, and the Swiss franc. In the short term the Australian dollar will continue to decline, but later this decade it has a very bright future and the US dollar will hold up well over the next few years. Having fallen 30-40% in recent years, it won't fall much further in the near term. However, over the long term, the US dollar will be seriously affected by its government's inability to get a grip on its debt, which by some accounts amount to twelve trillion, if you include Washington's future liabilities as well as its current ones, which now are close to four trillion. Gold's coming back with a bang as more and more investors realize that currencies are very unstable. And while the price of gold is still low at the moment, I'd start nibbling at bits here and there, if you have excess funds. I think the idea of having a few chunks of gold stashed away for a rainy day is quite a good idea. Further, it's one way for citizens to stash wealth out of sight of the authorities, who have a great incentive to pillage every dollar you have. But the era for buying things to hedge against inflation is not yet upon us, so there's no need to rush.

I have never been a great lover of real estate, but that is just my personal view. The reason I don't like it is because you have to look after it and you can't move it. Many people have all their wealth trapped in one house or real estate investment. That doesn't make for a free life; for many it is just a comfy prison to live in while you work all your life to service the mortgage. However, I can see a time where little homesteads of say five to

What Next?

thirty acres close to attractive, peaceful, rural towns will become very, very valuable. The migration from the big cities will accelerate at an ever quickening pace, becoming a stampede as people seek refuge at the margins, away from pollution, crime, and the neurotic environment of urban life.

The advent of sophisticated communication systems has allowed many to work from home, and much of the small commerce of the future will be homebased via modem, fax, satellite dishes, and whatever advances come along in fiber optic and laser technology. Gradually, we'll return to the olden days when families lived and worked together and mothers and fathers were around to communicate and influence their children in a positive way. It's great when children can see their parents working at home or nearby in their district. Work becomes real, and often the children can be involved, seeing what's happening, and understanding the correlation between concerted effort in the market place, creativity and money. The developments in this area are most encouraging in my view. Home based industry leads to a more peaceful and cohesive family life. It also increases employment in rural areas, improving the quality of life for everyone in the district. In addition, the rapid spread of small communes and rural collectives suits many people, and I think it's a great thing for people to live in harmony with nature, each helping the other, based on love and free flowing spiritual attitudes. The only types of collective I'm not keen on are the ones set up around cult figures; there's always a tendency for hanky-panky that doesn't honor individuals. Communities that respect each other's space and right to freedom are holy and good, and I feel they will thrive in the years to come. Many see the simple life as a blessing, not a denial of the ego and its need for excitement.

283

Politically, we're in for loads of fun. Presidents, governments, and leaders will come and go as regularly as you change your socks. Each will have a plan based on ego, designed to sustain the popular emotion. The plans won't work and they will be spun out of the ever quickening spiral. The turnover of these characters will become a fast moving spectacle—a three-ring circus —akin to the goings-on in Italy right now, where the so-called *Mani Pulite* (Clean Hands) investigation based in Milan is felling the echelons of Italian power left and right. Eight hundred and twenty-five bent politicians, crooked business-men, and petty Mafiosi have been indicted so far, and the final number may run to many thousands. The whole parliamentary system in Italy is being reformed as people demand more honest rulers.

Italy is very civilized—just a little bent. Things are much worse in other parts of our planet. There are so many people in power in the world today whose very existence is an affront to com-mon decency. What irks me a bit is that our governments pander to these bums for commercial and political reasons. It boggles my mind that the Olympic committee has accepted an application by the Chinese Government for Beijing to stage the Olympic games in the year 2000. The same Communist Party of China that has murdered millions of its people since it came to power. I don't have much respect for the Olympic committee, and all that brotherhood of man waffle sounds a bit phony to me. There seems a lot of politics involved.

Personally, I can hardly wait for the time when we shaft these modern repressive regimes and are allowed to call a spade a spade. Still, I'm happy to wait. I see improvement all the time, and groups like Amnesty International do a lot to highlight the problems. Unfortunately, while our leaders are so embroiled in their power trips they will never bring themselves to the spiritual stance that we require of them. However, as the power of spirit grows in the Planetary Group Soul there will be less and less space for evil leaders to exist. Still, I think America is very lucky to have a young President like Clinton, who has the benefit of an intelligent wife who works beside him. Some say he is as honest as the day is long, and although some of his promises only last one day, I still think he's quite genuine and he'll try to fix things. But don't hold your breath. His system is no different to that of others that came before him. Ego, emotion, power—power, emotion, ego. The problem with the American political system is that the President can't pass laws; legislative power rests with a corrupt and self-indulgent Congress which has been in the hands of the same political party for over forty years. Author P.J. O'Rourke calls it a Parliament of Whores, but that's not a fair description, as it gives working girls who offer love and value for money a bad name. Unless the Congress gets a big dose of reasonableness, I don't see real change coming to America for a while. However, having said that, realize that both major political parties in America are in a state of gradual decline, and eventually something new and different will result.

285

I have been all over America, and there are only four states I haven't visited—Vermont, the Dakotas and Alaska. I have a great faith in the American people—they have so much energy. The main things holding them back in my view are conservatism, lack of knowledge of the outside world and political gullibility. But economic difficulties and social problems will galvanize people into action. The fact that millions of Americans voted for the economic rationalism of Perot in the last election is a sign of things to come. America can never fix itself on the national level because it can't easily get rid of the Washington power base that controls everything. Meanwhile, it will have to tackle its problems at the local level, state by state.

When the problems get too enormous, you'll see the states shifting even further away from central control, which is why I believe America will eventually devolve into a number of separate parts. The only other alternative is a military coup to bang a few heads together and oust the Congress. It's a possibility, but remote. However, fifteen or twenty years from now a military takeover could become highly possible, if the government doesn't change its ways. Right now the idea of a coup seems nuts, but wait and see, as the debt begins to really bite and the ego-based Congress plays around doing nothing much, squirming as it attempts to sustain its power in deteriorating conditions. At the very heart of America the people are fair and reasonable—that's a fact I know to be true. From that reasonableness will come the healing. However, while Washington dominates the country, reasonableness will have to wait. Its time will come.

The devolution of the United States and the fall of the British-style status quo in Washington is quite some time off, but the devolution of Canada is around the corner. The main political parties in Canada are collapsing and regional parties are thriving. I can see a time when the various parts of Canada will go their separate ways. At best they will have some kind of loose confederation of Canadian States. That will be a very good thing for the Canadians, who have been under the thumb of the House of Windsor and the British North America Act (1867) for far too long. Why a massive and potentially wonderful, pristine nation like Canada would mess with an old queen from a distant land beats me. I think it's time for the Canadians to grow up and chuck out Ottawa and the Queen, and all that democratic piffle that's worthless to individual Canadians. It only seeks to screw them for every cent they've got. I think it best that the provinces and the indigenous Inuit should control and develop their affairs as they wish. It is only a matter of time before that comes about.

Everything is looking good. There are a few dark spots, but so what. I'm a bit suspicious that the current period of history between 1980 and 1993 seems like an exact replica of the period between 1920 and 1933. The nineteen twenties like the eighties was a boom time, there was a lot of speculation, rising stock markets, inflation, plenty of real estate hype, and a currency crisis in Europe. The German mark reached its final collapse in November, 1923.

What Next?

The twenties—like the eighties—was a fun time. It was an era of moral and sexual freedom. There was exciting music, new dances, shorter skirts, and an air of expectancy. Then the crash of 1929 brought on the Depression. Our crash of 1987 and excesses of the eighties followed the same path to unemployment and economic instability. The Nazis came to power in Germany in 1933 and there was a crisis of the British monarchy (as there is today) when Edward VIII abdicated in 1936 to marry the American divorcee Mrs. Simpson. The Spanish Civil War from 1936-1939 could be loosely compared to our modern Yugoslavian Civil war. There are many factors that fit and some that don't.

My only concern is that the ego of the status quo will plunge our economies into such a tailspin that the only way out is to have a jolly war. However, I think we are a bit more sensible now. Most citizens in the Western world would refuse to fight. The days when you could get the mass of ordinary people to march toward the machine guns in defense of the power structure is long gone. There does seem to be the makings of a new system for resolving issues within the United Nations, and while that's a good thing, I'm a bit suspicious that the United Nations may eventually be promoted as a world parliament to rubber stamp the dictates of a New World Order. You can see some of that already. UN resolutions that the American government likes are enforced while resolutions it doesn't like are ignored.

There is nothing much wrong with our Western world, other than we have developed a big deficit of energy. If you have millions of citizens who can't read or write properly, trying to exist in a technological world while competing against Asian countries (some of which spend over sixteen percent of their annual government income on education), then you are in for big trouble. Our societies have a lot of very powerful, very energetic men and women who create vast goodness and wealth, but in truth, we also have a high percentage of citizens that can't or are unwilling to contribute at any level.

Now, that fact wouldn't matter if those less able or willing would accept a humble slot in life and be content with that. But once you crank everyone's specialness, then you have to pay for the energy deficit in hard cash.

You have to call a spade a spade. Too many nonproductive people are sucking the real workers dry. Millions feed off the system, contributing little or nothing to a society that is required to sustain them. What little color and energy they do contribute is often wiped out by the mayhem of violence and crime that follows automatically when the ego can't legitimately acquire status and importance. Our modern system is a feeding frenzy of the ego, seeking a guarantee of the particle state without effort. There are no guarantees. People will have to learn that. To bankrupt your countries and place the whole Western world in terrible peril just to pander to people's importance is not wise. People are not anywhere near as important as we make them out to be. In the vastness of all things bright and beautiful, humans are not particularly significant. One day we'll wake up to that fact.

Look at our urban youth. Because a kid can do a groovy dance on a drain and throw a few balls through a hoop we think that's marvelous. But realistically, they have nothing to sell or offer a technological age. If we pump the kids with ego and give them no skills and no discipline, and if we don't teach them to generate energy, then the law of the jungle will prevail. It's not entirely the kids' fault; they will respond to whatever programming they receive. We teach them ego and the philosophy of the free ride, and they accept it.

It's no exaggeration to say that the urban youth of America are a plague on their people. The young that roam streets have no morals or qualms about feeding rapaciously off other citizens.

What Next?

It's all a part of the philosophy of self-indulgence that has become the Western disease. Why work for a pair of fancy running shoes when you can steal them?

Our education system is equally responsible because it panders to nonsense and lax attitudes, rather than results. Sure, we have marvelous universities and institutions of higher learning, but they won't do us much good if we don't discipline and educate those at the lower end of the scale. Otherwise, all the higher learning and productivity can't sustain the drag created by uselessness. So many children pass through our system without being able to read and write. Forty million Americans are functionally illiterate and many are armed. The state of Maryland has 4.7 million people and over three million registered guns. Add in a few unregistered ones and almost everyone's packin' a pistol. Mix that with a religion that underwrites laziness and ineptitude, that says that even the dysfunctional, totally spastic part of our society will be elevated and sustained while nothing will be required of them, and you have manufactured a Molotov cocktail. The urban plague of ego over legitimate activity is spreading via film and TV, from America to other countries. Look at Moss Side in Manchester, England; it's a no-go zone captured by armed gangs that strut a very important gait. In the same way as AIDS attacks the immune system, the urban pox destroys the moral fiber of our people and creates an atmosphere of hopelessness. People will tell you that the way to fix things is to spend more money, but that's heroin to the ego. It underwrites the weakness. Education and a shift in consciousness is the only healing that will work.

How long we want to play the ego's game is up to us, but I think it's best that we start to call it what it is: stuck up and totally inappropriate in the modern competitive climate. To fix our countries we each have to get off our high horse and get real. The governments will have to do the same. There is no overall national fix, only millions of personal ones. As spiritual ideals

win ground from egotistical ones, people will see that reasonableness is preferable to materialism. Parents who worked
hard to provide material benefits for their children are now
realizing that the cost of that effort often meant that their
children were emotionally neglected, unsupervised or sub-
contracted out to others. We can never really heal our children
until we reestablish parental responsibility and care. This may
mean families moving from less consumption to more love and
caring, but it is necessary. The process is already underway;
many families have begun to see that love and strong family
ties are more sustaining than just money and material benefits.
Further, I think the idea of males fathering children and then
dumping them and their mothers on the state is a social
misfortune that ought to be rectified by legislation and education. Laws should be passed requiring both parents to become
more responsible. Single parents living off the welfare state
ought to be required to attend their child's school and actively
participate in the education of their children.

Things are on the mend and conscious educators are trying to
bring a new wave of ideas to the classrooms, but the old system
has to run its course before people realize it doesn't work.
Reeducating a nation takes several generations—it's not
achieved overnight. Rationalism can only come in small bursts;
too much too soon and society runs amok. That's why it's very
important that governments take a more responsible fiscal
view. If economies ratchet down too quickly, we'll tumble
headlong into terminal realism, which many are not ready to
handle. Gentle realism is the way for the masses; fast realism is
the way for conscious individuals who want to grip their lives
on the hurry up. Everyone will have to go through the process
in the end. It's the only way back to sanity, and though rationalism is tough for people to take, it's very invigorating—it's the
start of the healing process. We have to teach our people to take
responsibility, and to think in terms of what they each contribute and offer to society. By involving people in their own
healing process, community by community as well as individu-

ally, people will shift from the egocentric view of "what can I get," to the broader more spiritual view of "what can I contribute." We have to show people the long-term worth of offering themselves in service to the healing of our societies.

The West is in for a bumpy ride while it gets the message, though. Temporarily, the Pacific Rim will inherit the earth—what bits it doesn't have already. It's not because the Asians have some special talent that we don't, but because they don't have the ego deficit we are obliged to sustain in the West. The British government spends forty-seven percent of its annual budget of £240 billion on benefits, pensions, and handouts, and almost nothing on research. What it does spend on research is almost entirely military. What chance has Britain got against Asian countries that spend little on handouts and massive amounts on education and research? In Asia where the family unit is still strong, the need for dumping your relatives on the government while you head for consumer heaven is not considered appropriate. Each looks after and takes responsibility for their own. This is possible because the old people don't demand so much as they do in the Western world. Looking after your family is not such a great burden. In the West we can't afford our grandfathers and grandmothers. But in the end, things will change and everyone will ratchet down their expectations, and the idea of a self-sustaining family unit will reemerge. That is the way it should be. It's time for us to return to filial responsibility and love, and we need to respect the old folk for their wisdom. We should care for them and involve them in our lives, rather than institutionalizing them to be cast aside. But they have to help by demanding less so that we are able to look after them.

I think it's best that we begin the healing voluntarily, rather than have it imposed upon us by economic circumstances, but only time will tell. As long as you understand the shift is inevitable, you can make changes to your life at a rate that is comfortable for you. If you do establish control and discipline over your life, I don't ever see you being a victim of circumstances or in trouble.

If you need more money, create more energy. If you are happy with a simple life, then make do with what you have. Enjoy the beauty of this wonderful planet on which we experience the immensity of this existence. In the end, everyone will have to ratchet down a little bit, as our economies can't sustain the pressure. In quietness and serenity, time slows down. You become more settled and more perceptive and more secure. It is the frantic activity of modern life that speeds up your perception of time, while destroying your subtle and precious etheric energy, forcing you to think of death and collapse.

People talk about earthquakes in California and Japan or the AIDS crisis as the coming stories of the nineties. In fact, these issues are secondary. The only story of the next ten years is the massive shift of consciousness that will take place as a result of economic pressure. The death of the ego and the rise of spirit in the hearts of people will be everywhere. It will be the greatest story of this age and the eventual liberator of our people.

Remember this, you don't have to be important or special or glamorous; all you actually need is success and pleasure from whatever it is that you choose to do with your life. You don't have to become something in the eyes of others, you only have to become something in your own reality. From this humble attitude flows a sweet serenity which comes naturally from personal healing and spiritual reconciliation.

Though people power is the driving force of the new millennium, it will not work if people power is used to create more importance and more energy deficits. People power should be used equitably, to show individuals how to liberate themselves. The spirit of reasonableness and cooperation requires each to contribute, rather than one group sustaining the rest. For the Planetary Group Soul of our people to come of age, each part of it will have to be stronger. Each must be taught that they have something to contribute, and they must want to do so.

Metaphysically you cannot raise people up by reaching down from above to pull them up. In doing so, their feet leave the ground and they lose touch with reality. The minute you let go they will fall. The only way we can successfully help people is for us to subjugate our individual egos and place ourselves underneath others to support and teach them, pushing them up from below. That is love, not just ego, emotion, and charity. Whereupon metaphysically, we temporarily act as their legs; they are grounded by the stability we offer until such time as they have the confidence and ability to stand on their own. Supporting and encouraging people through self-help and the shift from ego to spirit is the only system that will work in the long term.

It's just a mind shift. We can teach others, once we have understood it ourselves. The beauty of it all is that a spiritual revolution can take place without any violence and without anyone getting hurt. It's a click of the mind and a shift in attitude. Nothing else. It may take time. But twenty-five to fifty years is nothing in the eons mankind has to learn about itself.

The shift is already well underway, though it seems to me a little unsophisticated as yet. Many people have gone within, taking on new disciplines, sometimes for spiritual reasons, and some-times to consolidate their power to exert more muscle in the acquiring of the external particle state. There is nothing wrong with that. I like philosophies you can turn into cash, as long as they are real and true. But in the long run—that is, several decades—spirit will eventually collapse the importance of the external particle state and offer our people the spiritual and philosophical alternative of an internal particle state. This is a true reality, rather than one manufactured from a false premise.

I feel women have a vital role to play in the process. In the seventies and eighties, when women began to take back their power, the result was not a lot different to the male ego and its power needs. But now that women have gotten over their initial anger, demands and so forth, I think they can contribute to the overall spiritual feeling in a way that the men usually can't. I don't think the feminist movement should be a battle between the sexes. I think females have the opportunity to use their power to assert the spiritual qualities of life. We should continue to expand the process of men and women working in cooperation. The idea that you replace a male ego with a feminine one is unattractive to me. You just wind up with more of the same. I see the feminine role as the reasonable voice that carries the world ego, be it male or female, back to the simplicity of things and the joy of life. There is natural softness and beauty that many women have lost. However, the female is vitally important in the process of reestablishing spirit in the hearts of our people. She can now make her presence felt in all walks of life, and she can be the voice of the Planetary Group Soul, as Joan of Arc was the voice of the folk spirit of France. Whereas Joan of Arc crowned the ego king, for the political and military benefit of France, the modern woman can crown a spiritual king and queen, showing people a new way. Not based on weakness and deficit, but based on kindness, cooperation and understanding—different than before; each will be required to pull his or her weight. The spiritual Fringe Dwellers will also play a role. They have been to the mountain and back. They can show others the necessity for self-discipline and the beauty of inner serenity and personal reconciliation. They offer teaching by example, and they show others how to go beyond fear. The split that occurred between the Fringe Dweller's evolutionary curve and the imploding curve of tick-tock has created a gap. That distance, which on the surface looks like a disadvantage, is in fact, a help. It established observation. The Fringe Dwellers are there to be seen. They look a little weird to the mainstream, but as people adjust to create spiritual philosophies that are real and practical, more of the mainstream will follow. The mass of our people are fearful of accepting back their power and becoming independent, but that fear will lessen, and more people will see that independence is worth more than the materialism offered by dull jobs or the promise of a pension when you are old.

On a personal level, if you establish proper observation and develop the Inner You, eventually you'll create the synapse of energy needed to fuse the two parts of your self—both inner and outer. Then the overall strength of the spiritual unit that is the Total You will grow very quickly, and a complete healing takes place. For all intents and purposes you will be completely finished in this world and you can act or loaf, be or do, or some of both and lots of neither. Then you can show the same trick to others.

The occult historian Trevor Ravenscroft, who wrote *The Spear of Destiny*, told me before he died, some years ago, that early next century we would see the rebirth of sacred societies, like the Knights Templar. He said that what I call the Fringe Dwellers were the makings of an inner dimension of evolution which would create a new destiny within the Planetary Group Soul of humanity. He believed this age, which began two thousand years ago in Pisces, had run its course, and that the new Aquarian Age would materialize from the inner mind of those who had extricated themselves from the destiny of the masses, and the thoughts and dreams inherited from the old Piscean age and its vision.

When Trevor told me these things in a cafe in California, in 1985, I remember being fascinated, but I couldn't see how it would come about. Trevor was a brilliant man and he probably knew more about the legend of the Holy Grail and esoteric history than anyone else alive, but he also had a way of being over the top and jumping to absolute conclusions based on historical similarities, which are speculative at best. History can show us trends but it doesn't guarantee what will happen next. So when Ravenscroft said those things about the Grail and the sacred societies, I remember wondering if what he said was likely or even possible in a modern context. During the intervening years I have seen developments which suggest—to me anyway—that Trevor Ravenscroft was right.

The wounded brain of mankind has caused a spasticity in the world vision. When reasonableness and spirit swamp the ego it has to back off. It takes its loss of influence personally. The hurt lingers and clouds humanity's vision. Even if the mass of our people begin to fix their lives, there will always be the lingering recall of the ignominious humiliation the ego suffered. Only later generations with little or no recall, or those currently alive, who have rotated out of the tick-tock Piscean mind, have enough serenity, detachment, and spirit to override the wound the ego suffers.

It may take the mass of humanity a hundred years to transit from the old Piscean ideas to the new Aquarian ones. Right now our people have a tainted vision based on ideas inherited from hundreds, if not thousands of years ago. They can't see. The world vision is blinded by ego and truncated by the hurt the ego is going through. The destiny of mankind, which, after all, flows from the minds of the people is now poorly defined. The old Piscean vision is coming to a close and the new vision has not yet matured. That confuses people—they feel lost. So they don't believe there is a future. Most have a horizon that stretches a year or two at the most. The young have no horizon at all.

The problem is easily fixed, we just need to create a new vision to replace the old one. Technology has taken us into a future world, but the deep-rooted beliefs we hold are very old fashioned and many don't work well in the modern age.

The Piscean memory will not be able to exist in the new age. The future is another dimension into which it cannot cross, and so it has to die at the doorway of that place. This two thousand year period drawing to a close was dominated in the Western world by the vision of Christ on the cross, which, in effect, was a symbol of the death of the ego and the birth of spirit. It was a prophesy. Our people, in their sweet simplicity, took that message to read that death should be avoided at all costs. Physical well-being and the ego's survival became paramount. The translators of the vision said that we did not have to be responsible for our own reality, that the savior would bare the suffering, dying as he did, on the cross for us.

The fear of death and the emotional impact of the vision of Christ on the cross reminded simple people that the ego should never be allowed to suffer the same fate. But in accepting that idea, it allowed a few to control the spiritual vision of the whole, by offering rules and dogma that they said would guarantee the ego's well-being. And when the ego died, the personality contained therein—which they called the soul—was offered an immortality in heaven. That immortality was guaranteed if an individual would give up his or her freedom, to follow the rules and support the system. The psychic integrity of the idea had to be maintained for the overall safety and benefit of the survivalist premise. Opposition was vigorously rooted out.

The crown of thorns symbolized the wounded brain and the pain the ego suffers in the light of spirit. The spear that pierced the side of Christ was the emotional suffering the personality would experience in the death of the ego. The blood of Christ flowing from that wound was the etheric hemorrhaging that comes from the emotional impact of the ego's death, flowing as lost etheric energy that exists via the navel. The women standing under the cross symbolized the compassion of the spiritual *yin* essence that can do nothing to save the ego. All she can do is accept its body.

At its deepest level, the symbol of Christ on the cross told the story of the death of the ego. However, on the surface level it further established the importance of the ego/personality, which at that time was entirely embodied in male and masculine ways, and was proclaimed a god. The symbol of the savior on the cross established the Piscean vision in an emotional context. From that came individual rights and respect, and so the vision had great worth. But the vision could not totally empower people. It said the Savior would accept responsibility for people and keep them safe and guarantee them immortality in heaven. The emotional response and gratitude people felt for such a promise meant that they transferred their power to the savior, casting their fate upon their trust in the vision, rather than considering that they might control their lives. That is why modern New Age philosophies seem to fundamentalist Christians as antagonistic. The idea of an individual accepting their own power and taking responsibility for their life rather than placing it at the foot of Christ seems contradictory to Christian teachings. In fact, it is not. Part of the vision foretold that very process; the savior rose again after three days, leaving the world of ego to embrace the world of spirit. The Ascension is actually the birth of the Inner You expressed as the spiritual individualism of the inner particle state. I think Christianity will change dramatically once the vision is completed, and all the emotion is spent as the final events depicted in that vision come to pass. That may take a couple of hundred years, but eventually a new destiny or theme for humanity will be established out of a new vision.

So what people currently say is the new Aquarian vision, with its global abundance and guarantees for all, is in fact a vision that stems partly from the Piscean heritage. The concept of the brotherhood and sisterhood of mankind is a fine and correct idea, but it is currently based on the premise that we must make everyone important and should guarantee everyone via a global welfare state. To those that have not, shipments will be sent. Status and importance are still considered vital, and great efforts are made to raise everyone up while the modern vision still seeks the fulfillment of the promise made to us, whereby the Christ figure would accept responsibility for our weaknesses and fears (sins), intercede with God on our behalf, and grant us a good life and a more or less effortless immortality.

The spiritual Fringe Dwellers, and others who have detached to migrate out of the Piscean mind ahead of the rest of humanity, are those responsible for introducing a new vision. They are the only ones currently alive that are out and beyond the emotion of the Piscean recall. It may take a hundred years or more before the old Piscean ideals fade away, and it will definitely take time for the ego to go beyond the hurt it suffered. The memory of that hurt is transferred from generation to generation as sadness and remorse, forming a part of tribal history. Eventually, humanity will evolve beyond the vision of the cross and the death of the ego. A new vision will replace it, establishing a new destiny for our people.

When the rest of humanity gets to the same place, the picture or future scenario that will become the destiny of the world, hundreds of years from now, will already be formulated in embryo, and our people will enter that destiny pattern *en masse* to give it true and complete reality. Today's consciousness raising not only helps with current circumstances, offering alternatives and hopefully showing the ego how to change without trauma, it also will serve our people two, three, even five hundred years from now.

The dimension that was Merlin and Camelot from which the legend was born, I believe existed over five hundred years before the Magna Carta was signed by King John, the brother of Richard the Lionheart, in 1215 A.D. The declaration gave voice to the rights of common people and it established justice and the right to a fair trial from which followed *Habeas Corpus,* the basis of our modern legal system. As singers sang in taverns of chivalry and the legend of Camelot, those ideals laid a foundation in the hearts and minds of what became the British people. Camelot sowed the seed of the Magna Carta, laying the foundations of change by affirming the right of people based in chivalry and honor and the equality of all mankind. Of course, there is a lot of difference between the equality of all mankind, which is noninfringing and respectful and, being responsible for all mankind, which comes from the emotional Piscean vision of the savior. So all of Camelot's ideals have not yet come to pass. Chivalry and honor have been lost in the chase for the particle state, and emotion has temporarily engulfed reasonableness. Our Aquarian vision must become more sophisticated and very different to the Piscean vision. Perhaps the new vision will show us a world after the death of the ego—a world of serenity and quietness and humble ideas that nourish the spirit. Certainly it will be a much less fearful vision, and perhaps we'll see the emergence of a new Camelot of some kind to reestablish chivalry and honor as a part of modern ideas.

That new vision will not become obvious until the current one has run its course. First, the overdraft of energy will have to be tackled. Our world can never come to love itself and reach stability and a new vision if our people are running a perpetual deficit. Weakness breeds fear; fear breeds unholy and unreasonable behavior.

Softly the presence of spirit changes your reality and offers you glimpses of the new. Spirit broadens you, so you move from concentrating on your personal needs to thinking about strengthening others by showing them how to take responsibility for themselves by creating energy. From there you may consider what help you might offer the folk spirit of your people, and from there your thoughts will drift to what might strengthen the Planetary Group Soul. You might consider not just what is beneficial at the present time, but what people might need three to five hundred years from now. Remembering, of course, that the help you offer must be on an energy level, you can never plough in and alter people's lives personally if they haven't asked you to help them, as that is an infringement upon them. Ravenscroft was right. It was just in his focusing in the near future that caused me to doubt. In looking at the future vision and the possible needs of our people hundreds of years from now, you can see how the rebirth of the sacred societies and the honor of the Knights Templar and the Ladies of the courts of old, could be used to reinvent the spirit of Camelot, to reaffirm a spiritual correctness that is much needed.

Such a dimension of Camelot would be inner and secret and hidden from view. While the vision of Camelot is always there in the eternal memory or *Akashic* record as it is sometimes called, it lays beyond the current evolution of the Planetary Group Soul, to be used at a later date. Don't expect it to be discussed on the morning talk show. By its very nature it can never be a part of power or glamour or even discoverable by the intellect. If it were made real once more, it would essentially exist beyond the event horizon of the current mind set. Its intrinsic *future state* precludes it from the perceptions of most people who would not see it with their current sight, clouded as that sight temporarily is. Meanwhile, I think it's time for the conscious people to stand up and be counted. We have to face the status quo eyeball to eyeball, and politely tell them, enough is enough. We want a new way. One that won't destroy our countries through financial excesses. We need a system that teaches our people to go from codependency to self-sufficiency, and we need policies that encourage sustainable growth with ecosystems that are at least neutral to the environment. We don't need hot air environmental politics. We need down-to-earth, back-to-basics, let's-get-real, politics. If our people will consume less and become more simple—less ego, more spirit; if we can develop a holy relationship between intellect and spirit, then we can develop self-sustaining renewable systems that will last forever. I don't believe the world has to fall apart for us to make that change. There is no crisis, at least none that we can't fix.

Somehow we have to learn to confront the Great Lies and stand with our finger in the air and with a nice loud, "Excuse me," to show the current system up for the hollow lie that it actually is. Once we let our leaders know we won't accept the falsehoods and puffery of the ego and that we want the truth, people will stop being frightened of the truth. They will stop the denial process and begin the healing process, which will be very refreshing and lots of fun. There is nothing more exhilarating than rolling up your sleeves to fix problems, rather than baring your chest to be a victim of them.

Now, maybe you don't have it in you to rise up and protest—some do, some don't—but if you can't, then at least talk to one person today from the authority of the Planetary Group Soul or from the folk spirit of your people and tell that person the truth of it all, suggest they make the shifts that you have already made. If you can't talk to one person a day, then one a week will do. And if that's not possible one a month or even one a year is fine. But in the end, spirit has to win. And you and I, and all our relations on the planet, with all our imperfections and insecurities and silly little foibles, will have to have the courage and self-confidence to become a voice for the ideal. And, one day somewhere, we have to walk up to the system and tell them of the dream and the sacred Mother and the Great Spirit in all things, and we will have to utter the truth, fearlessly speaking from the authority of that spirit and our hearts saying, "We want our people back—every man, woman, and child. We want them and we want them now!"

Disappearing Through
the Looking Glass

Appendix

A s a preliminary to this exercise do this: Every time you meditate practice mentally turning inside your body and walking out through the back of it, stretching to reach some point across the room behind you. That loosens you up.

When you feel you are ready for a shot at Disappearing Through the Looking Glass, commence the process by finding a large mirror, in the bathroom say, and take a moment to stare at yourself in it, making a strong mental note of the characteristics that you see reflected there. Really know that person. Next, find a comfy spot where you will not be disturbed and lie down with your head to the north and feet to the south and place yourself at a low brain speed—as close to trance or near trance as possible. Don't fall asleep.

Once at that level, recall the image in the mirror. In your mind's eye, walk back to the bathroom and look at the image that you remember being reflected in the mirror. Stare at it for a moment, then mentally walk into the mirror, rotating yourself as you do, so that you are now in the mirror image *facing back* into the bathroom.

The first thing you'll notice is that what you consider is the real you—that is, the person that was standing in the bathroom looking at itself in the mirror—is no longer there. *The bathroom is empty.*

Now the fun starts. Standing inside your mirror image looking back through the mirror into the bathroom, start walking *backward* away from that mirror. Make your retreat vigorous and aggressive, striding with a purposeful action. Your intention is to distance yourself from the back of the mirror that is on the bathroom wall, which exists, of course, in the 3-D world. Stepping back in this way you are attempting to establish the gap!

Take six to ten strides backward and then at high speed rotate the mirror image person who is doing the walking through a one hundred and eighty degree turn. So now, rather than facing the bathroom and the 3-D world as you stride away backward from it, you will have turned the inner person around and it will now have its back to the mirror and the bathroom. Continue aggressively walking away from the 3-D world. At this point, if the rotation has been performed correctly, and if your trance state is deep enough so that you are not distracted by your physical body and the ambiance in which it lies, you will, at the moment of rotation or slightly after it, lose recognition or perception of where your personality is. You will momentarily have disappeared. *Gone!*

You have stepped through a crack between two worlds, a place that is poised beyond the rotation, beyond the perception of your normal 3-D personality.

In stepping backward aggressively, you momentarily spread yourself out. The gap you establish is the distance between your personality in the entranced body and the hived-off personality temporarily in the inner, mirror person, who is striding away beyond the rotation. The feeling of losing your personality's precise location is a bit eerie, but it is a very mystical experience, and in doing, so, you train yourself for other things. I believe you strengthen your inner journey and you open yourself up to another world. If after the rotation is complete, you still know where you are, it's generally because the quality of your trance is not deep enough. However, if your trance is OK, but you are still not lost in the crack between the two worlds, then the fault lies in the rotation. Do this: Twist the mirror person back again so that it is now facing back towards the bathroom and take two or three steps *toward* the 3-D world. Then, suddenly and aggressively, twist away from the 3-D world once more and fearlessly stride away from it as you were doing before. Sometimes, fear gets you and won't allow you to perform the rotation correctly. Your 3-D personality holds on attempting to stop you from crossing a threshold it can't see beyond. It can't fathom the idea of your dumping it—not even for a moment.

307

If everything goes well the first time out, and it should, this is a relatively easy exercise to perform, you'll enter the *no-where* state each time you do it. You will know you are there because your personality will be temporarily wiped away—you won't be able to find it.

The Inner You that's performing the rotation is usually still blind at this stage. You may possibly have feelings, but no sight. Those feelings are usually quite faint, but from them you will know you are somewhere, even if you can't figure out where. That helps you to settle. If you can, resist the temptation to try and find yourself just yet. In the crack between these worlds is hidden a very great and marvelous secret. If you can control your fear and rest comfortably in the *no-where* state, you will touch upon that secret and unlock an energy that is not normally available to humans—an energy that I believe hasn't been in regular use for a thousand years and more.

Hovering between both the inner and outer worlds for even just a brief moment shows you a transcendence which will fill you with awe. It is here that the inner particle state will eventually exist. Rotating, in the way described, places you along a trajectory that penetrates that inner world—establishing you there. It forms an anchor point. It will show you many wonderful things, some beyond your wildest dreams.

Anyway, performing this exercise and losing yourself in the rotation says you are not scared to try unusual procedures as a part of your knowledge and quest.

Meanwhile, back at the ranch, where your body is laying entranced, something else of interest is happening. To the vision of a third party who say, silently comes upon your entranced body, you wouldn't be there. Of course, your body is still in the physical, it's just that an another person won't see you. This is because we are used to viewing people's physical body with their personalities shining through. This is true even in sleep, during which time your personality is expressed via the dream state. That expression, as in the waking state, radiates out through the etheric allowing us to see and notice people we are looking at. However, once the personality is temporarily gone, the etheric is very still and lacks motion. A person walking into the room would cast their eyes in your direction, and even though they may *look* at you they won't *see* you. The room will appear empty to them. The illusion of your not being there does not apply if the third party has been with you from the beginning of the trance for they would have seen you while your personality was active and so they would know you were there. In looking at your body they would see it.

The *no-where* state is placed on the other side of the rotation between our 3-D world and the near-death tube. Normally, when you meditate, the Inner You is in that world. The difference is that the outer you is not lost and so you know where you are and you know that you are meditating.

If the sensation of not having a precise idea where you are (or even knowing if you exist at all) bothers you, and you want to come back, put your concentration into where you remember your right hand to be and strongly desire to move it. As you do so, your external consciousness—that is entranced in the physical body—will gradually reawaken, and with it will come your normal perception of self. You'll be back home in the 3-D state.

There is no way of knowing how many humans have entered that *no-where* place, perhaps not many. However, once people realize they can move in and out of that dimension then gradually their experience permeates to others via the interconnection we all have. The boundary of human possibility, and the dream that flows from those possibilities, changes. Our people will dream of hitherto unknown things. That will benefit us all, and all the new, higher evolution that lies ahead of us will become possible and it will gradually be made manifest from the feelings of our brothers and sisters to be experienced, learned, and enjoyed.

Think of this: If a very great angel came upon you and it said, "Dream a silent dream of that which humanity will need and use in the year 2500 A.D." Your reaction predictably might be, why me? I'm not qualified. I have no experience in dreaming in this way. Now multiply your reaction by five billion people who are looking at today and tomorrow and think nothing of later on, and you can see that humanity has no solid future state.

Now stepping into *no-where* land and watching and feeling, you might easily see what humanity needs once the ego has burnt itself out. You can create that dream. Certainly, when humans get to the year 2500 A.D. they will change and strengthen the dream to suit themselves, but in the meantime the foundation is laid and a future state of spiritual worth is conceived and birthed in the same way as the visions of our ancestors gave rise to our current world.

So, it might as well be you and me, mate, and several tens of thousands of others that may take to the task. Someone has to do it, we are all equally unqualified. There aren't any qualified characters available, so it follows that the unqualified ones will have to do. Perhaps we are more qualified than we think. I imagine we don't need any special gifts to dream the big dream. We just have to be audacious, fearless, and unlimited in our approach. So let's step to it. After all, what else is happening Thursday?

Thank you for your time.

To-da-loo from Skippy the Kangaroo!

STUART WILDE

STUART WILDE

Photo... J. Rigler

World Tour

and

Seminar

Information

**Send for Stuart Wilde's information package which
includes his latest tours and seminar dates.**
In Australia, NewZealand, and Hong Kong:
White Dove International
Box 1914 N. Sydney NSW 2059 Australia
Phone: (02) 9092273 FAX: (02) 9098803

In Europe, Great Britian, and Eire:
Christiane Klehr, Christinelund #4720, Praesto Denmark
Phone: 45 55 99 3590   FAX: 45 55 99 3560

In Canada and the US
White Dove International
P.O. Box 1000, Taos NM 87571
Phone: 505- 758-0500 FAX: 505-758-2265

BOOKS BY STUART WILDE

Please ask for **Stuart Wilde** products, at your local bookstore. Should you have any difficulty, contact: White Dove to order by mail or by phone, and for the latest catalogue. White Dove, P.O. Box 1000, Taos, NM 87571. **Phone** 505-758-0500, **FAX** 505-758-2265

THE QUICKENING
ISBN 0-930603-22-2   **US$9.95**

The Quickening discusses the power of the ancient Warrior-Sages and it teaches the reader etheric (Life Force) and psychological techniques for consolidating his or her energy for that final push to the peak within the Self.

AFFIRMATIONS
ISBN 0-930603-36-2   **US$9.95**

This book, *Affirmations*, serves not so much to give you nice words to say to yourself, but as a magnificent and devastating battleplan, where you learn to expand the power you already have in order to win back absolute control of your life.

THE FORCE
ISBN 0-930603-00-1   **US$7.95**

The Force, like your Higher Self, is an energy that experiences evolution. It is massive, exhilarating, magnanimous beyond description~perhaps you might want to call it God. It is growing, dynamic and has an inner drive or desire to become more of itself...everything has the Force within.

MIRACLES
ISBN 0-930603-01-X   **US$4.50**

To create miracles, you have to be very clear about what it is you want. By being forthright and acting as if you have already obtained the object or condition that you desire, you create such a powerful energy that the Universal Law gives you what you want.

BOOKS BY STUART WILDE
CONTINUED

LIFE WAS NEVER MEANT TO BE A STRUGGLE
ISBN 0-930603-04-4   US$2.50
This amusing little book helps you identify the cause of struggle in your life and shows how to eliminate it quickly, through a concerted action plan. Your heritage is to be free. To achieve that you have to move gradually from struggle into free FLOW.

THE TRICK TO MONEY IS HAVING SOME
ISBN 0-930603-48-6   US$10.95
Stuart Wilde's money book, deals with the e.s.p. of easy money and the metaphysics of being in the right place at the right time, with the right idea and the right attitude. Like his other highly successful books, this work is chock full of useful information. His breezy and comical style make for effortless reading, as you plot your path to complete financial freedom.

THE SECRETS OF LIFE
ISBN 0-930603-03-6   US$9.95
The Secrets of Life is a collection of excerpts and quotes They form the basis of Stuart Wilde's "alternative philosophy" which has attracted such a large readership over the years.

WHISPERING WINDS OF CHANGE
ISBN 0-930603-45-1   US$12.95
Stuart Wilde's latest book. This work is full of compelling ideas, unusual perceptions and esoteric concepts for individuals who want to progress inwardly, while making a success of their lives in the external world. Stuart Wilde challenges us to stand outside the usual paradigms of consciousness as "fringe dwellers." He asks us to observe the dying throes of what he calls the "world ego"--- the embodiment of the manipulative and dominating force of the status quo.

VIDEOS FROM STUART WILDE

In Search of the Super Self
ISBN 0-930603-38-9 Single Video 76 Min.   US$34.95

This original and fast-moving video seminar gives you practical, esoteric techniques for thought-form empowerment. The difference between success and failure is often very little. Learn how subtle energies affect your life. Be aware that even a small shift in your metaphysical understanding can bring you almost instant rewards. Harness the power of your Life Force by identifying with it and develop a congruence with your infinite power that is almost unstoppable. By detaching from your weaknesses and concentrating all your energies on your heroic quest in life, that super-self within you moves from imagination into reality. Step up and enjoy!

Mastery of Money
ISBN 0-930603-37-0 Single Video 71 Min.   US$34.95

In this entertaining video seminar, lecturer-author Stuart Wilde talks about money as energy. It is a vital part of your spiritual quest, for you need money to buy life's experiences. Once you can see money as energy there is no limit to how much money you can acquire. Stuart's highly successful metaphysical approach shows you how to get into the flow of "easy-money". He discusses practical techniques on how to raise your energy quickly. Once you do, people will be naturally attracted to what you are. When they show up, bill'em.

Soul Mates
ISBN 0-930603-27-3 Single Video 100 Min.   US$34.95

In this delightful seminar, Stuart Wilde addresses the modern day problem of interpersonal relationships. He shows you in practical day-to-day terms how to create a powerful energy within you so that the soul mate you have or the one you pull to you will allow you to participate in an intimate and exciting expression of human relations. Learn an understanding of esoteric sexuality and use that energy to heal your life and pull from the inner resources of Life Force that exist everywhere.

SUBLIMINAL TAPES FROM STUART WILDE

The subliminal affirmations on these tapes are embedded in a musical background. Your conscious mind hears only the music while your subconscious mind, your motivating force, accepts the powerful affirmations. There is no talking or introduction to these tapes-just a full hour of energy-creating messages laid under inspirational new age music.

All Subliminals are Single Cassettes at US$11.95

ABUNDANCE
A Sack of Polished Emeralds
ISBN 0-930603-28-1
Abundance is so much a matter of how you feel. In order for you to pull more money into your life both your intellect and the *inner you* have to agree to accept more abundance.

CREATIVITY
Manifesting Your Creativity
ISBN 0-930603-40-0
Pure creativity is not learned. It is a matter of having the courage to develop it from within you and committing to a belief in yourself. Reprogram your mind with this subliminal tape to manifest the tangible successes that your creative splendor deserves.

COURAGE
I Can Do Anything
ISBN 0-930603-49-4
Fly like an eagle to the upper limits of your life! Dare to believe in your own power and watch the magic happen! Use this excellent tape to help you listen to your heart and to channel the rivers of power and energy already within you to make your dreams come true. There is no limit to what you can do.

DEEP SLEEP
ISBN 0-930603-29-X
This tape, with its peaceful affirmations, will help you get the rest you need. It also works while you are asleep, reinforcing the idea that you are in control of your sleeping patterns. It

will help you be more receptive to your other subliminal programs.

ENERGY
I Am Power
ISBN 0-930603-07-9
This High Energy subliminal tape, written and produced by Stuart Wilde, is especially designed to quickly create energy for you when needed.

FEMININITY
Feminine Spirituality
ISBN 0-930603043-5
A woman's true warrior power lies deep within her. This subliminal tape reprograms your mind to remember that! The natural power and beauty within you is limitless. Realign and heal with the spiritual energy of Mother Earth.

MORE LOVE
Tender Moments
ISBN 0-930603-21-4
This subliminal tape is especially designed to assist in opening yourself to receive and give more love. The subliminal affirmations are to help you pull that "special" person into your life or develop a greater sense of love and caring for those who are already around you.

OPPORTUNITIES
Pulling Opportunities Like Plums From A Tree
ISBN 0-930603-09-5
This subliminal tape is especially designed to pull opportunities to you by programming your mind to the possibility of new and exciting change.

SUBLIMINAL TAPES FROM STUART WILDE

RELEASING
Waving Good-bye, Leaving and Smiling
ISBN 0-930603-42-7
Releasing situations can be hard because the mind tends to hold on. Use this tape to get over the people, places, jobs and old energies that you feel you need to "step beyond." Give the past "the boot." Step into a new, happier and more prosperous life.

QUIT SMOKING
Release Smoking Forever
ISBN 0-930603-32-X
To release smoking forever takes effort and courage. These subliminal affirmations will help you create a powerful *inner* feeling that you are in fact a non-smoker and that you can release smoking forever.

SPIRITUAL HEALING
Healing Rays From A Higher Power
ISBN 0-930603-08-7
To heal your body your mind has to be inspired to do so. On this subliminal tape we call upon that Higher Power within us to grant us the energy we need to realign our body.

STRESS REDUCTION
ISBN 0-930603-39-7
Our bodies are naturally designed to cope with stress. However, in the hectic pace of the modern day we can become overwhelmed by the complexities of life. Use this tape to re-establish the natural balance inherent in mind, body and spirit.

WEIGHT LOSS
I Feel Thin
ISBN 0-930603-10-9
Dieting and looking good do not have to be a struggle with this very effective subliminal weight loss program. Reprogram your mind to lose weight effortlessly by listening to subliminal affirmations embedded in a musical background.

MASCULINITY
ISBN 0-930603-52-4
The spiritual male is confident of his sexuality and sensitive to the needs of others. He knows that his ability to be magnanimous is the touchstone of his spiritual growth. He aligns with his power and pulls to himself what he needs to meet his obligations as the "out-going" creator of the earth plane.

If your local bookstore does not carry the **Stuart Wilde** products listed, have them contact White Dove for a list of distributors. They may write to **White Dove International, Inc., P.O. Box 1000, Taos, NM 87571 USA** or call **505-758-0500, Fax 505-758-2265.**

WILDE CARDS
Retail Price US$1.95 each

Twenty-four of Stuart Wilde's personal favorite affirmations are now available as individual magnetic cards. These eye-catching, metallic-colored WILDE CARDS can be displayed in a prominent place in your daily life to help reaffirm these positive messages from the Wilde Man.

SELF-HELP TAPES FROM STUART WILDE

THE MASTERY OF MONEY
ISBN 0-930603-14-1
Four-Tape Series US$29.95
The Mastery of Money series is one of our very best sellers. Recorded live in Melbourne, Australia, this series looks at practical and esoteric techniques for *consciousness alignment* that allow you to step effortlessly into abundance.

MEDITATION
On The Edge
ISBN 0-930603-26-5
Two-Tape Series US$21.95
Side one of this two-tape series discusses how to get real value from your meditations and gives you techniques for expanding contact with the inner worlds and your Higher Self. Sides two, three and four are unusual guided meditations centering on Pulling Instant Power, Spiritual Healing, and Contacting the Reservoirs of Talent Deep Within.

THE MIND
The Power Of The Subconscious Mind
ISBN 0-930603-44-3 Single US$9.95
So much of your personal power lies dormant in the inner mind waiting for you to reclaim it. Listen to author Stuart Wilde talk to you about unleashing the awesome power of the shamanistic mind. Use the practical techniques he offers to whip-saw life into giving you what you want.

THIRTY-THREE STEPS BEYOND THE EARTH PLANE
ISBN 0-930603-19-2
Eight-Tape Series US$69.95
Many consider the *Thirty-Three Steps* to be Stuart Wilde's definitive work. The quality of the series and the catchy title have insured its popularity. The material discusses thirty-three ancient wisdoms drawn from the Tao and the teachings of the initiates of bygone ages.

TRANCE STATES
And Theta Brain Waves
ISBN 0-930603-20-6
Two-Tape Series US$21.95
The theta dimension is a source of inspiration and learning and it will bring you deeply in touch with your *inner guidance.* The first three sides of this series discuss the benefits of theta states. The fourth side is the theta metronome sound and a meditation exercise which will help you achieve theta effortlessly in your own meditation.

THE SUBTLE ART OF NEGOTIATING
ISBN 0-930603-55-9
Two-Tape Series US$21.95
Everything is negotiable. PROFIT, according to Stuart Wilde, is an acronym for the components of a strong negotiating position. Combine these components with an understanding of the subtle art of negotiating and you will place yourself powerfully on the high ground in all of you business and personal dealings.

DREAM POWER
ISBN 0-930603-54-0
Two-Tape Series US$21.95
We spend a third of our lives asleep, much of it dreaming. As a first step to better understanding your life and the relationships you are involved in, Stuart explains how to interpret and harness the power of your dreams.

DEVELOPING MORE SELF-CONFIDENCE
ISBN 0-930603-53-2
Two-tape Series US$21.95
Stuart shows you how to arrange your thinking to develop a sense of positive expectancy. Learn how to dominate the reality around you so the circumstances of your life become an affirmation of your ever-expanding self-confidence.